C-4892 CAREER EXAMINATION SERIES

This is your
PASSBOOK for...

Taxpayer Services Specialist IV

Test Preparation Study Guide
Questions & Answers

COPYRIGHT NOTICE

This book is SOLELY intended for, is sold ONLY to, and its use is RESTRICTED to individual, bona fide applicants or candidates who qualify by virtue of having seriously filed applications for appropriate license, certificate, professional and/or promotional advancement, higher school matriculation, scholarship, or other legitimate requirements of education and/or governmental authorities.

This book is NOT intended for use, class instruction, tutoring, training, duplication, copying, reprinting, excerption, or adaptation, etc., by:

1) Other publishers
2) Proprietors and/or Instructors of "Coaching" and/or Preparatory Courses
3) Personnel and/or Training Divisions of commercial, industrial, and governmental organizations
4) Schools, colleges, or universities and/or their departments and staffs, including teachers and other personnel
5) Testing Agencies or Bureaus
6) Study groups which seek by the purchase of a single volume to copy and/or duplicate and/or adapt this material for use by the group as a whole without having purchased individual volumes for each of the members of the group
7) Et al.

Such persons would be in violation of appropriate Federal and State statutes.

PROVISION OF LICENSING AGREEMENTS – Recognized educational, commercial, industrial, and governmental institutions and organizations, and others legitimately engaged in educational pursuits, including training, testing, and measurement activities, may address request for a licensing agreement to the copyright owners, who will determine whether, and under what conditions, including fees and charges, the materials in this book may be used them. In other words, a licensing facility exists for the legitimate use of the material in this book on other than an individual basis. However, it is asseverated and affirmed here that the material in this book CANNOT be used without the receipt of the express permission of such a licensing agreement from the Publishers. Inquiries re licensing should be addressed to the company, attention rights and permissions department.

All rights reserved, including the right of reproduction in whole or in part, in any form or by any means, electronic or mechanical, including photocopying, recording, or by any information storage and retrieval system, without permission in writing from the Publisher.

Copyright © 2025 by
National Learning Corporation

212 Michael Drive, Syosset, NY 11791
(516) 921-8888 • www.passbooks.com
E-mail: info@passbooks.com

PASSBOOK® SERIES

THE *PASSBOOK® SERIES* has been created to prepare applicants and candidates for the ultimate academic battlefield – the examination room.

At some time in our lives, each and every one of us may be required to take an examination – for validation, matriculation, admission, qualification, registration, certification, or licensure.

Based on the assumption that every applicant or candidate has met the basic formal educational standards, has taken the required number of courses, and read the necessary texts, the *PASSBOOK® SERIES* furnishes the one special preparation which may assure passing with confidence, instead of failing with insecurity. Examination questions – together with answers – are furnished as the basic vehicle for study so that the mysteries of the examination and its compounding difficulties may be eliminated or diminished by a sure method.

This book is meant to help you pass your examination provided that you qualify and are serious in your objective.

The entire field is reviewed through the huge store of content information which is succinctly presented through a provocative and challenging approach – the question-and-answer method.

A climate of success is established by furnishing the correct answers at the end of each test.

You soon learn to recognize types of questions, forms of questions, and patterns of questioning. You may even begin to anticipate expected outcomes.

You perceive that many questions are repeated or adapted so that you can gain acute insights, which may enable you to score many sure points.

You learn how to confront new questions, or types of questions, and to attack them confidently and work out the correct answers.

You note objectives and emphases, and recognize pitfalls and dangers, so that you may make positive educational adjustments.

Moreover, you are kept fully informed in relation to new concepts, methods, practices, and directions in the field.

You discover that you are actually taking the examination all the time: you are preparing for the examination by "taking" an examination, not by reading extraneous and/or supererogatory textbooks.

In short, this PASSBOOK®, used directedly, should be an important factor in helping you to pass your test.

TAXPAYER SERVICES SPECIALIST IV

DUTIES:
As a Taxpayer Services Specialist IV, you would manage the activities and operations of one or more sections within a bureau. You would be responsible for the supervision of Taxpayer Services Specialists III and lower-level staff performing technical activities such as program development and evaluation; identifying tax processing system requirements; testing of tax processing systems; provisioning of taxpayer contact center services; and resolving return processing errors, taxpayer protests, collections, and requests for refunds. You would evaluate proposed changes to existing legislation, regulations, forms, instructions and other Department publications to determine potential impact on bureau operations.

SUBJECT OF EXAMINATION:
The written test is designed to test for knowledge, skills, and/or abilities in such areas as:
1. **Analyzing and evaluating information** - These questions test for the ability to analyze, interpret, and draw reasonable conclusions from information presented in text, data, images or symbols. This may involve identifying a significant problem or issue; focusing on relevant data and text; identifying trends, relationships, and significant features; assessing relevant alternatives; suggesting or evaluating possible conclusions; and applying logical principles to information provided.
2. **Working and interacting with others** - These questions test for knowledge of how to effectively approach work and maintain professional relationships with others in the workplace. Each question presents a situation and a number of possible approaches for handling it. Question topics may include working with supervisors and coworkers, interacting with members of the public, handling conflict, and managing workplace demands and priorities. The questions are not specific to any job title or place of work.
3. **Understanding and applying administrative principles** - These questions test for knowledge of how to effectively manage and direct an organization or an organizational segment. These questions cover such areas as developing objectives, formulating policies, making decisions, forecasting and planning, developing personnel, organizing and coordinating work, communicating information, providing leadership, and delegating authority and responsibility.
4. **Administrative supervision** - These questions test for knowledge of the principles and practices involved in directing the activities of a large subordinate staff, including subordinate supervisors. Questions relate to the personal interactions between an upper level supervisor and his/her subordinate supervisors in the accomplishment of objectives. These questions cover such areas as assigning work to and coordinating the activities of several units, establishing and guiding staff development programs, evaluating the performance of subordinate supervisors, and maintaining relationships with other organizational sections.
5. **Understanding and interpreting written material** - These questions test how well you comprehend written material. You will be provided with brief reading selections and will be asked questions about the selections. All the information required to answer the questions will be presented in the selections; you will not be required to have any special knowledge relating to the subject areas of the selections
6. **Understanding and interpreting tabular material** - These questions test your ability to understand, analyze, and use the internal logic of data presented in tabular form. You may be asked to perform tasks such as completing tables, drawing conclusions from them, analyzing data trends or interrelationships, and revising or combining data sets. The concepts of rate, ratio, and proportion are tested. Mathematical operations are simple, and computational speed is not a major factor in the test.

HOW TO TAKE A TEST

I. YOU MUST PASS AN EXAMINATION

A. *WHAT EVERY CANDIDATE SHOULD KNOW*

Examination applicants often ask us for help in preparing for the written test. What can I study in advance? What kinds of questions will be asked? How will the test be given? How will the papers be graded?

As an applicant for a civil service examination, you may be wondering about some of these things. Our purpose here is to suggest effective methods of advance study and to describe civil service examinations.

Your chances for success on this examination can be increased if you know how to prepare. Those "pre-examination jitters" can be reduced if you know what to expect. You can even experience an adventure in good citizenship if you know why civil service exams are given.

B. *WHY ARE CIVIL SERVICE EXAMINATIONS GIVEN?*

Civil service examinations are important to you in two ways. As a citizen, you want public jobs filled by employees who know how to do their work. As a job seeker, you want a fair chance to compete for that job on an equal footing with other candidates. The best-known means of accomplishing this two-fold goal is the competitive examination.

Exams are widely publicized throughout the nation. They may be administered for jobs in federal, state, city, municipal, town or village governments or agencies.

Any citizen may apply, with some limitations, such as the age or residence of applicants. Your experience and education may be reviewed to see whether you meet the requirements for the particular examination. When these requirements exist, they are reasonable and applied consistently to all applicants. Thus, a competitive examination may cause you some uneasiness now, but it is your privilege and safeguard.

C. *HOW ARE CIVIL SERVICE EXAMS DEVELOPED?*

Examinations are carefully written by trained technicians who are specialists in the field known as "psychological measurement," in consultation with recognized authorities in the field of work that the test will cover. These experts recommend the subject matter areas or skills to be tested; only those knowledges or skills important to your success on the job are included. The most reliable books and source materials available are used as references. Together, the experts and technicians judge the difficulty level of the questions.

Test technicians know how to phrase questions so that the problem is clearly stated. Their ethics do not permit "trick" or "catch" questions. Questions may have been tried out on sample groups, or subjected to statistical analysis, to determine their usefulness.

Written tests are often used in combination with performance tests, ratings of training and experience, and oral interviews. All of these measures combine to form the best-known means of finding the right person for the right job.

II. HOW TO PASS THE WRITTEN TEST

A. NATURE OF THE EXAMINATION

To prepare intelligently for civil service examinations, you should know how they differ from school examinations you have taken. In school you were assigned certain definite pages to read or subjects to cover. The examination questions were quite detailed and usually emphasized memory. Civil service exams, on the other hand, try to discover your present ability to perform the duties of a position, plus your potentiality to learn these duties. In other words, a civil service exam attempts to predict how successful you will be. Questions cover such a broad area that they cannot be as minute and detailed as school exam questions.

In the public service similar kinds of work, or positions, are grouped together in one "class." This process is known as *position-classification*. All the positions in a class are paid according to the salary range for that class. One class title covers all of these positions, and they are all tested by the same examination.

B. FOUR BASIC STEPS

1) Study the announcement

How, then, can you know what subjects to study? Our best answer is: "Learn as much as possible about the class of positions for which you've applied." The exam will test the knowledge, skills and abilities needed to do the work.

Your most valuable source of information about the position you want is the official exam announcement. This announcement lists the training and experience qualifications. Check these standards and apply only if you come reasonably close to meeting them.

The brief description of the position in the examination announcement offers some clues to the subjects which will be tested. Think about the job itself. Review the duties in your mind. Can you perform them, or are there some in which you are rusty? Fill in the blank spots in your preparation.

Many jurisdictions preview the written test in the exam announcement by including a section called "Knowledge and Abilities Required," "Scope of the Examination," or some similar heading. Here you will find out specifically what fields will be tested.

2) Review your own background

Once you learn in general what the position is all about, and what you need to know to do the work, ask yourself which subjects you already know fairly well and which need improvement. You may wonder whether to concentrate on improving your strong areas or on building some background in your fields of weakness. When the announcement has specified "some knowledge" or "considerable knowledge," or has used adjectives like "beginning principles of..." or "advanced ... methods," you can get a clue as to the number and difficulty of questions to be asked in any given field. More questions, and hence broader coverage, would be included for those subjects which are more important in the work. Now weigh your strengths and weaknesses against the job requirements and prepare accordingly.

3) Determine the level of the position

Another way to tell how intensively you should prepare is to understand the level of the job for which you are applying. Is it the entering level? In other words, is this the position in which beginners in a field of work are hired? Or is it an intermediate or advanced level? Sometimes this is indicated by such words as "Junior" or "Senior" in the class title. Other jurisdictions use Roman numerals to designate the level – Clerk I, Clerk II, for example. The word "Supervisor" sometimes appears in the title. If the level is not indicated by the title, check the description of duties. Will you be working under very close supervision, or will you have responsibility for independent decisions in this work?

4) Choose appropriate study materials

Now that you know the subjects to be examined and the relative amount of each subject to be covered, you can choose suitable study materials. For beginning level jobs, or even advanced ones, if you have a pronounced weakness in some aspect of your training, read a modern, standard textbook in that field. Be sure it is up to date and has general coverage. Such books are normally available at your library, and the librarian will be glad to help you locate one. For entry-level positions, questions of appropriate difficulty are chosen – neither highly advanced questions, nor those too simple. Such questions require careful thought but not advanced training.

If the position for which you are applying is technical or advanced, you will read more advanced, specialized material. If you are already familiar with the basic principles of your field, elementary textbooks would waste your time. Concentrate on advanced textbooks and technical periodicals. Think through the concepts and review difficult problems in your field.

These are all general sources. You can get more ideas on your own initiative, following these leads. For example, training manuals and publications of the government agency which employs workers in your field can be useful, particularly for technical and professional positions. A letter or visit to the government department involved may result in more specific study suggestions, and certainly will provide you with a more definite idea of the exact nature of the position you are seeking.

III. KINDS OF TESTS

Tests are used for purposes other than measuring knowledge and ability to perform specified duties. For some positions, it is equally important to test ability to make adjustments to new situations or to profit from training. In others, basic mental abilities not dependent on information are essential. Questions which test these things may not appear as pertinent to the duties of the position as those which test for knowledge and information. Yet they are often highly important parts of a fair examination. For very general questions, it is almost impossible to help you direct your study efforts. What we can do is to point out some of the more common of these general abilities needed in public service positions and describe some typical questions.

1) General information

Broad, general information has been found useful for predicting job success in some kinds of work. This is tested in a variety of ways, from vocabulary lists to questions about current events. Basic background in some field of work, such as sociology or economics, may be sampled in a group of questions. Often these are principles which have become familiar to most persons through exposure rather than through formal training. It is difficult to advise you how to study for these questions; being alert to the world around you is our best suggestion.

2) Verbal ability

An example of an ability needed in many positions is verbal or language ability. Verbal ability is, in brief, the ability to use and understand words. Vocabulary and grammar tests are typical measures of this ability. Reading comprehension or paragraph interpretation questions are common in many kinds of civil service tests. You are given a paragraph of written material and asked to find its central meaning.

3) **Numerical ability**

Number skills can be tested by the familiar arithmetic problem, by checking paired lists of numbers to see which are alike and which are different, or by interpreting charts and graphs. In the latter test, a graph may be printed in the test booklet which you are asked to use as the basis for answering questions.

4) **Observation**

A popular test for law-enforcement positions is the observation test. A picture is shown to you for several minutes, then taken away. Questions about the picture test your ability to observe both details and larger elements.

5) **Following directions**

In many positions in the public service, the employee must be able to carry out written instructions dependably and accurately. You may be given a chart with several columns, each column listing a variety of information. The questions require you to carry out directions involving the information given in the chart.

6) **Skills and aptitudes**

Performance tests effectively measure some manual skills and aptitudes. When the skill is one in which you are trained, such as typing or shorthand, you can practice. These tests are often very much like those given in business school or high school courses. For many of the other skills and aptitudes, however, no short-time preparation can be made. Skills and abilities natural to you or that you have developed throughout your lifetime are being tested.

Many of the general questions just described provide all the data needed to answer the questions and ask you to use your reasoning ability to find the answers. Your best preparation for these tests, as well as for tests of facts and ideas, is to be at your physical and mental best. You, no doubt, have your own methods of getting into an exam-taking mood and keeping "in shape." The next section lists some ideas on this subject.

IV. KINDS OF QUESTIONS

Only rarely is the "essay" question, which you answer in narrative form, used in civil service tests. Civil service tests are usually of the short-answer type. Full instructions for answering these questions will be given to you at the examination. But in case this is your first experience with short-answer questions and separate answer sheets, here is what you need to know:

1) Multiple-choice Questions

Most popular of the short-answer questions is the "multiple choice" or "best answer" question. It can be used, for example, to test for factual knowledge, ability to solve problems or judgment in meeting situations found at work.

A multiple-choice question is normally one of three types—
- It can begin with an incomplete statement followed by several possible endings. You are to find the one ending which *best* completes the statement, although some of the others may not be entirely wrong.
- It can also be a complete statement in the form of a question which is answered by choosing one of the statements listed.

- It can be in the form of a problem – again you select the best answer.

Here is an example of a multiple-choice question with a discussion which should give you some clues as to the method for choosing the right answer:

When an employee has a complaint about his assignment, the action which will *best* help him overcome his difficulty is to
- A. discuss his difficulty with his coworkers
- B. take the problem to the head of the organization
- C. take the problem to the person who gave him the assignment
- D. say nothing to anyone about his complaint

In answering this question, you should study each of the choices to find which is best. Consider choice "A" – Certainly an employee may discuss his complaint with fellow employees, but no change or improvement can result, and the complaint remains unresolved. Choice "B" is a poor choice since the head of the organization probably does not know what assignment you have been given, and taking your problem to him is known as "going over the head" of the supervisor. The supervisor, or person who made the assignment, is the person who can clarify it or correct any injustice. Choice "C" is, therefore, correct. To say nothing, as in choice "D," is unwise. Supervisors have and interest in knowing the problems employees are facing, and the employee is seeking a solution to his problem.

2) True/False Questions

The "true/false" or "right/wrong" form of question is sometimes used. Here a complete statement is given. Your job is to decide whether the statement is right or wrong.

SAMPLE: A roaming cell-phone call to a nearby city costs less than a non-roaming call to a distant city.

This statement is wrong, or false, since roaming calls are more expensive.

This is not a complete list of all possible question forms, although most of the others are variations of these common types. You will always get complete directions for answering questions. Be sure you understand *how* to mark your answers – ask questions until you do.

V. RECORDING YOUR ANSWERS

Computer terminals are used more and more today for many different kinds of exams.
For an examination with very few applicants, you may be told to record your answers in the test booklet itself. Separate answer sheets are much more common. If this separate answer sheet is to be scored by machine – and this is often the case – it is highly important that you mark your answers correctly in order to get credit.
An electronic scoring machine is often used in civil service offices because of the speed with which papers can be scored. Machine-scored answer sheets must be marked with a pencil, which will be given to you. This pencil has a high graphite content which responds to the electronic scoring machine. As a matter of fact, stray dots may register as answers, so do not let your pencil rest on the answer sheet while you are pondering the correct answer. Also, if your pencil lead breaks or is otherwise defective, ask for another.

Since the answer sheet will be dropped in a slot in the scoring machine, be careful not to bend the corners or get the paper crumpled.

The answer sheet normally has five vertical columns of numbers, with 30 numbers to a column. These numbers correspond to the question numbers in your test booklet. After each number, going across the page are four or five pairs of dotted lines. These short dotted lines have small letters or numbers above them. The first two pairs may also have a "T" or "F" above the letters. This indicates that the first two pairs only are to be used if the questions are of the true-false type. If the questions are multiple choice, disregard the "T" and "F" and pay attention only to the small letters or numbers.

Answer your questions in the manner of the sample that follows:

32. The largest city in the United States is
    A. Washington, D.C.
    B. New York City
    C. Chicago
    D. Detroit
    E. San Francisco

1) Choose the answer you think is best. (New York City is the largest, so "B" is correct.)
2) Find the row of dotted lines numbered the same as the question you are answering. (Find row number 32)
3) Find the pair of dotted lines corresponding to the answer. (Find the pair of lines under the mark "B.")
4) Make a solid black mark between the dotted lines.

VI. BEFORE THE TEST

Common sense will help you find procedures to follow to get ready for an examination. Too many of us, however, overlook these sensible measures. Indeed, nervousness and fatigue have been found to be the most serious reasons why applicants fail to do their best on civil service tests. Here is a list of reminders:

- Begin your preparation early – Don't wait until the last minute to go scurrying around for books and materials or to find out what the position is all about.
- Prepare continuously – An hour a night for a week is better than an all-night cram session. This has been definitely established. What is more, a night a week for a month will return better dividends than crowding your study into a shorter period of time.
- Locate the place of the exam – You have been sent a notice telling you when and where to report for the examination. If the location is in a different town or otherwise unfamiliar to you, it would be well to inquire the best route and learn something about the building.
- Relax the night before the test – Allow your mind to rest. Do not study at all that night. Plan some mild recreation or diversion; then go to bed early and get a good night's sleep.
- Get up early enough to make a leisurely trip to the place for the test – This way unforeseen events, traffic snarls, unfamiliar buildings, etc. will not upset you.
- Dress comfortably – A written test is not a fashion show. You will be known by number and not by name, so wear something comfortable.

- Leave excess paraphernalia at home – Shopping bags and odd bundles will get in your way. You need bring only the items mentioned in the official notice you received; usually everything you need is provided. Do not bring reference books to the exam. They will only confuse those last minutes and be taken away from you when in the test room.
- Arrive somewhat ahead of time – If because of transportation schedules you must get there very early, bring a newspaper or magazine to take your mind off yourself while waiting.
- Locate the examination room – When you have found the proper room, you will be directed to the seat or part of the room where you will sit. Sometimes you are given a sheet of instructions to read while you are waiting. Do not fill out any forms until you are told to do so; just read them and be prepared.
- Relax and prepare to listen to the instructions
- If you have any physical problem that may keep you from doing your best, be sure to tell the test administrator. If you are sick or in poor health, you really cannot do your best on the exam. You can come back and take the test some other time.

VII. AT THE TEST

The day of the test is here and you have the test booklet in your hand. The temptation to get going is very strong. Caution! There is more to success than knowing the right answers. You must know how to identify your papers and understand variations in the type of short-answer question used in this particular examination. Follow these suggestions for maximum results from your efforts:

1) Cooperate with the monitor

The test administrator has a duty to create a situation in which you can be as much at ease as possible. He will give instructions, tell you when to begin, check to see that you are marking your answer sheet correctly, and so on. He is not there to guard you, although he will see that your competitors do not take unfair advantage. He wants to help you do your best.

2) Listen to all instructions

Don't jump the gun! Wait until you understand all directions. In most civil service tests you get more time than you need to answer the questions. So don't be in a hurry. Read each word of instructions until you clearly understand the meaning. Study the examples, listen to all announcements and follow directions. Ask questions if you do not understand what to do.

3) Identify your papers

Civil service exams are usually identified by number only. You will be assigned a number; you must not put your name on your test papers. Be sure to copy your number correctly. Since more than one exam may be given, copy your exact examination title.

4) Plan your time

Unless you are told that a test is a "speed" or "rate of work" test, speed itself is usually not important. Time enough to answer all the questions will be provided, but this does not mean that you have all day. An overall time limit has been set. Divide the total time (in minutes) by the number of questions to determine the approximate time you have for each question.

5) Do not linger over difficult questions

If you come across a difficult question, mark it with a paper clip (useful to have along) and come back to it when you have been through the booklet. One caution if you do this – be sure to skip a number on your answer sheet as well. Check often to be sure that you have not lost your place and that you are marking in the row numbered the same as the question you are answering.

6) Read the questions

Be sure you know what the question asks! Many capable people are unsuccessful because they failed to *read* the questions correctly.

7) Answer all questions

Unless you have been instructed that a penalty will be deducted for incorrect answers, it is better to guess than to omit a question.

8) Speed tests

It is often better NOT to guess on speed tests. It has been found that on timed tests people are tempted to spend the last few seconds before time is called in marking answers at random – without even reading them – in the hope of picking up a few extra points. To discourage this practice, the instructions may warn you that your score will be "corrected" for guessing. That is, a penalty will be applied. The incorrect answers will be deducted from the correct ones, or some other penalty formula will be used.

9) Review your answers

If you finish before time is called, go back to the questions you guessed or omitted to give them further thought. Review other answers if you have time.

10) Return your test materials

If you are ready to leave before others have finished or time is called, take ALL your materials to the monitor and leave quietly. Never take any test material with you. The monitor can discover whose papers are not complete, and taking a test booklet may be grounds for disqualification.

VIII. EXAMINATION TECHNIQUES

1) Read the general instructions carefully. These are usually printed on the first page of the exam booklet. As a rule, these instructions refer to the timing of the examination; the fact that you should not start work until the signal and must stop work at a signal, etc. If there are any *special* instructions, such as a choice of questions to be answered, make sure that you note this instruction carefully.

2) When you are ready to start work on the examination, that is as soon as the signal has been given, read the instructions to each question booklet, underline any key words or phrases, such as *least, best, outline, describe* and the like. In this way you will tend to answer as requested rather than discover on reviewing your paper that you *listed without describing*, that you selected the *worst* choice rather than the *best* choice, etc.

3) If the examination is of the objective or multiple-choice type – that is, each question will also give a series of possible answers: A, B, C or D, and you are called upon to select the best answer and write the letter next to that answer on your answer paper – it is advisable to start answering each question in turn. There may be anywhere from 50 to 100 such questions in the three or four hours allotted and you can see how much time would be taken if you read through all the questions before beginning to answer any. Furthermore, if you come across a question or group of questions which you know would be difficult to answer, it would undoubtedly affect your handling of all the other questions.

4) If the examination is of the essay type and contains but a few questions, it is a moot point as to whether you should read all the questions before starting to answer any one. Of course, if you are given a choice – say five out of seven and the like – then it is essential to read all the questions so you can eliminate the two that are most difficult. If, however, you are asked to answer all the questions, there may be danger in trying to answer the easiest one first because you may find that you will spend too much time on it. The best technique is to answer the first question, then proceed to the second, etc.

5) Time your answers. Before the exam begins, write down the time it started, then add the time allowed for the examination and write down the time it must be completed, then divide the time available somewhat as follows:
    - If 3-1/2 hours are allowed, that would be 210 minutes. If you have 80 objective-type questions, that would be an average of 2-1/2 minutes per question. Allow yourself no more than 2 minutes per question, or a total of 160 minutes, which will permit about 50 minutes to review.
    - If for the time allotment of 210 minutes there are 7 essay questions to answer, that would average about 30 minutes a question. Give yourself only 25 minutes per question so that you have about 35 minutes to review.

6) The most important instruction is to *read each question* and make sure you know what is wanted. The second most important instruction is to *time yourself properly* so that you answer every question. The third most important instruction is to *answer every question*. Guess if you have to but include something for each question. Remember that you will receive no credit for a blank and will probably receive some credit if you write something in answer to an essay question. If you guess a letter – say "B" for a multiple-choice question – you may have guessed right. If you leave a blank as an answer to a multiple-choice question, the examiners may respect your feelings but it will not add a point to your score. Some exams may penalize you for wrong answers, so in such cases *only*, you may not want to guess unless you have some basis for your answer.

7) Suggestions
    a. Objective-type questions
        1. Examine the question booklet for proper sequence of pages and questions
        2. Read all instructions carefully
        3. Skip any question which seems too difficult; return to it after all other questions have been answered
        4. Apportion your time properly; do not spend too much time on any single question or group of questions

5. Note and underline key words – *all, most, fewest, least, best, worst, same, opposite,* etc.
6. Pay particular attention to negatives
7. Note unusual option, e.g., unduly long, short, complex, different or similar in content to the body of the question
8. Observe the use of "hedging" words – *probably, may, most likely,* etc.
9. Make sure that your answer is put next to the same number as the question
10. Do not second-guess unless you have good reason to believe the second answer is definitely more correct
11. Cross out original answer if you decide another answer is more accurate; do not erase until you are ready to hand your paper in
12. Answer all questions; guess unless instructed otherwise
13. Leave time for review

b. Essay questions
1. Read each question carefully
2. Determine exactly what is wanted. Underline key words or phrases.
3. Decide on outline or paragraph answer
4. Include many different points and elements unless asked to develop any one or two points or elements
5. Show impartiality by giving pros and cons unless directed to select one side only
6. Make and write down any assumptions you find necessary to answer the questions
7. Watch your English, grammar, punctuation and choice of words
8. Time your answers; don't crowd material

8) Answering the essay question

Most essay questions can be answered by framing the specific response around several key words or ideas. Here are a few such key words or ideas:

M's: manpower, materials, methods, money, management
P's: purpose, program, policy, plan, procedure, practice, problems, pitfalls, personnel, public relations

a. Six basic steps in handling problems:
1. Preliminary plan and background development
2. Collect information, data and facts
3. Analyze and interpret information, data and facts
4. Analyze and develop solutions as well as make recommendations
5. Prepare report and sell recommendations
6. Install recommendations and follow up effectiveness

b. Pitfalls to avoid
1. *Taking things for granted* – A statement of the situation does not necessarily imply that each of the elements is necessarily true; for example, a complaint may be invalid and biased so that all that can be taken for granted is that a complaint has been registered

2. *Considering only one side of a situation* – Wherever possible, indicate several alternatives and then point out the reasons you selected the best one
3. *Failing to indicate follow up* – Whenever your answer indicates action on your part, make certain that you will take proper follow-up action to see how successful your recommendations, procedures or actions turn out to be
4. *Taking too long in answering any single question* – Remember to time your answers properly

IX. AFTER THE TEST

Scoring procedures differ in detail among civil service jurisdictions although the general principles are the same. Whether the papers are hand-scored or graded by machine we have described, they are nearly always graded by number. That is, the person who marks the paper knows only the number – never the name – of the applicant. Not until all the papers have been graded will they be matched with names. If other tests, such as training and experience or oral interview ratings have been given, scores will be combined. Different parts of the examination usually have different weights. For example, the written test might count 60 percent of the final grade, and a rating of training and experience 40 percent. In many jurisdictions, veterans will have a certain number of points added to their grades.

After the final grade has been determined, the names are placed in grade order and an eligible list is established. There are various methods for resolving ties between those who get the same final grade – probably the most common is to place first the name of the person whose application was received first. Job offers are made from the eligible list in the order the names appear on it. You will be notified of your grade and your rank as soon as all these computations have been made. This will be done as rapidly as possible.

People who are found to meet the requirements in the announcement are called "eligibles." Their names are put on a list of eligible candidates. An eligible's chances of getting a job depend on how high he stands on this list and how fast agencies are filling jobs from the list.

When a job is to be filled from a list of eligibles, the agency asks for the names of people on the list of eligibles for that job. When the civil service commission receives this request, it sends to the agency the names of the three people highest on this list. Or, if the job to be filled has specialized requirements, the office sends the agency the names of the top three persons who meet these requirements from the general list.

The appointing officer makes a choice from among the three people whose names were sent to him. If the selected person accepts the appointment, the names of the others are put back on the list to be considered for future openings.

That is the rule in hiring from all kinds of eligible lists, whether they are for typist, carpenter, chemist, or something else. For every vacancy, the appointing officer has his choice of any one of the top three eligibles on the list. This explains why the person whose name is on top of the list sometimes does not get an appointment when some of the persons lower on the list do. If the appointing officer chooses the second or third eligible, the No. 1 eligible does not get a job at once, but stays on the list until he is appointed or the list is terminated.

X. HOW TO PASS THE INTERVIEW TEST

The examination for which you applied requires an oral interview test. You have already taken the written test and you are now being called for the interview test – the final part of the formal examination.

You may think that it is not possible to prepare for an interview test and that there are no procedures to follow during an interview. Our purpose is to point out some things you can do in advance that will help you and some good rules to follow and pitfalls to avoid while you are being interviewed.

What is an interview supposed to test?

The written examination is designed to test the technical knowledge and competence of the candidate; the oral is designed to evaluate intangible qualities, not readily measured otherwise, and to establish a list showing the relative fitness of each candidate – as measured against his competitors – for the position sought. Scoring is not on the basis of "right" and "wrong," but on a sliding scale of values ranging from "not passable" to "outstanding." As a matter of fact, it is possible to achieve a relatively low score without a single "incorrect" answer because of evident weakness in the qualities being measured.

Occasionally, an examination may consist entirely of an oral test – either an individual or a group oral. In such cases, information is sought concerning the technical knowledges and abilities of the candidate, since there has been no written examination for this purpose. More commonly, however, an oral test is used to supplement a written examination.

Who conducts interviews?

The composition of oral boards varies among different jurisdictions. In nearly all, a representative of the personnel department serves as chairman. One of the members of the board may be a representative of the department in which the candidate would work. In some cases, "outside experts" are used, and, frequently, a businessman or some other representative of the general public is asked to serve. Labor and management or other special groups may be represented. The aim is to secure the services of experts in the appropriate field.

However the board is composed, it is a good idea (and not at all improper or unethical) to ascertain in advance of the interview who the members are and what groups they represent. When you are introduced to them, you will have some idea of their backgrounds and interests, and at least you will not stutter and stammer over their names.

What should be done before the interview?

While knowledge about the board members is useful and takes some of the surprise element out of the interview, there is other preparation which is more substantive. It *is* possible to prepare for an oral interview – in several ways:

1) Keep a copy of your application and review it carefully before the interview

This may be the only document before the oral board, and the starting point of the interview. Know what education and experience you have listed there, and the sequence and dates of all of it. Sometimes the board will ask you to review the highlights of your experience for them; you should not have to hem and haw doing it.

2) Study the class specification and the examination announcement

Usually, the oral board has one or both of these to guide them. The qualities, characteristics or knowledges required by the position sought are stated in these documents. They offer valuable clues as to the nature of the oral interview. For example, if the job involves supervisory responsibilities, the announcement will usually indicate that knowledge of modern supervisory methods and the qualifications of the candidate as a supervisor will be tested. If so, you can expect such questions, frequently in the form of a hypothetical situation which you are expected to solve. NEVER go into an oral without knowledge of the duties and responsibilities of the job you seek.

3) Think through each qualification required

Try to visualize the kind of questions you would ask if you were a board member. How well could you answer them? Try especially to appraise your own knowledge and background in each area, *measured against the job sought*, and identify any areas in which you are weak. Be critical and realistic – do not flatter yourself.

4) Do some general reading in areas in which you feel you may be weak

For example, if the job involves supervision and your past experience has NOT, some general reading in supervisory methods and practices, particularly in the field of human relations, might be useful. Do NOT study agency procedures or detailed manuals. The oral board will be testing your understanding and capacity, not your memory.

5) Get a good night's sleep and watch your general health and mental attitude

You will want a clear head at the interview. Take care of a cold or any other minor ailment, and of course, no hangovers.

What should be done on the day of the interview?

Now comes the day of the interview itself. Give yourself plenty of time to get there. Plan to arrive somewhat ahead of the scheduled time, particularly if your appointment is in the fore part of the day. If a previous candidate fails to appear, the board might be ready for you a bit early. By early afternoon an oral board is almost invariably behind schedule if there are many candidates, and you may have to wait. Take along a book or magazine to read, or your application to review, but leave any extraneous material in the waiting room when you go in for your interview. In any event, relax and compose yourself.

The matter of dress is important. The board is forming impressions about you – from your experience, your manners, your attitude, and your appearance. Give your personal appearance careful attention. Dress your best, but not your flashiest. Choose conservative, appropriate clothing, and be sure it is immaculate. This is a business interview, and your appearance should indicate that you regard it as such. Besides, being well groomed and properly dressed will help boost your confidence.

Sooner or later, someone will call your name and escort you into the interview room. *This is it.* From here on you are on your own. It is too late for any more preparation. But remember, you asked for this opportunity to prove your fitness, and you are here because your request was granted.

What happens when you go in?

The usual sequence of events will be as follows: The clerk (who is often the board stenographer) will introduce you to the chairman of the oral board, who will introduce you to the other members of the board. Acknowledge the introductions before you sit down. Do not be surprised if you find a microphone facing you or a stenotypist sitting by. Oral interviews are usually recorded in the event of an appeal or other review.

Usually the chairman of the board will open the interview by reviewing the highlights of your education and work experience from your application – primarily for the benefit of the other members of the board, as well as to get the material into the record. Do not interrupt or comment unless there is an error or significant misinterpretation; if that is the case, do not hesitate. But do not quibble about insignificant matters. Also, he will usually ask you some question about your education, experience or your present job – partly to get you to start talking and to establish the interviewing "rapport." He may start the actual questioning, or turn it over to one of the other members. Frequently, each member undertakes the questioning on a particular area, one in which he is perhaps most competent, so you can expect each member to participate in the examination. Because time is limited, you may also expect some rather abrupt switches in the direction the questioning takes, so do not be upset by it. Normally, a board member will not pursue a single line of questioning unless he discovers a particular strength or weakness.

After each member has participated, the chairman will usually ask whether any member has any further questions, then will ask you if you have anything you wish to add. Unless you are expecting this question, it may floor you. Worse, it may start you off on an extended, extemporaneous speech. The board is not usually seeking more information. The question is principally to offer you a last opportunity to present further qualifications or to indicate that you have nothing to add. So, if you feel that a significant qualification or characteristic has been overlooked, it is proper to point it out in a sentence or so. Do not compliment the board on the thoroughness of their examination – they have been sketchy, and you know it. If you wish, merely say, "No thank you, I have nothing further to add." This is a point where you can "talk yourself out" of a good impression or fail to present an important bit of information. Remember, *you close the interview yourself*.

The chairman will then say, "That is all, Mr. _____, thank you." Do not be startled; the interview is over, and quicker than you think. Thank him, gather your belongings and take your leave. Save your sigh of relief for the other side of the door.

How to put your best foot forward

Throughout this entire process, you may feel that the board individually and collectively is trying to pierce your defenses, seek out your hidden weaknesses and embarrass and confuse you. Actually, this is not true. They are obliged to make an appraisal of your qualifications for the job you are seeking, and they want to see you in your best light. Remember, they must interview all candidates and a non-cooperative candidate may become a failure in spite of their best efforts to bring out his qualifications. Here are 15 suggestions that will help you:

1) Be natural – Keep your attitude confident, not cocky

If you are not confident that you can do the job, do not expect the board to be. Do not apologize for your weaknesses, try to bring out your strong points. The board is interested in a positive, not negative, presentation. Cockiness will antagonize any board member and make him wonder if you are covering up a weakness by a false show of strength.

2) Get comfortable, but don't lounge or sprawl

Sit erectly but not stiffly. A careless posture may lead the board to conclude that you are careless in other things, or at least that you are not impressed by the importance of the occasion. Either conclusion is natural, even if incorrect. Do not fuss with your clothing, a pencil or an ashtray. Your hands may occasionally be useful to emphasize a point; do not let them become a point of distraction.

3) Do not wisecrack or make small talk

This is a serious situation, and your attitude should show that you consider it as such. Further, the time of the board is limited – they do not want to waste it, and neither should you.

4) Do not exaggerate your experience or abilities
In the first place, from information in the application or other interviews and sources, the board may know more about you than you think. Secondly, you probably will not get away with it. An experienced board is rather adept at spotting such a situation, so do not take the chance.

5) If you know a board member, do not make a point of it, yet do not hide it
Certainly you are not fooling him, and probably not the other members of the board. Do not try to take advantage of your acquaintanceship – it will probably do you little good.

6) Do not dominate the interview
Let the board do that. They will give you the clues – do not assume that you have to do all the talking. Realize that the board has a number of questions to ask you, and do not try to take up all the interview time by showing off your extensive knowledge of the answer to the first one.

7) Be attentive
You only have 20 minutes or so, and you should keep your attention at its sharpest throughout. When a member is addressing a problem or question to you, give him your undivided attention. Address your reply principally to him, but do not exclude the other board members.

8) Do not interrupt
A board member may be stating a problem for you to analyze. He will ask you a question when the time comes. Let him state the problem, and wait for the question.

9) Make sure you understand the question
Do not try to answer until you are sure what the question is. If it is not clear, restate it in your own words or ask the board member to clarify it for you. However, do not haggle about minor elements.

10) Reply promptly but not hastily
A common entry on oral board rating sheets is "candidate responded readily," or "candidate hesitated in replies." Respond as promptly and quickly as you can, but do not jump to a hasty, ill-considered answer.

11) Do not be peremptory in your answers
A brief answer is proper – but do not fire your answer back. That is a losing game from your point of view. The board member can probably ask questions much faster than you can answer them.

12) Do not try to create the answer you think the board member wants
He is interested in what kind of mind you have and how it works – not in playing games. Furthermore, he can usually spot this practice and will actually grade you down on it.

13) Do not switch sides in your reply merely to agree with a board member
Frequently, a member will take a contrary position merely to draw you out and to see if you are willing and able to defend your point of view. Do not start a debate, yet do not surrender a good position. If a position is worth taking, it is worth defending.

14) Do not be afraid to admit an error in judgment if you are shown to be wrong

The board knows that you are forced to reply without any opportunity for careful consideration. Your answer may be demonstrably wrong. If so, admit it and get on with the interview.

15) Do not dwell at length on your present job

The opening question may relate to your present assignment. Answer the question but do not go into an extended discussion. You are being examined for a *new* job, not your present one. As a matter of fact, try to phrase ALL your answers in terms of the job for which you are being examined.

Basis of Rating

Probably you will forget most of these "do's" and "don'ts" when you walk into the oral interview room. Even remembering them all will not ensure you a passing grade. Perhaps you did not have the qualifications in the first place. But remembering them will help you to put your best foot forward, without treading on the toes of the board members.

Rumor and popular opinion to the contrary notwithstanding, an oral board wants you to make the best appearance possible. They know you are under pressure – but they also want to see how you respond to it as a guide to what your reaction would be under the pressures of the job you seek. They will be influenced by the degree of poise you display, the personal traits you show and the manner in which you respond.

ABOUT THIS BOOK

This book contains tests divided into Examination Sections. Go through each test, answering every question in the margin. We have also attached a sample answer sheet at the back of the book that can be removed and used. At the end of each test look at the answer key and check your answers. On the ones you got wrong, look at the right answer choice and learn. Do not fill in the answers first. Do not memorize the questions and answers, but understand the answer and principles involved. On your test, the questions will likely be different from the samples. Questions are changed and new ones added. If you understand these past questions you should have success with any changes that arise. Tests may consist of several types of questions. We have additional books on each subject should more study be advisable or necessary for you. Finally, the more you study, the better prepared you will be. This book is intended to be the last thing you study before you walk into the examination room. Prior study of relevant texts is also recommended. NLC publishes some of these in our Fundamental Series. Knowledge and good sense are important factors in passing your exam. Good luck also helps. So now study this Passbook, absorb the material contained within and take that knowledge into the examination. Then do your best to pass that exam.

EXAMINATION SECTION

EXAMINATION SECTION
TEST 1

DIRECTIONS: Each question or incomplete statement is followed by several suggested answers or completions. Select the one that BEST answers the question or completes the statement. *PRINT THE LETTER OF THE CORRECT ANSWER IN THE SPACE AT THE RIGHT.*

1. When conducting a needs assessment for the purpose of education planning, an agency's FIRST step is to identify or provide
    A. a profile of population characteristics
    B. barriers to participation
    C. existing resources
    D. profiles of competing resources

    1.____

2. Research has demonstrated that of the following, the MOST effective medium for communicating with external publics is(are)
    A. video news releases   B. television
    C. radio   D. newspapers

    2.____

3. Basic ideas behind the effort to influence the attitudes and behaviors of a constituency include each of the following EXCEPT the idea that
    A. words, rather than actions or events, are most likely to motivate
    B. demands for action are a usual response
    C. self-interest usually figures heavily into public involvement
    D. the reliability of change programs is difficult to assess

    3.____

4. An agency representative is trying to craft a pithy message to constituents in order to encourage the use of agency program resources.
    Choosing an audience for such messages is easiest when the message
    A. is project- or behavior-based   B. is combined with other messages
    C. is abstract   D. has a broad appeal

    4.____

5. Of the following factors, the MOST important to the success of an agency's external education or communication programs is the
    A. amount of resources used to implement them
    B. public's prior experiences with the agency
    C. real value of the program to the public
    D. commitment of the internal audience

    5.____

6. A representative for a state agency is being interviewed by a reporter from a local news network. The representative is being asked to defend a program that is extremely unpopular in certain parts of the municipality.
    When a constituency is known to be opposed to a position, the MOST useful communication strategy is to present

    6.____

A. only the arguments that are consistent with constituents' views
B. only the agency's side of the issue
C. both sides of the argument as clearly as possible
D. both sides of the argument, omitting key information about the opposing position

7. The MOST significant barriers to effective agency community relations include
   I. widespread distrust of communication strategies
   II. the media's "watchdog" stance
   III. public apathy
   IV. statutory opposition

   The CORRECT answer is:
   A. I only   B. I and II   C. II and III   D. III and IV

8. In conducting an education program, many agencies use workshops and seminars in a classroom setting.
   Advantages of classroom-style teaching over other means of educating the public include each of the following, EXCEPT
   A. enabling an instructor to verify learning through testing and interaction with the target audience
   B. enabling hands-on practice and other participatory learning techniques
   C. ability to reach an unlimited number of participants in a given length of time
   D. ability to convey the latest, most up-to-date information

9. The _____ model of community relations is characterized by an attempt to persuade the public to adopt the agency's point of view.
   A. two-way symmetric
   B. two-way asymmetric
   C. public information
   D. press agency/publicity

10. Important elements of an internal situation analysis include the
    I. list of agency opponents
    II. communication audit
    III. updated organizational almanac
    IV. stakeholder analysis

    The CORRECT answer is:
    A. I and II   B. I, II, and III   C. II and III   D. I, II, III and IV

11. Government agency information efforts typically involve each of the following objectives, EXCEPT to
    A. implement changes in the policies of government agencies to align with public opinion
    B. communicate the work of agencies
    C. explain agency techniques in a way that invites input from citizens
    D. provide citizen feedback to government administrators

12. Factors that are likely to influence the effectiveness of an educational campaign include the
    I. level of homogeneity among intended participants
    II. number and types of media used
    III. receptivity of the intended participants
    IV. level of specificity in the message or behavior to be taught

    The CORRECT answer is:
    A. I and II   B. I, II, and III   C. II and III   D. I, II, III, and IV

13. An agency representative is writing instructional objectives that will later help to measure the effectiveness of an educational program.
    Which of the following verbs, included in an objective, would be MOST helpful for the purpose of measuring effectiveness?
    A. Know   B. Identify   C. Learn   D. Comprehend

14. A state education agency wants to encourage participation in a program that has just received a boost through new federal legislation. The program is intended to include participants from a wide variety of socioeconomic and other demographic characteristics. The agency wants to launch a broad-based program that will inform virtually every interested party in the state about the program's new circumstances.
    In attempting to deliver this message to such a wide-ranging constituency, the agency's BEST practice would be to
    A. broadcast the same message through as many different media channels as possible
    B. focus on one discrete segment of the public at a time
    C. craft a message whose appeal is as broad as the public itself
    D. let the program's achievements speak for themselves and rely on word-of-mouth

15. Advantages associated with using the World Wide Web as an educational tool include
    I. an appeal to younger generations of the public
    II. visually-oriented, interactive learning
    III. learning that is not confined by space, time, or institutional association
    IV. a variety of methods for verifying use and learning

    The CORRECT answer is:
    A. I only   B. I and II   C. I, II, and III   D. I, II, II, and IV

16. In agencies involved in health care, community relations is a critical function because it
    A. serves as an intermediary between the agency and consumers
    B. generates a clear mission statement for agency goals and priorities
    C. ensures patient privacy while satisfying the media's right to information
    D. helps marketing professionals determine the wants and needs of agency constituents

17. After an extensive campaign to promote its newest program to constituents, an agency learns that most of the audience did not understand the intended message.
    MOST likely, the agency has
    A. chosen words that were intended to inform, rather than persuade
    B. not accurately interpreted what the audience really needed to know
    C. overestimated the ability of the audience to receive and process the message
    D. compensated for noise that may have interrupted the message

17.____

18. The necessary elements that lead to conviction and motivation in the minds of participants in an educational or information program include each of the following, EXCEPT the _____ of the message.
    A. acceptability   B. intensity
    C. single-channel appeal   D. pervasiveness

18.____

19. Printed materials are often at the core of educational programs provided by public agencies.
    The PRIMARY disadvantage associated with print is that it
    A. does not enable comprehensive treatment of a topic
    B. is generally unreliable in term of assessing results
    C. is often the most expensive medium available
    D. is constrained by time

19.____

20. Traditional thinking on public opinion holds that there is about _____ percent of the public who are pivotal to shifting the balance and momentum of opinion—they are concerned about an issue, but not fanatical, and interested enough to pay attention to a reasoned discussion.
    A. 2   B. 10   C. 33   D. 51

20.____

21. One of the most useful guidelines for influencing attitude change among people is to
    A. invite the target audience to come to you, rather than approaching them
    B. use moral appeals as the primary approach
    C. use concrete images to enable people to see the results of behaviors or indifference
    D. offer tangible rewards to people for changes in behavior

21.____

22. An agency is attempting to evaluate the effectiveness of its educational program. For this purpose, it wants to observe several focus groups discussing the same program.
    Which of the following would NOT be a guideline for the use of focus groups?
    A. Focus groups should only include those who have participated in the program.
    B. Be sure to accurately record the discussion.
    C. The same questions should be asked at each focus group meeting.
    D. It is often helpful to have a neutral, non-agency employee facilitate discussions.

22.____

23. Research consistently shows that _____ is the determinant most likely to make a newspaper editor run a news release.
    A. novelty B. prominence C. proximity D. conflict

24. Which of the following is NOT one of the major variables to take into account when considering a population-needs assessment?
    A. State of program development   B. Resources available
    C. Demographics   D. Community attitudes

25. The FIRST step in any communications audit is to
    A. develop a research instrument
    B. determine how the organization currently communicates
    C. hire a contractor
    D. determine which audience to assess

KEY (CORRECT ANSWERS)

1.	A	11.	A
2.	D	12.	D
3.	A	13.	B
4.	A	14.	B
5.	D	15.	C
6.	C	16.	A
7.	D	17.	B
8.	C	18.	C
9.	B	19.	B
10.	C	20.	B

21. C
22. A
23. C
24. C
25. D

TEST 2

DIRECTIONS: Each question or incomplete statement is followed by several suggested answers or completions. Select the one that BEST answers the question or completes the statement. *PRINT THE LETTER OF THE CORRECT ANSWER IN THE SPACE AT THE RIGHT.*

1. A public relations practitioner at an agency has just composed a press release highlighting a program's recent accomplishments and success stories.
   In pitching such releases to print outlets, the practitioner should
   I. e-mail, mail, or send them by messenger
   II. address them to "editor" or "news director"
   III. have an assistant call all media contacts by telephone
   IV. ask reporters or editors how they prefer to receive them

   The CORRECT answer is:
   A. I and II   B. I and IV   C. II, III, and IV   D. III only

2. The "output goals" of an educational program are MOST likely to include
   A. specified ratings of services by participants on a standardized scale
   B. observable effects on a given community or clientele
   C. the number of instructional hours provided
   D. the number of participants served

3. An agency wants to evaluate satisfaction levels among program participants, and mails out questionnaires to everyone who has been enrolled in the last year.
   The PRIMARY problem associated with this method of evaluative research is that it
   A. poses a significant inconvenience for respondents
   B. is inordinately expensive
   C. does not allow for follow-up or clarification questions
   D. usually involves a low response rate

4. A communications audit is an important tool for measuring
   A. the depth of penetration of a particular message or program
   B. the cost of the organization's information campaigns
   C. how key audiences perceive an organization
   D. the commitment of internal stakeholders

5. The "ABCs" of written learning objectives include each of the following, EXCEPT
   A. Audience   B. Behavior   C. Conditions   D. Delineation

6. When attempting to change the behaviors of constituents, it is important to keep in mind that
   I. most people are skeptical of communications that try to get them to change their behaviors
   II. in most cases, a person selects the media to which he exposes himself
   III. people tend to react defensively to messages or programs that rely on fear as a motivating factor
   IV. programs should aim for the broadest appeal possible in order to include as many participants as possible

   The CORRECT answer is:
   A. I and II   B. I, II and III   C. II and III   D. I, II, III, and IV

7. The "laws" of public opinion include the idea that it is
   A. useful for anticipating emergencies
   B. not sensitive to important events
   C. basically determined by self-interest
   D. sustainable through persistent appeals

8. Which of the following types of evaluations is used to measure public attitudes before and after an information/educational program?
   A. Retrieval study   B. Copy test
   C. Quota sampling   D. Benchmark study

9. The PRIMARY source for internal communications is(are) usually
   A. flow charts   B. meetings
   C. voice mail   D. printed publications

10. An agency representative is putting together informational materials—brochures and a newsletter—outlining changes in one of the state's biggest benefits programs.
    In assembling print materials as a medium for delivering information to the public, the representative should keep in mind each of the following trends:
    I. For various reasons, the reading capabilities of the public are in general decline
    II. Without tables and graphs to help illustrate the changes, it is unlikely that the message will be delivered effectively
    III. Professionals and career-oriented people are highly receptive to information written in the form of a journal article or empirical study
    IV. People tend to be put off by print materials that use itemized and bulleted (●) lists

    The CORRECT answer is:
    A. I and II   B. I, II and III   C. II and III   D. I, II, III, and IV

11. Which of the following steps in a problem-oriented information campaign would typically be implemented FIRST?
    A. Deciding on tactics
    B. Determining a communications strategy
    C. Evaluating the problem's impact
    D. Developing an organizational strategy

12. A common pitfall in conducting an educational program is to
    A. aim it at the wrong target audience
    B. overfund it
    C. leave it in the hands of people who are in the business of education, rather than those with expertise in the business of the organization
    D. ignore the possibility that some other organization is meeting the same educational need for the target audience

13. The key factors that affect the credibility of an agency's educational program include
    A. organization
    B. scope
    C. sophistication
    D. penetration

14. Research on public opinion consistently demonstrates that it is
    A. easy to move people toward a strong opinion on anything, as long as they are approached directly through their emotions
    B. easier to move people away from an opinion they currently hold than to have them form an opinion about something they have not previously cared about
    C. easy to move people toward a strong opinion on anything, as long as the message appeals to their reason and intellect
    D. difficult to move people toward a strong opinion on anything, no matter what the approach

15. In conducting an education program, many agencies use meetings and conferences to educate an audience about the organization and its programs. Advantages associated with this approach include
    I. a captive audience that is known to be interested in the topic
    II. ample opportunities for verifying learning
    III. cost-efficient meeting space
    IV. the ability to provide information on a wider variety of subjects

    The CORRECT answer is:
    A. I and II   B. I, III and IV   C. II and III   D. I, II, III and IV

16. An agency is attempting to evaluate the effectiveness of its educational programs. For this purpose, it wants to observe several focus groups discussing particular programs.
    For this purpose, a focus group should never number more than _____ participants.
    A. 5   B. 10   C. 15   D. 20

17. A _____ speech is written so that several agency members can deliver it to different audiences with only minor variations.
    A. basic   B. printed   C. quota   D. pattern

18. Which of the following statements about public opinion is generally considered to be FALSE?
    A. Opinion is primarily reactive rather than proactive.
    B. People have more opinions about goals than about the means by which to achieve them.
    C. Facts tend to shift opinion in the accepted direction when opinion is not solidly structured.
    D. Public opinion is based more on information than desire.

19. An agency is trying to promote its educational program.
    As a general rule, the agency should NOT assume that
    A. people will only participate if they perceive an individual benefit
    B. promotions need to be aimed at small, discrete groups
    C. if the program is good, the audience will find out about it
    D. a variety of methods, including advertising, special events, and direct mail, should be considered

20. In planning a successful educational program, probably the first and most important question for an agency to ask is:
    A. What will be the content of the program?
    B. Who will be served by the program?
    C. When is the best time to schedule the program?
    D. Why is the program necessary?

21. Media kits are LEAST likely to contain
    A. fact sheets   B. memoranda
    C. photographs with captions D. news releases

22. The use of pamphlets and booklets as media for communication with the public often involves the disadvantage that
    A. the messages contained within them are frequently nonspecific
    B. it is difficult to measure their effectiveness in delivering the message
    C. there are few opportunities for people to refer to them
    D. color reproduction is poor

23. The MOST important prerequisite of a good educational program is an
    A. abundance of resources to implement it
    B. individual staff unit formed for the purpose of program delivery
    C. accurate needs assessment
    D. uneducated constituency

24. After an education program has been delivered, an agency conducts a program evaluation to determine whether its objectives have been met.
General rules about how to conduct such an education program valuation include each of the following, EXCEPT that it
   A. must be done immediately after the program has been implemented
   B. should be simple and easy to use
   C. should be designed so that tabulation of responses can take place quickly and inexpensively
   D. should solicit mostly subjective, open-ended responses if the audience was large

25. Using electronic media such as television as means of educating the public is typically recommended ONLY for agencies that
   I. have a fairly simple message to begin with
   II. want to reach the masses, rather than a targeted audience
   III. have substantial financial resources
   IV. accept that they will not be able to measure the results of the campaign with much precision

   The CORRECT answer is:
   A. I and II   B. I, II and III   C. II and IV   D. I, II, III and IV

KEY (CORRECT ANSWERS)

1.	B		11.	C
2.	C		12.	D
3.	D		13.	A
4.	C		14.	D
5.	D		15.	B
6.	B		16.	B
7.	C		17.	D
8.	D		18.	D
9.	D		19.	C
10.	A		20.	D

21. B
22. B
23. C
24. D
25. D

EXAMINATION SECTION
TEST 1

DIRECTIONS: Each question or incomplete statement is followed by several suggested answers or completions. Select the one that BEST answers the question or completes the statement. *PRINT THE LETTER OF THE CORRECT ANSWER IN THE SPACE AT THE RIGHT.*

1. A group member who starts out at the same level as other group members and is able to move into a leadership position within that group would be described as what kind of a leader?
   A. Autocratic   B. Democratic   C. Emergent   D. Informal

   1.____

2. Your boss is only effective as the leader of your department when you and your coworkers are motivated experts on the topic at hand. If any of you do not really have expertise in a given field, his leadership falters somewhat. What type of leader is your boss?
   A. Laissez-faire   B. Technical   C. Democratic   D. Autocratic

   2.____

3. If a leader is in charge of an inexperienced group that does not have the appropriate information and proficiency to successfully complete a task, which of the following approaches should the leader use in order for success to follow within the group?
   A. Yelling   B. Delegating   C. Participating   D. Selling

   3.____

4. If you are a democratic leader, which of the following styles will be reflective of your leadership technique?
   A. Participating   B. Telling   C. Yelling   D. Delegating

   4.____

5. In producing equality in group member participation, which of the following should a leader NOT do?
   A. Make a statement or ask a question after each person in the group has said something
   B. Avoid taking a position during disagreements
   C. Limit comments to specific individuals within the group
   D. Control dominating speakers

   5.____

6. Social capital is BEST defined as
   A. social connections that help us make more money
   B. social connections that improve our lives
   C. a type of connection that experts believe is becoming more common in Europe than the United States.
   D. none of the above

   6.____

7. Communication is not simply sending a message. It is creating true
   A. connectivity   B. understanding
   C. empathy   D. power

   7.____

11

8. Of the following, which is NOT a part of the speech communication process?
   A. Feedback
   B. Central idea
   C. Interference
   D. Ethics

9. You are leading a meeting and afterwards your colleagues tell you they didn't quite understand what you were communicating verbally and nonverbally to them. Which part of the communication process do you need to work on?
   A. Channel
   B. Main idea
   C. Message
   D. Specific purpose

10. If nonverbal messages contradict verbal symbols, you are sending what kind of message to your public?
    A. Clear
    B. Mixed
    C. Controversial
    D. Negative

11. Which of the following would a public speaker use to deliver verbal symbols?
    A. Words
    B. Gestures
    C. Tone
    D. Facial expression

12. You are in the process of taking a course on interacting with the public. Your instructor starts talking about "the pathway" used to transmit a message. He explains that "the pathway" is better known as a
    A. link
    B. loop
    C. transmitter
    D. channel

13. You finish an informational meeting with members of a community concerning a new park that will be built nearby. Afterwards, you are seeking feedback from them. Which of the following would NOT be a form of helpful feedback to you?
    A. Listeners raise their hands to point out a mistake
    B. Videotape the presentation
    C. Have colleagues and/or friends critique your presentation
    D. Hand out evaluation forms to listeners and have them fill it out after the presentation

14. Many public speaking experts have often repeated the famous quote, "A yawn is a silent _____," which references the quality of engagement within a presentation.
    A. rudeness
    B. insult
    C. shout
    D. protest

15. If a child is running around during your speech and making a lot of noise, what type of interference would that be?
    A. Situational
    B. External
    C. Internal
    D. Intentional

16. According to multiple recent surveys, of the five biggest mistakes that speakers make during a presentation, which one is the WORST?
    A. Being poorly prepared
    B. Trying to cover too much in one speech
    C. Failing to tailor a speech to the needs and interests of the audience
    D. Being boring

17. One of your colleagues has been asked to lead a meeting, and she confides   17.____
    in you that she suffers from excessive stage fright. Which of the following
    areas should you advise her to focus on to prevent her fear?
    A. Preparation   B. Self-confidence
    C. Experience   D. Sense of humor

18. When interacting with the public, which of the following elements should you   18.____
    NEVER imagine before engaging in public speaking?
    A. Effective delivery   B. Nervousness
    C. Possibility of failure   D. Success

19. A spokesperson is giving a speech to community members and you are evaluating   19.____
    him. You notice he tends to focus too much on himself and not enough on his
    audience. What is one piece of advice you can give him so he can shift his
    focus more to his audience?
    A. Change his amount of eye contact   B. Work on facial expressions
    C. Alter his style of speaking   D. All of the above

20. Most experts agree that the best way to eliminate excess energy would be   20.____
    to do all of the following EXCEPT
    A. using visual aids
    B. gripping the lectern
    C. walking to the right and left occasionally
    D. making gestures

21. A woman has lived in Newville her whole life. Recently, the Newville   21.____
    public works department made a policy change that angered her since it
    completely rearranged her schedule. She calls you on the phone and displays
    her displeasure with your department's recent policy change. What is the
    FIRST response you should have toward her?
    A. Interrupt her to say you cannot discuss the situation until she calms down
    B. Apologize to her that she has been negatively affected by the public
       works department
    C. Listen to her and demonstrate comprehension of her situation and why
       she was upset by your department's action
    D. Give her a detailed explanation of the reasons for the policy change

22. Which of the following is generally TRUE regarding public opinion?   22.____
    A. It is hard to move people toward a strong opinion on anything
    B. It is easy to move people toward a strong opinion on anything
    C. Most public relations are devoted to repairing negative public opinion
       about individuals
    D. It is easier than previously thought to move people away from an opinion
       they hold

23. Influencing a community member's attitude really comes down to which of the   23.____
    following?
    A. Journalism   B. Public relations
    C. Social psychology   D. Social action groups

24. If you attend a town hall meeting in which community members will bring up issues that require you to explain why your organization made the decisions it made, you will need to persuade them using evidence that is virtually indisputable. Which type of evidence should you stick to when explaining answers to the public?
    A. Facts
    B. Personal experience
    C. Emotions
    D. Using what appeals to the target public

25. In the last decade, especially after all the organizational and governmental scandals, public institutions must do which of the following in order to be successful?
    A. Work hard to earn and sustain favorable public opinion
    B. Trust the instincts expressed by the general public
    C. Be cognizant of the media's power
    D. Place the needs of the executives ahead of the needs of the public and other constituents

KEY (CORRECT ANSWERS)

1.	C		11.	A
2.	A		12.	D
3.	B		13.	A
4.	D		14.	C
5.	A		15.	B
6.	B		16.	C
7.	B		17.	A
8.	D		18.	B
9.	C		19.	D
10.	B		20.	B

21. C
22. D
23. B
24. A
25. A

TEST 2

DIRECTIONS: Each question or incomplete statement is followed by several suggested answers or completions. Select the one that BEST answers the question or completes the statement. *PRINT THE LETTER OF THE CORRECT ANSWER IN THE SPACE AT THE RIGHT.*

1. Unique attributes of the Internet that people can enjoy include all of the following EXCEPT
    A. immediacy
    B. low cost
    C. pervasiveness
    D. value for building one-to-one human relationships

    1.____

2. Which of the following is a reason that social media can be more effective than traditional means of advertising and communication?
    A. When someone mentions your brand in social media, there is much more potential for other people to notice
    B. It is easier to decipher tone and purpose through Twitter or Facebook than through personal communication
    C. Most of the people who would be interested in your brand or service are comfortable and familiar with using social media
    D. Almost anyone can step into a media relations role if primarily using social media, because it is easy to communicate effectively through social media platforms

    2.____

3. You are tasked with building publicity for the upcoming reveal of a new art installation in the town you work in. Your boss tells you to contact journalists, reporters and bloggers to help spread the word. Which of the following would be the MOST effective way of getting the media to help build coverage?
    A. Send out a mass e-mail to any media members in the area detailing the art installation and why you need coverage for it
    B. Call each media outlet and find out who would most likely cover and build publicity for your project. Then reach out to them either face-to-face or through a phone call
    C. Using Twitter, tweet at the media members and introduce yourself and your art installation and ask them to help spread the word
    D. None of the above

    3.____

4. When using written communication, which of the following is a MAJOR challenge of writing to listeners?
    A. Providing lots of statistics
    B. Grabbing the attention of the listener quickly
    C. Providing information that is easily reviewed
    D. Presenting lots of incidentals

    4.____

5. In order to communicate well in writing, which of the following pieces of advice sounds good but doesn't actually help you?
   A. Write material for all audiences rather than focusing on one
   B. Think before writing
   C. Write simply and with clarity
   D. Write and rewrite until you have a polished, finished product

6. You send out a public newsletter that details a project that your team is currently working on. One week later, an employee on your team tells you she has received multiple phone calls from confused constituents claiming that the newsletter's readability was low. When you send out a corrected newsletter, you need to make sure that your communication is easy to
   A. read   B. hear   C. edit   D. comprehend

7. You work for a biomedical company as a public outreach advocate. One day, an exciting e-mail circulates internally that states one of your scientists has discovered a cure for leukemia and your supervisor tasks you with writing the release. When writing the release, the newsworthy element inherent in the story is
   A. oddity   B. conflict   C. impact   D. proximity

8. When communicating with the public through the Internet, news releases
   A. should not be sent via e-mail
   B. should be succinct
   C. should be sent via "snail mail"
   D. none of the above

9. What is the MAJOR advantage of organizational publications? Their ability to
   A. give sponsoring organizations a means of uncontrolled communications
   B. deliver specific, detailed information to narrowly defined target publics
   C. avoid the problems typically associated with two-way media
   D. provide a revenue source for sponsoring organizations

10. You are confronted by a question from a reporter that you do not know the answer to. What should you do?
    A. Give them other information you are certain is right
    B. Tell them that information is "off the record" and will be distributed later
    C. Say "no comment" rather than look like you're uninformed
    D. Admit that you don't know but promise to provide the information later

11. Often times, an organization will run situation analysis before they share information with the public. Which one of these "internal factors" is usually associated with a situational analysis?
    A. A communication audit   B. Community focus groups
    C. A list of media contacts   D. Strategy suggestions

12. When you are hired, your first task is to start a process of identifying who are involved and affected by a situation central to your organization. This process is MOST commonly referred to as a(n)
    A. situation interview
    B. communication audit
    C. exploratory survey
    D. stakeholder analysis

12.____

13. Once a public outreach plan is in the summative evaluation phase, which of the following is generally associated with it?
    A. Impact
    B. Implementation
    C. Attitude change
    D. Preparation

13.____

14. Which of the following Internet-related challenges is MOST significant in the public relations field?
    A. Finding stable, cost-effective internet provides
    B. Representing clients using new social media environments
    C. Staying abreast of changing technology
    D. Training staff to use social media

14.____

15. Which of the following BEST defines a public issue? Any
    A. problem that brings a public lawsuit
    B. concern that is of mutual distress to competitors
    C. issue that is of mutual concern to an organization and its stakeholders
    D. problem that is not a concern to an organization and/or one of its stakeholders

15.____

16. A handful of people are posting misleading and/or negative information about your organization. What is the MOST proactive approach to handling this situation?
    A. Buy up enough shares in the site where the negative posts are, and prevent those users from posting again
    B. Post anonymous comments on the sites to help combat the negativity
    C. Prepare news releases that discredit the inaccuracies
    D. Make policy changes to address complaints highlighted on the sites

16.____

17. Your supervisor has recently asked you to review present and future realities for interacting with the public. Why is it important to continually review these?
    A. It helps develop your vision statement
    B. It helps interpret trends for management
    C. It helps construe the organization's business plan
    D. To know what path the company should pursue

17.____

18. You are the community relations director for the public water utility plant that has been the focus of a group of activists who are opposed to the addition of fluoride to drinking water. These objectors are not only at the plant each day, but they are also very active on social media inciting negativity towards the practice. As the director of the plant, you have overwhelming evidence that contradicts what the protestors are arguing. You want to combat their social media with your own internet plan. Which of the following is the MOST appropriate action for you to take?
    A. Use utility employees to write the blog, posing as healthcare professionals
    B. Reach out to medical professionals to volunteer to tweet and message community members under their own identities, but with no reference to the utility company
    C. Write a blog yourself, identifying yourself as an employee, and quote the scientific opinions of a variety of sources
    D. Pay for medical professionals to respond through the internet, identifying the utility as their sponsor, but without disclosing the compensation

19. You have recently completed an advertising campaign to help assuage the anger of the community at changes in the upcoming summer program for the city. Which of the following measurements would be MOST effective for evaluating the campaign's impact on audience attitude?
    A. A content analysis of media coverage
    B. Studying blog postings about the issue
    C. Analyzing pre- and post-numbers of people signed up for the summer programs
    D. Conducting a pre- and post-analysis of public opinions

20. In order to measure how policy changes will affect the public, you recommend that your supervisors first run a focus group for research. They like the idea, but want you to be in charge of running the group. Which of the following should you keep in mind as you form the focus group?
    A. Participants need to be randomly selected
    B. Make sure participants are radically different from one another so you get a range of opinions
    C. Include at least seven or more people in the group. Otherwise, the sample is too small to draw any conclusions.
    D. Formulate a research plan and use it as a script so you can make sure the results are ones that will work for you and your supervisors

21. The public university has recently come under fire for not offering enough tuition savings options for students. You have been hired to help promote the programs they offer including new savings programs. What is the MOST appropriate first step for you to take?
    A. Research pricing and development costs for the services
    B. Develop a survey to discover which factors impact families' savings
    C. Conduct a situation analysis to gain better understanding of the issues
    D. Hold a focus group to determine which messages would be most effective for your program

22. After receiving feedback from the public on a new program, you are concerned that the results have been tainted by courtesy bias. You plan on sending out a new questionnaire, but you need to make sure the bias is discouraged in it. Which of the following techniques will be MOST effective at decreasing the partiality?
    A. Make questionnaire responses confidential
    B. Employ an outside firm to run the survey
    C. Offer a larger range of responses in the survey
    D. Both "A" and "C"

23. You have just relocated from Omaha, Nebraska to a branch in Chicago, Illinois. In order to communicate well while in Chicago, you must remember that
    A. most publics have the same needs
    B. all publics are most interested only in technology you are using
    C. each audience has its own special needs and require different types of communication
    D. all audiences' needs overlap

24. Recently, the Parks and Recreation Department has come under fire because it has been accused of too much marketing and not enough public relations. Which of the following, if true, would lend credibility to these accusations?
    A. Employees are focused on signing citizens up for as many different camps and activities available over the summer as possible
    B. Management consistently tries to send appreciation gifts to members of the community when they have volunteered or attending an activity sponsored by the Park district
    C. Weekly meetings are held to determine how to best improve the Park district's image as it relates to consumers
    D. Parks and Recreation is primarily focused on making sure the public enjoys their activities and trusts them to put on educational programs for the children

25. During your speech, a community member stands up and accuses you of "spinning" a story. Which of the following BEST describes their accusation?
    A. You are relating a message through an agreed-upon ethical practice within the public relations community
    B. You are twisting a message to create performance where there is none
    C. You are trying to preserve hard-earned credibility
    D. You are providing the media with balanced and accurate information

KEY (CORRECT ANSWERS)

1.	D	11.	A
2.	A	12.	D
3.	C	13.	A
4.	B	14.	C
5.	D	15.	C
6.	D	16.	B
7.	C	17.	A
8.	B	18.	C
9.	B	19.	D
10.	D	20.	A

21. C
22. D
23. C
24. A
25. B

TEST 3

DIRECTIONS: Each question or incomplete statement is followed by several suggested answers or completions. Select the one that BEST answers the question or completes the statement. *PRINT THE LETTER OF THE CORRECT ANSWER IN THE SPACE AT THE RIGHT.*

1. In order to be successful in relating to the public, all of the following are vital EXCEPT
   A. performance
   B. relationship building
   C. formal education
   D. diversity of experience

   1.____

2. Which of the following is TRUE of communicating well regarding public relations experts?
   A. It will differentiate you and your role from others with special skills in the organization you work for
   B. It should be handled delicately in order to avoid upsetting stakeholders
   C. It is not as important as looking fashionable
   D. It is less important than understanding bureaucratic peculiarities

   2.____

3. You are critiquing a staffer who will lead an important meeting in two days and you note that she keeps using words that are steeped with connotation. You tell her to be careful of these words. Why?
   A. They transmit meaning too clearly, and you always want to leave wiggle room in your meaning
   B. They transmit the dictionary definition of a word that makes for a boring presentation
   C. They transmit meaning with an emotional overtone that could lead to misunderstanding in an overall message
   D. They lend themselves to stereotyping

   3.____

4. If you are trying to avoid biasing your intended audience, which of the following factors could help with that?
   A. Symbols
   B. Objective reporting by media
   C. Semantics
   D. Peers

   4.____

5. Of the following, which trait is MOST desirable when working with the public?
   A. Having the "gift for gab"
   B. Being an elite strategist
   C. Being able to leap organizational boundaries
   D. Performing well, especially in crises

   5.____

6. Which of the following areas is likely to see continual growth in the practice of public relations?
   A. Healthcare
   B. Social media
   C. Law enforcement
   D. None of the above

   6.____

7. What is the MOST commonly used public relations tactic?
   A. A news release
   B. A special event
   C. A PSA (public service announcement)
   D. A full feature news article

8. You have just been assigned to help with a new advertising campaign that will promote the new services offered by your organization. One major component of the new campaign will focus on publicity through photographs. Knowing you need to get this part of the project right, which of the following is the BEST tip to remember when taking PR photos?
   A. Don't use action shots because they usually wind up blurry
   B. Make sure there is good contrast and sharp detail
   C. Ensure that the product/services are the biggest thing(s) in the photo
   D. Photograph multiple people rather than only one

9. Which of the following situations would merit holding a press conference?
   A. When a corporation is restructured
   B. When a new public relations employee has been hired
   C. When information is of minor relevance to a specific audience
   D. When there is a new product to be released

10. On average, how long should an announcement to the public last on the radio?
    A. 2 minutes   B. 20 seconds   C. 1 minute   D. 10 seconds

11. In educating the public, you need to develop a PR plan and analyze each situation that could arise. Which of the following should NOT be a part of the analysis?
    A. Research   B. Message crafting
    C. Creating a problem statement   D. Asking the 5 W's and the H

12. You are in charge of promoting an event in the near future, but social media is unavailable to you at this time. Which of the following is the BEST way to get your message out to the media and, therefore, the public?
    A. An Op-Ed piece in the local newspaper
    B. A press conference
    C. A newsletter
    D. A news release

13. In the past few months, you and your colleagues have been accused of "doublespeak". Which of the following excerpts from presentations you have used could you defend and explain why it would NOT be an example of "doublespeak"?
    A. You called combat "fighting"
    B. Fred referred to genocide as "ethnic cleansing"
    C. Your boss referred to recent layoffs as "downsizing"
    D. Susie called the janitor a "custodial engineer"

14. In relating to the public, which of the following reflects key words in defining modern day PR? 14.____
    A. Deliberate, public interest, management function
    B. Persuasive, manipulative, improvisation
    C. Management, technical, flexible
    D. Influential, creative, evaluative

15. How is educating and relating to the public different from being a journalist, marketing agent, or advertiser? 15.____
    A. It is more focused on advocacy
    B. It is about getting "free" press coverage
    C. It is about building relationships with various demographics
    D. All of the above

16. Of the following, what is the BEST tactic for learning employee attitudes? 16.____
    A. Internal communications audit
    B. Research
    C. Conference meeting
    D. Both A and B

17. When releasing news to the public, you should make sure it reads at a _____-grade reading level. 17.____
    A. 5th
    B. 12th
    C. 9th
    D. 7th

18. If you are using a euphemism that actually changes the meaning/impact of a concept you are trying to relay, what is that called? 18.____
    A. Insider language
    B. Doublespeak
    C. Stylizing
    D. Plagiarism

19. Which of the following should be included in a public relations campaign if you want to ensure people will hear, understand, and believe your message? 19.____
    A. Repetition
    B. Imagery
    C. Thoroughness
    D. Acceptance

20. In PR, what is it called when you track coverage and compare it over a period of time? 20.____
    A. Bookmarking
    B. Benchmarking
    C. Comparison analysis
    D. Correspondence

21. What is a baseline study PRIMARILY used for? 21.____
    A. To determine changes in audience perception and attitude
    B. To figure out how well your company is doing in the marketplace compared to your competitors
    C. To find out the cost of buying space taken up by a particular article if that article is an advertisement
    D. None of the above

22. Of the following people, who would BEST be considered a modern role model for successful public relations?   22._____
    A. Phineas T. Barnum (Barnum and Bailey)
    B. Ivy Lee
    C. Andrew Jackson
    D. Sir Walter Raleigh

23. If your organization has recently participated in a "publicity stunt," what type of PR strategy have you just used?   23._____
    A. Community   B. Lobbying
    C. News management   D. Crisis management

24. You tell your supervisor that you want to start using video press releases. When he presses you to explain why, you tell him that you want to take advantage of the fact that   24._____
    A. many news agencies don't review them ahead of broadcasting
    B. most reporters hired to create them have contacts within the industry
    C. they cover stories that some local news organizations cannot
    D. the production value may be better than those at local stations

25. A _____ is a type of news leak in which the source reveals large policy changes are on the table.   25._____
    A. disclosure   B. hook   C. exclusive   D. trial balloon

KEY (CORRECT ANSWERS)

1. C
2. B
3. C
4. B
5. D

6. B
7. A
8. B
9. D
10. C

11. B
12. D
13. A
14. A
15. D

16. D
17. C
18. B
19. A
20. B

21. A
22. B
23. C
24. C
25. D

TEST 4

DIRECTIONS: Each question or incomplete statement is followed by several suggested answers or completions. Select the one that BEST answers the question or completes the statement. *PRINT THE LETTER OF THE CORRECT ANSWER IN THE SPACE AT THE RIGHT.*

1. The Facial Feedback Hypothesis is a popular nonverbal theory that is BEST defined as
   A. people mirroring each other's facial expressions
   B. emotions leading to certain facial expressions
   C. facial expression can lead to the experience of certain emotions
   D. looking into a mirror while making a facial expression can cause one to change their facial expression

   1.____

2. Of the following, which is NOT recognized as a function of smiling?
   A. It provides feedback.
   B. It signals disinterest.
   C. It helps establish rapport.
   D. It signals attentiveness.

   2.____

3. When facial expressions are limited by cultural expectations, that is referred to as
   A. display rules
   B. syntactic displays
   C. adaptors
   D. interaction intensification

   3.____

4. Of the following, which is recognized as part of the six basic emotions across cultures globally?
   A. Guilt
   B. Happiness
   C. Fear
   D. Both B and C

   4.____

5. Which kinds of communication scenarios are more likely to see leadership roles develop from?
   A. Small group
   B. Intrapersonal communication
   C. Face-to-face public communication
   D. Text messaging

   5.____

6. Which of the following highlights the key difference between small group communication and organizational communication?
   A. Feedback is easier and more immediate in organizational.
   B. Communication is more informal in small group communication.
   C. The message is easier to adapt to the specific needs of the receiver in organizational communication.
   D. People are more spread out in small group communication.

   6.____

7. Which of the following would be an example of mediated communication?
   A. A principal addresses the student body in a speech.
   B. Two friends communicate while they work together in class.
   C. An employee texts his coworkers to see if they want to hang out after work.
   D. Three friends joke with one another while attending a concert.

   7.____

8. Which of the following is FALSE concerning the way interpersonal relationships can affect us physically?
   A. Without interpersonal relationships, we can become sick
   B. These interpersonal relationships are necessary for humans; according to most research, humans raised in isolation are less healthy than those raised with others
   C. Humans are not the only mammals that need relationships in order to survive and thrive
   D. Interpersonal relationships are necessary until about age 12, but not later in adulthood

9. Which of the following is a characteristic of public relationships as they compare to private relationships?
   A. Intrinsic rewards
   B. Normative rules
   C. Use of particularistic knowledge
   D. Small number of intimates

10. When someone asks how you know they were angry, it is likely they fall into which style of facial expressions?
    A. Withholder
    B. Revealer
    C. Frozen-affect expressor
    D. Unwitting expressor

11. The theory of expectancy violations is BEST defined as
    A. nonverbal behavior reciprocated based primarily on positive or negative valence and the perceived reward value of the other person
    B. the process of intimacy exchange within a dyad relationship
    C. a social rule that says we should repay in kind what another has provided us
    D. none of the above

12. If an employee has a very good idea of what is and is not socially acceptable in any given situation, which kind of linguistic competence is she strong in?
    A. Phonemic   B. Syntactic   C. Pragmatic   D. Semantic

13. Which of the following would NOT be considered sexist language?
    A. Although a girl, Sonia is very brave.
    B. A gorgeous model, Johnny also likes to use his surfboard on the weekends.
    C. Jimmy's brother is a male nurse.
    D. None; all are considered to be sexist.

14. What is it called when individual experience, and NOT conventional agreement, creates meaning?
    A. Small talk communication
    B. Denotative meaning
    C. Connotative meaning
    D. Self-reflexive communication

15. Which of the following kinds of communication do students spend the MOST time engaged in?
    A. Listening   B. Writing   C. Reading   D. Speaking

16. Which of the following would be evidence of active listening?
    A. Maintain eye contact
    B. Nodding and making eye contact
    C. Asking for clarification
    D. All of the above

17. When listening in an evaluative context, which of the following must be done for it to be considered successful?
    A. Precisely disseminate stimuli in a message
    B. Comprehend the intended meaning of a message
    C. Make critical assessments of the accuracy of the facts in a message
    D. All of the above

18. A friend visits one day and tells you she thinks her husband is cheating on her with his ex-wife. She tells you she doesn't know what to do because she can't imagine living without him. If you wanted to paraphrase, which of the following BEST exemplifies that?
    A. "You are feeling insecure because you don't have a very good relationship with your husband."
    B. "You're afraid your husband is seeing his ex-wife behind your back; you don't know what to do; and you can't live without him."
    C. "You're afraid that your husband may still have feelings for his ex-wife and you're afraid you'll lose him."
    D. "Don't worry; his ex-wife is not back with him. You're just being paranoid."

19. When we form impressions of others, when might the recency effect impact our assessments? If we
    A. focus on our own feelings instead of the feelings of others
    B. are motivated to be more accurate or expect to be held accountable for our own perceptions
    C. engage in self-monitoring of our behaviors
    D. employ the discounting rule

20. Which of the following BEST defines a "modal self"?
    A. The ideal person for a social order
    B. A person who does not go to extremes
    C. The kind of self valued in the 20th century but not the 21st century
    D. The person who monitors his own behavior in social situations

21. Which of the following is TRUE of today's society?
    A. People are less selfish than they have ever been.
    B. People spend most of their time trying to be a single, unitary self.
    C. People have many short-lived relationships leading to their notions of themselves changing easily.
    D. People try to be frugal, honorable, and self-sacrificing.

22. A man's childhood consisted of a dismissing attachment style. Which of the following behaviors will he MOST likely exhibit as an adult?
    A. Anxiousness and ambivalence
    B. Obsessive friendliness and dependence
    C. Autonomy and distance from others
    D. Rhetorical sensitivity

23. When practicing self-disclosure, which of the following is a good rule of thumb?
    A. Be sure to disclose more than your partner
    B. Reserve your most important disclosures for people you know well
    C. Ignore the style of disclosure; the only thing that is important is content
    D. All of the above

24. During your first meeting as project leader, you approach your group and inform them that John will serve as your assistant project leader. He will be responsible for chairing team meetings and establishing the agenda. When John is given this formal leadership position, what type of power does he have over the other members of the project?
    A. Legitimate   B. Reward   C. Expert   D. Punishment

25. If you bring an employee to lead a project because she is knowledgeable and skilled in the area the project focuses on, what type of power does she possess?
    A. Legitimate   B. Reward   C. Referent   D. Expert

KEY (CORRECT ANSWERS)

1. C
2. B
3. A
4. D
5. A

6. B
7. C
8. D
9. B
10. D

11. A
12. C
13. D
14. C
15. A

16. D
17. C
18. B
19. D
20. A

21. C
22. C
23. B
24. A
25. D

COMMUNICATION

EXAMINATION SECTION
TEST 1

DIRECTIONS: Each question or incomplete statement is followed by several suggested answers or completions. Select the one that BEST answers the question or completes the statement. *PRINT THE LETTER OF THE CORRECT ANSWER IN THE SPACE AT THE RIGHT.*

1. In some agencies the counsel to the agency head is given the right to bypass the chain of command and issue orders directly to the staff concerning matters that involve certain specific processes and practices.
   This situation MOST nearly illustrates the principle of _____ authority.
   A. the acceptance theory of
   B. multiple-linear
   C. splintered
   D. functional

   1._____

2. It is commonly understood that communication is an important part of the administrative process.
   Which of the following is NOT a valid principle of the communication process in administration?
   A. The channels of communication should be spontaneous.
   B. The lines of communication should be as direct and as short as possible.
   C. Communications should be authenticated.
   D. The persons serving in communications centers should be competent.

   2._____

3. Of the following, the one factor which is generally considered LEAST essential to successful committee operations is
   A. stating a clear definition of the authority and scope of the committee
   B. selecting the committee chairman carefully
   C. limiting the size of the committee to four persons
   D. limiting the subject matter to that which can be handled in group discussion

   3._____

4. Of the following, the failure by line managers to accept and appreciate the benefits and limitations of a new program or system VERY FREQUENTLY can be traced to the
   A. budgetary problems involved
   B. resultant need to reduce staff
   C. lack of controls it engenders
   D. failure of top management to support its implementation

   4._____

5. If a manager were thinking about using a committee of subordinates to solve an operating problem, which of the following would generally NOT be an advantage of such use of the committee approach?
   A. Improved coordination
   B. Low cost
   C. Increased motivation
   D. Integrated judgment

   5._____

31

6. Every supervisor has many occasions to lead a conference or participate in a conference of some sort.
Of the following statements that pertain to conferences and conference leadership, which is generally considered to be MOST valid?
   A. Since World War II, the trend has been toward fewer shared decisions and more conferences.
   B. The most important part of a conference leader's job is to direct discussion.
   C. In providing opportunities for group interaction, management should avoid consideration of its past management philosophy.
   D. A good administrator cannot lead a good conference if he is a poor public speaker.

6.____

7. Of the following, it is usually LEAST desirable for a conference leader to
   A. call the name of a person after asking a question
   B. summarize proceedings periodically
   C. make a practice of repeating questions
   D. ask a question without indicating who is to reply

7.____

8. Assume that, in a certain organization, a situation has developed in which there is little difference in status or authority between individuals.
Which of the following would be the MOST likely result with regard to communication in this organization?
   A. Both the accuracy and flow of communication will be improved.
   B. Both the accuracy and flow of communication will substantially decrease.
   C. Employees will seek more formal lines of communication.
   D. Neither the flow nor the accuracy of communication will be improved over the former hierarchical structure.

8.____

9. The main function of many agency administrative officers is "information management." Information that is received by an administrative officer may be classified as active or passive, depending upon whether or not it requires the recipient to take some action.
Of the following, the item received which is clearly the MOST active information is
   A. an appointment of a new staff member
   B. a payment voucher for a new desk
   C. a press release concerning a past event
   D. the minutes of a staff meeting

9.____

10. Of the following, the one LEAST considered to be a communication barrier is
    A. group feedback   B. charged words
    C. selective perception D. symbolic meanings

10.____

3 (#1)

11. Management studies support the hypothesis that, in spite of the tendency of employees to censor the information communicated to their supervisor, subordinates are more likely to communicate problem-oriented information UPWARD when they have a
    A. long period of service in the organization
    B. high degree of trust in the supervisor
    C. high educational level
    D. low status on the organizational ladder

    11.____

12. Electronic data processing equipment can produce more information faster than can be generated by any other means.
    In view of this, the MOST important problem faced by management at present is to
    A. keep computers fully occupied
    B. find enough computer personnel
    C. assimilate and properly evaluate the information
    D. obtain funds to establish appropriate information systems

    12.____

13. A well-designed management information system essentially provides each executive and manager the information he needs for
    A. determining computer time requirements
    B. planning and measuring results
    C. drawing a new organization chart
    D. developing a new office layout

    13.____

14. It is generally agreed that management policies should be periodically reappraised and restated in accordance with current conditions.
    Of the following, the approach which would be MOST effective in determining whether a policy should be revised is to
    A. conduct interviews with staff members at all levels in order to ascertain the relationship between the policy and actual practice
    B. make proposed revisions in the policy and apply it to current problems
    C. make up hypothetical situations using both the old policy and a revised version in order to make comparisons
    D. call a meeting of top level staff in order to discuss ways of revising the policy

    14.____

15. Your superior has asked you to notify division employees of an important change in one of the operating procedures described in the division manual. Every employee presently has a copy of this manual.
    Which of the following is normally the MOST practical way to get the employees to understand such a change?
    A. Notify each employee individually of the change and answer any questions he might have
    B. Send a written notice to key personnel, directing them to inform the people under them

    15.____

33

C. Call a general meeting, distribute a corrected page for the manual, and discuss the change
D. Send a memo to employees describing the change in general terms and asking them to make the necessary corrections in their copies of the manual

16. Assume that the work in your department involves the use of any technical terms.
In such a situation, when you are answering inquiries from the general public, it would usually be BEST to
   A. use simple language and avoid the technical terms
   B. employ the technical terms whenever possible
   C. bandy technical terms freely, but explain each term in parentheses
   D. apologize if you are forced to use a technical term

17. Suppose that you receive a telephone call from someone identifying himself as an employee in another city department who asks to be given information which your own department regards as confidential.
Which of the following is the BEST way of handling such a request?
   A. Give the information requested, since your caller as official standing
   B. Grant the request, provided the caller gives you a signed receipt
   C. Refuse the request, because you have no way of knowing whether the caller is really who he claims to be
   D. Explain that the information is confidential and inform the caller of the channels he must go through to have the information released to him

18. Studies show that office employees place high importance on the social and human aspects of the organization. What office employees like best about their jobs is the kind of people with whom they work. So strive hard to group people who are most likely to get along well together.
Based on this information, it is MOST reasonable to assume that office workers are most pleased to work in a group which
   A. is congenial   B. has high productivity
   C. allows individual creativity D. is unlike other groups

19. A certain supervisor does not compliment members of his staff when they come up with good ideas. He feels that coming up with good ideas is part of the job and does not merit special attention.
This supervisor's practice is
   A. *poor*, because recognition for good ideas is a good motivator
   B. *poor*, because the staff will suspect that the supervisor has no good ideas of his own
   C. *good*, because it is reasonable to assume that employees will tell their supervisor of ways to improve office practice
   D. *good*, because the other members of the staff are not made to seem inferior by comparison

20. Some employees of a department have sent an anonymous letter containing many complaints to the department head.
    Of the following, what is this MOST likely to show about the department?
    A. It is probably a good place to work.
    B. Communications are probably poor.
    C. The complaints are probably unjustified.
    D. These employees are probably untrustworthy.

21. Which of the following actions would usually be MOST appropriate for a supervisor to take after receiving an instruction sheet from his superior explaining a new procedure which is to be followed?
    A. Put the instruction sheet aside temporarily until he determines what is wrong with the old procedure.
    B. Call his superior and ask whether the procedure is one he must implement immediately.
    C. Write a memorandum to the superior asking for more details.
    D. Try the new procedure and advise the superior of any problems or possible improvements.

22. Of the following, which one is considered the PRIMARY advantage of using a committee to resolved a problem in an organization?
    A. No one person will be held accountable for the decision since a group of people was involved.
    B. People with different backgrounds give attention to the problem.
    C. The decision will take considerable time so there is unlikely to be a decision that will later be regretted.
    D. One person cannot dominate the decision-making process.

23. Employees in a certain office come to their supervisor with all their complaints about the office and the work. Almost every employee has had at least one minor complaint at some time.
    The situation with respect to complaints in this office may BEST be described as probably
    A. *good*; employees who complain care about their jobs and work hard
    B. *good*; grievances brought out into the open can be corrected
    C. *bad*; only serious complaints should be discussed
    D. *bad*; it indicates the staff does not have confidence in the administration

24. The administrator who allows his staff to suggest ways to do their work will usually find that
    A. this practice contributes to high productivity
    B. the administrator's ideas produce greater output
    C. clerical employees suggest inefficient work methods
    D. subordinate employees resent performing a management function

25. The MAIN purpose for a supervisor's questioning the employees at a conference he is holding is to
    A. stress those areas of information covered but not understood by the participants
    B. encourage participants to think through the problem under discussion
    C. catch those subordinates who are not paying attention
    D. permit the more knowledgeable participants to display their grasp of the problems being discussed

KEY (CORRECT ANSWERS)

1.	D		11.	B
2.	A		12.	C
3.	C		13.	B
4.	D		14.	A
5.	B		15.	C
6.	B		16.	A
7.	C		17.	D
8.	D		18.	A
9.	A		19.	A
10.	A		20.	B

21.	D
22.	B
23.	B
24.	A
25.	B

TEST 2

DIRECTIONS: Each question or incomplete statement is followed by several suggested answers or completions. Select the one that BEST answers the question or completes the statement. *PRINT THE LETTER OF THE CORRECT ANSWER IN THE SPACE AT THE RIGHT.*

1. For a superior to use *consultative supervision* with his subordinates effectively, it is ESSENTIAL that he
    A. accept the fact that his formal authority will be weakened by the procedure
    B. admit that he does not know more than all his men together and that his ideas are not always best
    C. utilize a committee system so that the procedure is orderly
    D. make sure that all subordinates are consulted so that no one feels left out

    1.____

2. The *grapevine* is an informal means of communication in an organization. The attitude of a supervisor with respect to the grapevine should be to
    A. ignore it since it deals mainly with rumors and sensational information
    B. regard it as a serious danger which should be eliminated
    C. accept it as a real line of communication which should be listened to
    D. utilize it for most purposes instead of the official line of communication

    2.____

3. The supervisor of an office that must deal with the public should realize that planning in this type of work situation
    A. is useless because he does not know how many people will request service or what service they will request
    B. must be done at a higher level but that he should be ready to implement the results of such planning
    C. is useful primarily for those activities that are not concerned with public contact
    D. is useful for all the activities of the office, including those that relate to public contact

    3.____

4. Assume that it is your job to receive incoming telephone calls. Those calls which you cannot handle yourself have to be transferred to the appropriate office.
    If you receive an outside call for an extension line which is busy, the one of the following which you should do FIRST is to
    A. interrupt the person speaking on the extension and tell him a call is waiting
    B. tell the caller the line is busy and let him know every thirty seconds whether or not it is free
    C. leave the caller on "hold" until the extension is free
    D. tell the caller the line is busy and ask him if he wishes to wait

    4.____

5. Your superior has subscribed to several publications directly related to your division's work, and he has asked you to see to it that the publications are circulated among the supervisory personnel in the division. There are eight supervisors involved.
The BEST method of insuring that all eight see these publications is to
   A. place the publication in the division's general reference library as soon as it arrives
   B. inform each supervisor whenever a publication arrives and remind all of them that they are responsible for reading it
   C. prepare a standard slip that can be stapled to each publication, listing the eight supervisors and saying, "Please read, initial your name, and pass along"
   D. send a memo to the eight supervisors saying that they may wish to purchase individual subscriptions in their own names if they are interested in seeing each issue

5.____

6. Your superior has telephoned a number of key officials in your agency to ask whether they can meet at a certain time next month. He has found that they can all make it, and he has asked you to confirm the meeting.
Which of the following is the BEST way to confirm such a meeting?
   A. Note the meeting on your superior's calendar.
   B. Post a notice of the meeting on the agency bulletin board.
   C. Call the officials on the day of the meeting to remind them of the meeting.
   D. Write a memo to each official involved, repeating the time and place of the meeting.

6.____

7. Assume that a new city regulation requires that certain kinds of private organizations file information forms with your department. You have been asked to write the short explanatory message that will be printed on the front cover of the pamphlet containing the forms and instructions.
Which of the following would be the MOST appropriate way of beginning this message?
   A. Get the readers' attention by emphasizing immediately that there are legal penalties for organizations that fail to file before a certain date.
   B. Briefly state the nature of the enclosed forms and the types of organizations that must file.
   C. Say that your department is very sorry to have to put organizations to such an inconvenience.
   D. Quote the entire regulation adopted by the city, even if it is quite long and is expressed din complicated legal language.

7.____

8. Suppose that you have been told to make up the vacation schedule for the 18 employees in a particular unit. In order for the unit to operate effectively, only a few employees can be on vacation at the same time.
Which of the following is the MOST advisable approach in making up the schedule?
   A. Draw up a schedule assigning vacations in alphabetical order
   B. Find out when the supervisors want to take their vacations, and randomly assign whatever periods are left to the non-supervisory personnel

8.____

C. Assign the most desirable times to employees of longest standing and the least desirable times to the newest employees
D. Have all employees state their own preference, and then work out any conflicts in consultation with the people involved

9. Assume that you have been asked to prepare job descriptions for various positions in your department.
   Which of the following are the basic points that should be covered in a *job description*?
   A. General duties and responsibilities of the position, with examples of day-to-day tasks
   B. Comments on the performances of present employees
   C. Estimates of the number of openings that may be available in each category during the coming year
   D. Instructions for carrying out the specific tasks assigned to your department

9.____

10. Of the following, the biggest DISADVANTAGE in allowing a free flow of communications in an agency is that such a free flow
    A. decreases creativity
    B. increases the use of the *grapevine*
    C. lengthens the chain of command
    D. reduces the executive's power to direct the flow of information

10.____

11. A downward flow of authority in an organization is one example of _____ communication.
    A. horizontal   B. informal   C. circular   D. vertical

11.____

12. Of the following, the one that would MOST likely block effective communication is
    A. concentration only on the issues at hand
    B. lack of interest or commitment
    C. use of written reports
    D. use of charts and graphs

12.____

13. An ADVANTAGE of the *lecture* as a teaching tool is that it
    A. enables a person to present his ideas to a large number of people
    B. allows the audience to retain a maximum of the information given
    C. holds the attention of the audience for the longest time
    D. enables the audience member to easily recall the main points

13.____

14. An ADVANTAGE of the *small-group* discussion as a teaching tool is that
    A. it always focuses attention on one person as the leader
    B. it places collective responsibility on the group as a whole
    C. its members gain experience by summarizing the ideas of others
    D. each member of the group acts as a member of a team

14.____

15. The one of the following that is an ADVANTAGE of a *large-group* discussion, when compared to a small-group discussion, is that the large-group discussion
    A. moves along more quickly than a small-group discussion
    B. allows its participants to feel more at ease, and speak out more freely
    C. gives the whole group a chance to exchange ideas on a certain subject at the same occasion
    D. allows its members to feel a greater sense of personal responsibility

15.____

KEY (CORRECT ANSWERS)

1.	D	6.	D	11.	D
2.	C	7.	B	12.	B
3.	D	8.	D	13.	A
4.	D	9.	A	14.	D
5.	C	10.	D	15.	C

EXAMINATION SECTION

TEST 1

DIRECTIONS: Each question or incomplete statement is followed by several suggested answers or completions. Select the one that BEST answers the question or completes the statement. *PRINT THE LETTER OF THE CORRECT ANSWER IN THE SPACE AT THE RIGHT.*

1. Managing conflict effectively by avoiding no-win situations, positively influencing the actions of others and using _____ strategies are what make a great leader. 1.____
    A. persuasive   B. ambiguous   C. prosecution   D. performance

2. In today's business world, collaboration will bring together people from distinct backgrounds. These collaborative groups may not share common norms, morals or _____, but they can offer unique _____. 2.____
    A. vocabulary; perspectives
    B. salaries; vocabulary
    C. modifications; insights
    D. perspectives; salaries

3. E-mail is a great tool for communication; however, which of the following should you be careful of when in electronic communication with a colleague? 3.____
    A. Font size
    B. E-mail length
    C. Font color
    D. Tone of voice

4. A formal relationship can BEST be described as 4.____
    A. regulated by procedures or directives
    B. personal and relaxed
    C. emotionally distant and very uncomfortable
    D. confusing and unproductive

5. John is in a meeting with his supervisor ad coworkers. He is thinking about what he's going to have for dinner that night when his boss asks him a question. John can repeat back what his supervisor said, but he cannot retain what was said during the meeting. 5.____
    This is a classic example of failing to
    A. focus at work
    B. effectively listen
    C. leave personal plans outside the workplace
    D. care about meetings

6. A person's choice of _____ can directly affect communication. 6.____
    A. clothing   B. food   C. hygiene   D. words

7. Why is it important to relax when communicating with team members? 7.____
    A. Relaxing always means having better ideas.
    B. People will automatically like you more if you are relaxed.

C. If you are nervous, you may talk too quickly and make it hard for others to understand your message or directive.
D. No one likes someone who is always working, so it is important to relax and not work too hard.

8. In order to show you are genuinely interested in what others have to say, you should
   A. tell them how nice they are
   B. repeat what they say back to them
   C. nod and find something to compliment them about
   D. ask questions and seek clarification from them

9. Jack and James are always arguing with one another. Their supervisor calls each one in separately to talk to them. He asks Jack to think about things from James' point of view and he asks James to do the same for Jack.
   What is the supervisor trying to get each person to do?
   A. Get along   B. Be positive
   C. Communicate effectively   D. Empathize

10. When working in groups, disagreements
    A. should be avoided at all costs
    B. are often a healthy way of building understanding and camaraderie
    C. lead coworkers to hate one another and the company they work for
    D. don't happen if the supervisor chooses the right people to work together

11. If things go wrong in a group situation, it is important to AVOID
    A. the boss   B. disagreements or arguments
    C. scapegoating   D. being polite and fair to one another

12. If you are a listener who likes to hear the rationale behind a message, your listening style would be described as _____ style.
    A. results   B. process   C. reasons   D. eye contact

13. Which of the following BEST describes a psychological barrier in communication?
    A. Molly is so stressed about her paying for her mortgage that she can't focus at work right now.
    B. John doesn't understand a lot of the terms the IT specialist used in an e-mail sent out to everyone.
    C. Jerry is a little older and has a hard time hearing everything so sometimes he misses parts of a conversation.
    D. Linda doesn't want to be at the company for longer than a few months, so she doesn't really try too hard to fit in.

14. Body language, also known as _____, is really important when building rapport with coworkers and communicating effectively.
    A. verbal language   B. kinesthetic
    C. non-verbal communication D. facial expressions

15. Which of the following might be a good example of someone who has a "closed" posture?
    A. Hands are apart on the arms of the chair.
    B. His/her arms are folded.
    C. They are directly facing you.
    D. They barely speak above a whisper.

15.____

16. Which of the following can eye contact be used for?
    A. To give and receive feedback
    B. To let someone know when it is their turn to speak
    C. To communicate how you feel about someone
    D. All of the above

16.____

17. Which of the following is NOT a form of non-verbal communication?
    A. Crossing your arms when talking to someone
    B. Using space within the room in a conversation
    C. Clearing your throat before you speak]
    D. Saying "10-4" when asked if you understand

17.____

18. Your best friend has just been hired at the company you work for. You notice he has come into work on several occasions after staying out late the night before. His work has not suffered yet, but you fear it will.
    Which of the following actions should you take to help prevent future problems?
    A. Do nothing; he's your friend but it is his life
    B. Try to talk to him and help him see the importance of not creating bad habits.
    C. Talk to your supervisor and tell him your friend isn't suitable for the job
    D. Tell your friend to change his ways or to quit

18.____

19. Interacting with coworkers can be positively or negatively affected by _____ when someone's previous biases and assumptions shape their reactions in future situations.
    A. racism   B. past experience
    C. interpersonal skills   D. active listening

19.____

20. Which of the following scenarios BEST describes a person who is being subjective?
    A. Sally is fair and honest when she listens to coworkers. She does not take sides and wants the best solution to the problem.
    B. Mike doesn't like Steve, because he thinks Steve is only out for himself. Still, Steve offers valuable insights, so Mike tries not to let personal feelings get in the way of working together.
    C. Jamie is dating Veronica's ex and Veronica just found out. Now, Veronica immediately shoots down anything Jamie suggests during a meeting as irrational and superfluous.
    D. None of the above

20.____

21. Which important communications tem is MOST closely defined as "the quality of a sound governed by the rate of vibrations producing it; the degree of highness or lowness of a tone"?
    A. Tone
    B. Pitch
    C. Effective communication
    D. Rationalization

22. _____ is when a person tries to make an imprudent and reckless action seem reasonable.
    A. Projection
    B. Self-deception
    C. Past experience
    D. Rationalization

23. When holding conversations with coworkers, you should
    A. do most of the talking
    B. let others do most of the talking
    C. try to split time between talking and listening
    D. zone out and wait for the meeting to finish

24. A new hire just arrived and you are meeting her for the first time. Which of the following actions is MOST appropriate?
    A. Walk up and introduce yourself with a smile and a handshake
    B. Wait for her to come and introduce herself
    C. Approach her and offer a hug to make her feel welcome
    D. Ignore the new hire; she is likely your competition

25. If you are the type of listener who likes to discuss concepts or issues in detail, you would MOST likely fall under which listening style?
    A. Process
    B. Reasons
    C. Results
    D. None of the above

KEY (CORRECT ANSWERS)

1.	A		11.	C
2.	A		12.	C
3.	D		13.	A
4.	A		14.	C
5.	B		15.	B
6.	D		16.	D
7.	C		17.	D
8.	D		18.	B
9.	D		19.	B
10.	B		20.	C

21. B
22. D
23. C
24. A
25. A

TEST 2

DIRECTIONS: Each question or incomplete statement is followed by several suggested answers or completions. Select the one that BEST answers the question or completes the statement. *PRINT THE LETTER OF THE CORRECT ANSWER IN THE SPACE AT THE RIGHT.*

1. Which of the following is an example of the BEST practice when communicating in the workplace?
    A. You are horrible with remembering names so you try to use nicknames to cover up for your poor memory.
    B. You only pay attention to the names of people who you work for or who you deem to be "important."
    C. You try to remember everyone's names and use them whenever possible.
    D. None of the above

1._____

2. Words of civility such as "please" and "thank you" should be used _____ when conversing with coworkers and business partners.
    A. always   B. sometimes   C. rarely   D. never

2._____

3. When communicating with others, one should _____ stand as close to them as possible and make body contact in order to get an important point across.
    A. always   B. sometimes   C. rarely   D. never

3._____

4. The MOST appropriate way to end a conversation is to
    A. seek a mutual resolution, but leave abruptly if it continues
    B. find a way to wrap up the conversation so the other person knows it is time to move on
    C. look impatient so hopefully the person will get the hint
    D. tell the other person the conversation should end

4._____

5. Another name for interpersonal communication in an office setting is
    A. peer-to-peer communication   B. mass communication
    C. virtual reality   D. e-mailing

5._____

6. Of the following statements, choose the one you feel is the MOST correct.
    A. Devoid of interpersonal communication, people become sick.
    B. Communication is not completely needed for humans.
    C. People are the only animals that need to have relationships in order to survive.
    D. Important communication is not really relevant until after you become an adult.

6._____

7. John is giving a presentation on ways to communicate effectively with peers. He is having trouble deciding on what to say in his speech.
   Which of the following statements should he AVOID using?
    A. Always try to understand another person's point of view or perspective
    B. Try to imagine what someone is going to say before they actually say it

7._____

C. Be aware of how non-verbal cues like eye contact and body language affect how your message is received
D. Both B and C

8. Which of the following would MOST affect our perception of communication with coworkers?
   A. Past experiences
   B. Marital problems
   C. Rumors spread about coworkers
   D. None of the above

9. Many people think of communication as both _____ and _____ messages.
   A. formal; informal
   B. hearing; listening
   C. sending; receiving
   D. finding; decoding

10. Why is context important in communication?
    A. It's important to know which buttons to push in order to get what you want.
    B. Saying something to one person may not have the same effect as saying it to someone else.
    C. Context is only important if you are worried about what others think.
    D. None of the above

11. If your brother is normally bright and talkative during the summer, but you notice he gets quiet and subdued in the winter, the MOST likely communication context he is dealing with would be
    A. relational   B. cultural   C. inner   D. physical

12. _____ is an example of a negative nonverbal action you can take.
    A. Smiling
    B. Using a tone of voice that matches your message
    C. Maintaining eye contact
    D. Slumping your shoulders

13. Cultural context can BEST be described as
    A. what people think of as it relates to the event they are participating in (i.e., wedding versus a funeral)
    B. the connection between a father and his son
    C. rules and patterns of Americans versus the Japanese
    D. thoughts, feelings, and sensations inside a person's head

14. Which of the following BEST describes feedback?
    A. Staring at the speaker while he talks
    B. Nodding and smiling while listening to a speaker
    C. Standing an appropriate distance away so the speaker does not get uncomfortable
    D. Trying to speak while the other person is speaking because you have something more important to say

15. Being able to communicate more effectively can be improved upon by
    A. continually making an effort to be as flexible as possible when talking to others
    B. committing to one style of speaking until you master it
    C. using the same style of correspondence as the person with whom you are speaking
    D. always using the opposite style of communication from the person you are speaking to

16. John walks up to Sally and compliments her on the dress she wore to work today. In his mind, John was just being friendly, but Sally went to her manager and filed a harassment charge against John.
    This miscommunication could MOST easily be classified as an error in what?
    A. Reality   B. Perception   C. Friendship   D. Loyalty

17. If a speaker's tone is flat and monotone, which of the following is the MOST likely reaction that listeners will have?
    They will
    A. enthused by the message
    B. enjoy the message but not be overly excited about it
    C. be polite and interested but will not seem very engaged
    D. be bored and uninterested in the message

18. When Steve speaks to his group about his ideas, he generally has a higher pitch to his voice and gesticulates frequently.
    This lead his team members to believe that Steve
    A. is enthusiastic and has great ideas for the group
    B. has had too much caffeine and needs to relax
    C. is trying to show off for the boss and make them look bad
    D. is extremely smart and great at his job

19. _____ is used when a person wants to add stress to key words in communication. It lets the audience understand the mood or feelings of particular words or phrases.
    A. Anger   B. Tone   C. Perception   D. Inflection

20. If Barry tells Bill that his haircut looks "great" and Bill can tell Barry is being insincere, which of the following tones is Barry MOST likely using?
    A. Affectionate B. Apologetic   C. Threatening   D. Sarcastic

21. As a supervisor, it is important that everyone clearly comprehends everything you communicate to them.
    In order to ensure this happens, which of the following things should you avoid?
    A. Overusing jargon
    B. Explaining something more than once
    C. Speaking slowly and annunciating everything
    D. Having meetings in the morning

22. If your supervisor is looking down at the ground or has his back to you as he is speaking, it MOST clearly indicates to those who are listening to him that the supervisor
    A. is shy and doesn't like speaking in front of people
    B. is disinterested and doesn't care what he's talking about
    C. is approachable and friendly
    D. dislikes his job and wants to get out as soon as possible

22.____

23. Interpersonal communication helps you
    A. know what others are thinking
    B. turn into an inspiring speaker, especially in public
    C. learn about yourself
    D. communicate with the general public

23.____

24. In general, people who smile more are perceived as
    A. devious   B. friendly
    C. attractive   D. easy to manipulate

24.____

25. If your supervisor constantly takes advantage of you and expresses his or her opinion often at the expense of you or other workers, which communication style are they MOST likely using?
    A. Nonassertive   B. Assertive   C. Aggressive   D. Peacemaking

25.____

KEY (CORRECT ANSWERS)

1.	C	11.	D
2.	A	12.	D
3.	D	13.	C
4.	B	14.	B
5.	A	15.	A
6.	A	16.	B
7.	B	17.	D
8.	A	18.	A
9.	C	19.	D
10.	B	20.	D

21. A
22. B
23. D
24. B
25. C

EXAMINATION SECTION
TEST 1

DIRECTIONS: Each question or incomplete statement is followed by several suggested answers or completions. Select the one that BEST answers the question or completes the statement. *PRINT THE LETTER OF THE CORRECT ANSWER IN THE SPACE AT THE RIGHT.*

1. It is often desirable for an administrator to consult, during the planning process, the persons to be affected by those plans.
   Of the following, the MAJOR justification for such consultation is that it recognizes the
   A. fact that participating in horizontal planning is almost always more effective than participating in vertical planning
   B. principle of participation and the need for a sense of belonging as a means of decreasing resistance and developing support
   C. principle that lower-level administrators normally are more likely than higher-level administrators to emphasize longer-range goals
   D. fact that final responsibility for the approval of plans should be placed in committees not individuals

1.____

2. In evaluating performance and, if necessary, correcting what is being done to assure attainment of results according to plan, it is GENERALLY best for the administrator to do which one of the following?
   A. Make a continual effort to increase the number of written control reports prepared
   B. Thoroughly investigate in equal detail all possible deviations indicated by comparison of performance to expectation
   C. Decentralize, within an operating unit or division, the responsibility for correcting deviations
   D. Concentrate on the exceptions, or outstanding variations, from the expected results or standards

2.____

3. Generally, changes in the ways in which the supervisors and employees in an organization do things are MORE likely to be welcomed by them when the changes
   A. threaten the security of the supervisors than when they do not
   B. are inaugurated after prior change has been assimilated than when they are inaugurated before other major changes have been assimilated
   C. follow a series of failures in changes when they follow a series of successful changes
   D. are dictated by personal order rather than when they result from an application of previously established impersonal principles

3.____

4. For sound organization relationships, of the following, it is generally MOST desirable that
   A. authority and responsibility be segregated from each other, in order to facilitate control
   B. the authority of a manager should be commensurate with his responsibility, and vice versa
   C. authority be defined as the obligation of an individual to carry out assigned activities to the best of his or her ability
   D. clear recognition be given to the fact that delegation of authority benefits only the manager who delegates it

5. In utilizing a checklist of questions for general managerial planning, which one of the following generally is the FIRST question to be asked and answered?
   A. Where will it take place?
   B. How will it be done?
   C. Why must it be done?
   D. Who will do it?

6. Of the following, it is USUALLY best to set administrative objectives so that they are
   A. at a level that is unattainable, so that administrators will continually be strongly motivated
   B. at a level that is attainable, but requires some stretching and reaching by administrators trying to attain them
   C. stated in qualitative rather than quantitative terms whenever a choice between the two is possible
   D. stated in a general and unstructured manner, to permit each administrator maximum freedom in interpreting them

7. In selecting from among administrative alternatives, three general bases for decisions are open to the manager – experience, experimentation, and research and analysis. Of the following, the best argument AGAINST primary reliance upon experimentation as the method of evaluating administrative alternatives is that experimentation is
   A. generally the most expensive of the three techniques
   B. almost always legally prohibited in procedural matters
   C. possible only in areas where results may be easily duplicated by other experimenters at any time
   D. an approach that requires information on scientific method seldom available to administrators

8. The administrator who utilizes the techniques of operations research, linear programming and simulation in making an administrative decision should MOST appropriately be considered to be using the techniques of _____ analysis.
   A. intuitive   B. quantitative
   C. nonmathematical   D. qualitative

9. When an additional organizational level is added within a department, that department has MOST directly manifested
   A. horizontal growth
   B. horizontal shrinkage
   C. vertical growth
   D. vertical shrinkage

9.____

10. Of the following, the one which GENERALLY is the most intangible planning factor is
    A. budget dollars allocated to a function
    B. square feet of space for office use
    C. number of personnel in various clerical titles
    D. emotional impact of a proposed personnel policy among employees

10.____

11. Departmentation by function is the same as, or most similar to, departmentation by
    A. equipment
    B. clientele
    C. territory
    D. activity

11.____

12. Such verifiable factors as turnover, absenteeism or volume of grievances would generally BEST assist in measuring the effectiveness of a program to improve
    A. forms control
    B. employee morale
    C. linear programming
    D. executive creativity

12.____

13. An organization increases the number of subordinates reporting to a manager up to the point where incremental savings in costs, better communication and morale, and other factors equal incremental losses in effectiveness of control, direction and similar factors. This action MOST specifically employs the technique of
    A. role playing
    B. queuing theory
    C. marginal analysis
    D. capital standards analysis

13.____

14. The term *computer hardware* is MOST likely to refer to
    A. machines and equipment
    B. Ethernet and USB cables
    C. training manuals
    D. word processing and spreadsheet programs

14.____

15. Determining what is being accomplished, that is, evaluating the performance and, if necessary, applying corrective measures so that performance takes place according to plans is MOST appropriately called management
    A. actuating
    B. planning
    C. controlling
    D. motivating

15.____

16. Of the following, the BEST overall technique for choosing from among several alternative public programs proposed to try to achieve the same broad objective generally is _____ analysis.
    A. random-sample
    B. input
    C. cost-effectiveness
    D. output

17. When the success of a plan in achieving specific program objectives is measured against that plan's costs, the measure obtained is most directly that of the plan's
    A. pervasiveness
    B. control potential
    C. primacy
    D. efficiency

18. Generally, the degree to which an organization's planning will be coordinated varies MOST directly with the degree to which
    A. the individuals charged with executing plans are better compensated than those charged with developing and evaluating plans
    B. the individuals charged with planning understand and agree to utilize consistent planning premises
    C. a large number of position classification titles have been established for those individuals charged with organizational planning functions
    D. subordinate unit objectives are allowed to control the overall objectives of the departments of which such subordinate units are a part

19. The responsibility for specific types of decisions generally is BEST delegated to
    A. the highest organizational level at which there is an individual possessing the ability, desire, impartiality and access to relevant information needed to make these decisions
    B. the lowest organizational level at which there is an individual possessing the ability, desire, impartiality and access to relevant information needed to make these decisions
    C. a group of executives, rather than a single executive, if these decisions deal with an emergency
    D. the organizational level midway between that which will have to carry out these decisions and that which will have to authorize the resources for their implementation

20. The process of managing by objectives is MOST likely to lead to a situation in which the
    A. goal accomplishment objectives of managers tend to have a longer timespan as one goes lower down the line in an organization
    B. establishment of quantitative goals for staff positions is generally easier than the establishment of quantitative goals for line positions
    C. development of objectives requires the manager to think of the way he will accomplish given results, and of the organization, personnel and resources that he will need
    D. superiors normally develop and finally approve detailed goals for subordinates without any prior consultation with either those subordinates or with the top-level executives responsible for the longer-run objectives of the organization

21. As used with respect to decision making, the application of scientific method to the study of alternatives in a problem situation, with a view to providing a quantitative basis for arriving at an optimum solution in terms of the goals sought is MOST appropriately called
    A. simple number departmentation
    B. geographic decentralization
    C. operations research
    D. trait rating

21._____

22. Assume that a bureau head proposes that final responsibility and authority for all planning within the bureau is to be delegated to one employee who is to be paid at the level of an assistant division head in that bureau.
    Of the following, the MOST appropriate comment about this proposal is that it's
    A. *improper*, mainly because planning does not call for someone at such a high level
    B. *improper*, mainly because responsibility for a basic management function such as planning may not properly be delegated as proposed
    C. *proper*, mainly because ultimate responsibility for all bureau planning is best placed as proposed
    D. *proper*, mainly because every well-managed bureau should have a full-time planning officer

22._____

23. Of the following, the MOST important reason that participation has motivating effects is generally that it gives to the individual participating
    A. a recognition of his or her desire to feel important and to contribute to achievement of worthwhile goals
    B. an opportunity to participate in work that is beyond the scope of the class specification for his or her title
    C. a secure knowledge that his or her organization's top leadership is as efficient as possible considering all major circumstances
    D. the additional information likely to be crucial to his or her promotion

23._____

24. Of the following, the MOST essential characteristic of an effective employee suggestion system is that
    A. suggestions be submitted upward through the chain of command
    B. suggestions be acted upon promptly so that employees may be promptly informed of what happens to their submitted suggestions
    C. suggesters be required to sign their names on the material sent to the actual evaluators for evaluation
    D. suggesters receive at least 25% of the agency's savings during the first two years after their suggestions have been accepted and put into effect by the agency

24._____

25. Two organizations have the same basic objectives and the same total number of employees. The span of authority of each intermediate manager is narrower in one organization than it is in the other. It is MOST likely that the organization in which each intermediate manager has a narrower span of authority will have
   A. fewer intermediate managers
   B. more organizational levels
   C. more managers reporting to a larger number of intermediate supervisors
   D. more characteristics of a *flat* organizational structure

25.____

KEY (CORRECT ANSWERS)

1.	B	11.	D
2.	D	12.	B
3.	B	13.	C
4.	B	14.	A
5.	C	15.	C
6.	B	16.	C
7.	A	17.	D
8.	B	18.	B
9.	C	19.	B
10.	D	20.	C

21. C
22. B
23. A
24. B
25. B

TEST 2

DIRECTIONS: Each question or incomplete statement is followed by several suggested answers or completions. Select the one that BEST answers the question or completes the statement. *PRINT THE LETTER OF THE CORRECT ANSWER IN THE SPACE AT THE RIGHT.*

1. Which one of the following BEST expresses the essence of the merit idea or system in public employment?
    A. A person's worth to the organization—the merit of his or her attributes and capacities—is the governing factor in his or her selection, assignment, pay, recognition, advancement and retention
    B. Written tests of the objective type are the only fair way to select on a merit basis from among candidates for open-competitive appointment to positions within the merit system
    C. Employees who have qualified for civil service positions shall have lifetime tenure during good behavior in those positions regardless of changes in public programs
    D. Periodic examinations with set date limits within which all persons desiring to demonstrate their merit may apply, shall be publicly advertised and held for all promotional titles

1.____

2. Of the following, the promotion selection policy generally considered MOST antithetical to the merit concept is the promotion selection policy which
    A. is based solely on objective tests of competence
    B. is based solely on seniority
    C. may require a manager to lose his or her best employee to another part of the organization
    D. permits operating managers collectively to play a significant role in promotion decisions

2.____

3. Of the following, the problems encountered by government establishments which are MOST likely to make extensive delegation of authority difficult to effectuate tend to be problems of
    A. accountability and ensuring uniform administration
    B. line and staff relationships within field offices
    C. generally employee opposition to such delegation of authority and to the subsequent record-keeping activities
    D. use of the management-by-objectives approach

3.____

4. The major decisions as to which jobs shall be created and who shall carry which responsibilities should GENERALLY be made by
    A. budgetary advisers
    B. line managers
    C. classification specialists
    D. peer-level rating committees

4.____

5. The ultimate controlling factor in structuring positions in the public service, MOST generally, should be the
   A. possibility of providing upgrading for highly productive employees
   B. collective bargaining demands initially made by established public employee unions
   C. positive motivational effects upon productivity resulting from an inverted pyramid job structure
   D. effectiveness of the structuring in serving the mission of the organization

6. Of the following, the most usual reason for unsatisfactory line-staff relationships is
   A. inept use of the abilities of staff personnel by line management
   B. the higher salaries paid to line officials
   C. excessive consultation between line officials and staff officials at the same organizational level
   D. a feeling among the staff members that only lower-level line members appreciate their work

7. Generally, an employee receiving new information from a fellow employee is MOST likely to
   A. forget the new information if it is consistent with his or her existing beliefs much more easily than he or she forgets the new information if it is inconsistent with existing beliefs
   B. accept the validity of the new information if it is consistent with his or her existing beliefs more readily than he or she accepts the validity of the new information if it is inconsistent with existing beliefs
   C. have a less accurate memory of the new information if it is consistent with his or her existing beliefs than he or she has of the new information if it is inconsistent with existing beliefs
   D. ignore the new information if it is consistent with his or her existing beliefs more often than he or she ignores the new information if it is inconsistent with existing beliefs

8. Virtually all of us use this principle in our human communications – perhaps without realizing it. In casual conversations, we are alert for cues to whether we are understood (e.g., attentive nods from the other person). Similarly, an instructor is always interested in reactions among those to whom he is giving instruction. The effective administrator is equally conscious of the need to determine his or her subordinates' reactions to what he or she is trying to communicate.
   The principle referred to in the above selection is MOST appropriately called
   A. cognitive dissonance   B. feedback
   C. negative reinforcement   D. noise transmission

9. Of the following, the PRINCIPAL function of an *ombudsman* generally is to
    A. review departmental requests for new data processing equipment so as to reduce duplication
    B. receive and investigate complaints from citizens who are displeased with the actions or non-actions of administrative officials and try to effectuate warranted remedies
    C. review proposed departmental reorganizations in order to advise the chief executive whether or not they are in accordance with the latest principles of proper management structuring
    D. presiding over courts of the judiciary convened to try *sitting* judges

10. Of the following, the MOST valid reason for recruiting an intermediate-level administrator from outside an agency, rather than from within the agency, normally is to
    A. improve the public image of the agency as a desirable place in which to be employed
    B. reduce the number of potential administrators who must be evaluated prior to filling the position
    C. minimize the morale problems arising from frequent internal staff upgradings
    D. obtain fresh ideas and a fresh viewpoint on agency problems

11. A MAJOR research finding regarding employee absenteeism is that
    A. absenteeism is likely to be higher on hot days
    B. male employees tend to be absent more than female employees
    C. the way an employee is treated as a definite bearing on absenteeism
    D. the distance employees have to travel is one of the most important factors in absenteeism

12. Of the following, the supervisory behavior that is of GREATEST benefit to the organization is exhibited by supervisors who
    A. are strict with subordinates about following rules and regulations
    B. encourage subordinates to be interested in the work
    C. are willing to assist with subordinates' work on most occasions
    D. get the most done with available staff and resources

13. The management of time is one of the critical aspects of any supervisor's performance.
    Therefore, in evaluating a subordinate from the viewpoint of how he manages time, a supervisor should rate HIGHEST the subordinate who
    A. concentrates on each task as he undertakes it
    B. performs at a standard and predictable pace under all circumstances
    C. takes shortened lunch periods when he is busy
    D. tries to do two things simultaneously

14. A MAJOR research finding regarding employee absenteeism is that
    A. absenteeism is likely to be higher on hot days
    B. male employees tend to be absent more than female employees
    C. the way an employee is treated as a definite bearing on absenteeism
    D. the distance employees have to travel is one of the most important factors in absenteeism

15. Of the following, the supervisory behavior that is of GREATEST benefit to the organization is exhibited by supervisors who
    A. are strict with subordinates about following rules and regulations
    B. encourage subordinates to be interested in the work
    C. are willing to assist with subordinates' work on most occasions
    D. get the most done with available staff and resources

16. In order to maintain a proper relationship with a worker who is assigned to staff rather than line functions, a line supervisor should
    A. accept all recommendations of the staff worker
    B. include the staff worker in the conferences called by the supervisor for his subordinates
    C. keep the staff worker informed of developments in the area of his staff assignment
    D. require that the staff worker's recommendations be communicated to the supervisor through the supervisor's own superior

17. Of the following, the GREATEST disadvantage of placing a worker in a staff position under the direct supervision of the supervisor whom he advises is the possibility that the
    A. staff worker will tend to be insubordinate because of a feeling of superiority over the supervisor
    B. staff worker will tend to give advice of the type which the supervisor wants to hear or finds acceptable
    C. supervisor will tend to be mistrustful of the advice of a worker of subordinate rank
    D. supervisor will tend to derive little benefit from the advice because to supervise properly he should know at least as much as his subordinate

18. One factor which might be given consideration in deciding upon the optimum span of control of a supervisor over his immediate subordinates is the position of the supervisor in the hierarchy of the organization.
It is generally considered proper that the number of subordinates immediately supervised by a higher, upper echelon, supervisor
    A. is unrelated to and tends to form no pattern with the number of supervised by lower level supervisors
    B. should be about the same as the number supervised by a lower level supervisor
    C. should be larger than the number supervised by a lower level supervisor
    D. should be smaller than the number supervised by a lower level supervisor

18.____

19. Assume that you are a supervisor and have been assigned to assist the head of a large agency unit. He asks you to prepare a simple, functional organization chart of the unit.
Such a chart would be USEFUL for
    A. favorably impressing members of the public with the important nature of the agency's work
    B. graphically presenting staff relationships which may indicate previously unknown duplications, overlaps, and gaps in job duties
    C. motivating all employees toward better performance because they will have a better understanding of job procedures
    D. subtly and inoffensively making known to the staff in the unit that you are now in a position of responsibility

19.____

20. In some large organizations, management's traditional means of learning about employee dissatisfaction has been in the *open door policy*.
This policy USUALLY means that
    A. management lets it be known that a management representative is generally available to discuss employees' questions, suggestions, and complaints
    B. management sets up an informal employee organization to establish a democratic procedure for orderly representation of employees
    C. employees are encouraged to attempt to resolve dissatisfactions at the lowest possible level of authority
    D. employees are provided with an address or box so that they may safely and anonymously register complaints

20.____

KEY (CORRECT ANSWERS)

1.	B	11.	A
2.	A	12.	D
3.	D	13.	A
4.	B	14.	C
5.	A	15.	D
6.	A	16.	C
7.	B	17.	B
8.	B	18.	D
9.	D	19.	B
10.	C	20.	A

EXAMINATION SECTION
TEST 1

DIRECTIONS: Each question or incomplete statement is followed by several suggested answers or completions. Select the one that BEST answers the question or completes the statement. *PRINT THE LETTER OF THE CORRECT ANSWER IN THE SPACE AT THE RIGHT.*

1. In many instances, managers deliberately set up procedures and routines that more than one department or more than one employee is required to complete and verify an entire operation or transaction.
   The MAIN reason for establishing such routines is generally to
   A. minimize the chances of gaps and deficiencies in feedback of information to management
   B. expand the individual employee's vision and concern for broader organizational objectives
   C. provide satisfaction of employees' social and egoistic needs through teamwork and horizontal communications
   D. facilitate internal control designed to prevent errors, whether intentional or accidental

   1.____

2. Committees—sometimes referred to as boards, commissions, or task forces—are widely used in government to investigate certain problems or to manage certain agencies.
   Of the following, the MOST serious limitation of the committee approach to management in government is that
   A. it reflects government's inability to delegate authority effectively to individual executives
   B. committee members do not usually have similar backgrounds, experience, and abilities
   C. it promotes horizontal communication at the expense of vertical communication
   D. the spreading out of responsibility to a committee often results in a willingness to settle for weak, compromise solutions

   2.____

3. Of the following, the BEST reason for replacing methods of committees on a staggered or partial basis rather than replacing all members simultaneously is that this practice
   A. gives representatives of different interest groups a chance to contribute their ideas
   B. encourages continuity of policy since retained members are familiar with previous actions
   C. prevents the interpersonal frictions from building up and hindering the work of the group
   D. improves the quality of the group's recommendations and decisions by stimulating development of new ideas

   3.____

4. Assume that in considering a variety of actions to take to solve a given problem, a manager decides to take no action at all.
   According to generally accepted management practice, such a decision would be
   A. *proper*, because under normal circumstances it is better to make no decision
   B. *improper*, because inaction would be rightly construed as shunning one's responsibilities
   C. *proper*, since this would be a decision which might produce more positive results than the other alternatives
   D. *improper*, since such a solution would delay corrective action and exacerbate the problem

4._____

5. Some writers in the field of management assume that when a newly promoted manager has been informed by his superior about the subordinates he is to direct and the extent of his authority, that is all that is necessary.
   However, thereafter, this new manager should realize that, for practical purposes, his authority will be effective ONLY when
   A. he accepts full responsibility for the actions of his subordinates
   B. his subordinates are motivated to carry out their assignments
   C. it derives from acceptable personal attributes rather than from his official position
   D. he exercises it in an authoritarian manner

5._____

6. A newly appointed manager is assigned to assist the head of a small developing agency handling innovative programs. Although this manager is a diligent worker, he does not delegate authority to middle- and lower-echelon supervisors.
   The MOST important reason why it would be desirable to change this attitude toward delegation is because otherwise
   A. he may have to assume more responsibility for the actions of his subordinates than is implied in the authority delegated to him
   B. his subordinates will tend to produce innovative solutions on their own
   C. the agency will become a decentralized type of organization in which he cannot maintain adequate controls
   D. he may not have time to perform other essential tasks

6._____

7. All types of organizations and all functions within them are to varying degrees affected today by the need to understand the application of computer systems to management practices.
   The one of the following purposes for which such systems would be MOST useful is to
   A. lower the costs of problem-solving by utilizing data that is already in the agency's control system correlated with new data
   B. stabilize basic patterns of the organization into long-term structures and relationships
   C. give instant solutions to complex problems
   D. affect savings in labor costs for office tasks involving non-routine complex problems

7._____

8. Compared to individual decision-making, group decision-making is burdened with the DISADVANTAGE of
   A. making snap judgments
   B. pressure to examine all relevant elements of the problem
   C. greater motivation needed to implement the decision
   D. the need to clarify problems for the group participants

9. Assume that a manager in an agency, faced with a major administrative problem, has developed a number of alternative solutions to the problem. Which of the following would be MOST effective in helping the manager make the best decision?
   A. *Experience*, because a manager can distill from the past the fundamental reasons for success or failure since the future generally duplicates the past
   B. *Experimentation*, because it is the method used in scientific inquiry and can be tried out economically in limited areas
   C. *Research analysis*, because it is generally less costly than most other methods and involves the interrelationships among the more critical factors that bear upon the goal sought
   D. *Value forecasting*, because it assigns numerical significance to the values of alternative tangible and intangible choices and indicates the degree of risk involved in each choice

10. Management information systems operate more effectively for managers than mere data tabulating systems because information systems
    A. eliminate the need for managers to tell information processors what is required
    B. are used primarily for staff rather than line functions
    C. are less expensive to operate than manual methods of data collection
    D. present and utilize data in a meaningful form

11. Project-type organizations are in widespread use today because they offer a number of advantages.
    The MOST important purpose of the project organization is to
    A. secure a higher degree of coordination than could be obtained in a conventional line structure
    B. provide an orderly way of phrasing projects in and out of organizations
    C. expedite routine administrative processes
    D. allow for rapid assessment of the status of any given project and its effect on agency productivity

12. A manager adjusts his plans for future activity by reviewing information about the performance of his subordinates.
    This is an application of the process of
    A. human factor impact   B. coordinated response
    C. feedback communication   D. reaction control

13. From the viewpoint of the manager in an agency, the one of the following which is the MOST constructive function of a status system or a rank system based on employee performance is that the system
    A. makes possible effective communication, thereby lessening social distances between organizational levels
    B. is helpful to employees of lesser ability because it provides them with an incentive to exceed their capacities
    C. encourages the employees to attain or exceed the goals set for them by the organization
    D. diminishes friction in assignment and work relationships of personnel

14. Some managers ask employees who have been newly hired by their agency and then assigned to their divisions or units such questions as: *What are your personal goals? What do you expect from your job? Why do you want to work for this organization?*
    For a manager to ask these questions is GENERALLY considered
    A. *inadvisable*; these questions should have been asked prior to hiring the employee
    B. *inadvisable*; the answers will arouse subjective prejudices in the manager before he sees what kind of work the employee can do
    C. *advisable*; this approach indicates to the employee that the manager is interested in him as an individual
    D. *advisable*; the manager can judge how much of a disparity exists between the employee's goals and the agency's goals

15. Assume that you have prepared a report to your superior recommending a reorganization of your staff to eliminate two levels of supervision. The total number of employees would remain the same, with the supervisors of the two eliminated levels taking on staff assignments.
    In your report, which one of the following should NOT be listed as an expected result of such a reorganization?
    A. Fewer breakdowns and distortions in communications to staff
    B. Greater need for training
    C. Broader opportunities for development of employee skills
    D. Fewer employee errors due to exercise of closer supervision and control

16. *Administration* has often been criticized as being unproductive in the sense that it seems far removed from the end products of an organization.
    According to modern management thought, this criticism, for the most part, is
    A. *invalid*, because administrators make it possible for subordinates to produce goods or services by directing coordination, and controlling their activities
    B. *valid*, because most subordinates usually do the work required to produce goods and services with only general direction from their immediate superiors
    C. *invalid*, because administrators must see to all of the details associated with the production of services
    D. *valid*, because administrators generally work behind the scenes and are mainly concerned with long-range planning

17. A manager must be able to evaluate the relative importance of his decisions and establish priorities for carrying them out.
Which one of the following factors bearing on the relative importance of making a decision would indicate to a manager that he can delegate that decision to a subordinate or give it low priority? The
    A. decision concerns a matter on which strict confidentiality must be maintained
    B. community impact of the decision is great
    C. decision can be easily changed
    D. decision commits the agency to heavy expenditure of funds

18. Suppose that you are responsible for reviewing and submitting to your superior the monthly reports from ten field auditors. Despite your repeated warnings to these auditors, most of them hand in their reports close to or after the deadline dates, so that you have no time to return them for revision and find yourself working overtime to make the necessary corrections yourself. The deadline dates for the auditors' reports and your report cannot be changed.
Of the following, the MOST probable cause for this continuing situation is that
    A. these auditors need retraining in the writing of this type of report
    B. possible disciplinary action as a result of the delay by the auditors has not been impressed upon them
    C. the auditors have had an opportunity to provide you with feedback to explain the reasons for the delays
    D. you, as the manager, have not used disciplinary measures of sufficient severity to change their behavior

19. Assume that an agency desiring to try out a *management-by-objectives* program has set down the guidelines listed below to implement this activity. Which one of these guidelines is MOST likely to present obstacles to the success of this type of program?
    A. Specific work objectives should be determined by top management for employees at all levels.
    B. Objectives should be specific, attainable, and preferably measurable as to units, costs, ratios, time, etc.
    C. Standards of performance should be either qualitative or quantitative, preferably quantitative.
    D. There should be recognition and rewards for successful achievement or objectives.

20. Of the following, the MOST meaningful way to express productivity where employees work a standard number of hours each day is in terms of the relationship between man-
    A. hours expended and number of work-units needed to produce the final product
    B. days expended and goods and services produced
    C. days and energy expended
    D. days expended and number of workers

21. Agencies often develop productivity indices for many of their activities. 21.____
Of the following, the MOST important use for such indices is generally to
   A. measure the agency's output against its own performance
   B. improve quality standards while letting productivity remain unchanged
   C. compare outputs of the agency with outputs in private industry
   D. determine manpower requirements

22. The MOST outstanding characteristic of staff authority, such as that of a public 22.____
relations officer in an agency, as compared with line authority, is generally accepted to be
   A. reliance upon personal attributes
   B. direct relationship to the primary objectives of the organization
   C. absence of the right to direct or command
   D. responsibility for attention to technical details

23. In the traditional organization structure, there are often more barriers to 23.____
upward communication than to downward communication.
From the viewpoint of a manager whose goal is to overcome obstacles to communication, this situation should be
   A. *accepted*; the downward system is the more important since it is highly directive, giving necessary orders, instructions, and procedures
   B. *changed*; the upward system should receive more emphasis than the downward system, which represents stifling bureaucratic authority
   C. *accepted*; it is generally conceded that upward systems supply enough feedback for control purposes necessary to the organization's survival
   D. *changed*; research has generally verified the need for an increase in upward communications to supply more information about employees' ideas, attitudes, and performance

24. A principal difficulty in productivity measurement for local government services 24.____
is in defining and measuring output, a problem familiar to managers. A measurement that merely looks good, but which may be against the public interest, is another serious problem. Managers should avoid encouraging employees to take actions that lead to such measurements.
In accordance with the foregoing statement, it would be MOST desirable for a manager to develop a productivity measure that
   A. correlates the actual productivity measure with impact on benefit to the citizenry
   B. does not allow for a mandated annual increase in productivity
   C. firmly fixes priorities for resource allocations
   D. uses numerical output, by itself, in productivity incentive plans

25. For a manager, the MOST significant finding of the Hawthorne studies and 25.____
experiments is that an employee's productivity is affected MOST favorably when the
   A. importance of tasks is emphasized and there is a logical arrangement of work functions

B. physical surroundings and work conditions are improved
C. organization has a good public relations program
D. employee is given recognition and allowed to participate in decision-making

KEY (CORRECT ANSWERS)

1.	D		11.	A
2.	D		12.	C
3.	B		13.	C
4.	C		14.	A
5.	B		15.	D
6.	D		16.	A
7.	A		17.	C
8.	D		18.	D
9.	C		19.	A
10.	D		20.	B

21.	A
22.	C
23.	D
24.	A
25.	D

TEST 2

DIRECTIONS: Each question or incomplete statement is followed by several suggested answers or completions. Select the one that BEST answers the question or completes the statement. *PRINT THE LETTER OF THE CORRECT ANSWER IN THE SPACE AT THE RIGHT.*

1. Which one of the following is generally accepted by managers as the MOST difficult aspect of a training program in staff supervision?
   A. Determining training needs of the staff
   B. Evaluating the effectiveness of the courses
   C. Locating capable instructors to teach the courses
   D. Finding adequate space and scheduling acceptable times for all participants

   1.____

2. Assume that, as a manager, you have decided to start a job enrichment program with the purpose of making jobs more varied and interesting in an effort to increase the motivation of a certain group of workers in your division.
   Which one of the following should generally NOT be part of this program?
   A. Increasing the accountability of these individuals for their own work
   B. Granting additional authority or job freedom to these employees in their job activities
   C. Mandating increased monthly production goals for this group of employees
   D. Giving each of these employees a complete unit of work

   2.____

3. Both employer and employee have an important stake in effective preparation for retirement.
   According to modern management thinking, the one of the following which is probably the MOST important aspect of a sound pre-retirement program is to
   A. make assignments that utilize the employee's abilities fully
   B. reassign the employee to a less demanding position in the organization for the last year or two he is on the job
   C. provide the employee with financial data and other facts that would be pertinent to his retirement planning
   D. encourage the employee to develop interests and hobbies which are connected with the job

   3.____

4. The civil service system generally emphasizes a policy of *promotion-from-within*. Employees in the direct line of promotion in a given occupational group are eligible for promotion to the next higher title in that occupational group. Which one of the following is LEAST likely to occur as a result of this policy and practice?
   A. Training time will be saved since employees in higher-level positions are already familiar with many agency rules, regulations, and procedures.
   B. The recruitment section will be able to show prospective employees that there are distinct promotional opportunities.

   4.____

C. Employees will be provided with a clear-cut picture as to their possible career ladder.
D. Employees will be encouraged to seek broad-based training and education to enhance their promotability.

5. From a management point of view, the MAIAN drawback of seniority as opposed to merit as a basis for granting pay increases to workers is that a pay increase system based on seniority
   A. is favored by unions
   B. upsets organizational status relationships
   C. may encourage mediocre performance by employees
   D. is more difficult to administer than a merit plan

6. One of the actions that is often taken against employees in the non-uniformed forces who are accused of misconduct on the job is suspension without pay. The MOST justifiable reason for taking such action is to
   A. ease an employee out of the agency
   B. enable an investigation to be conducted into the circumstances of the offense
   C. improve the performance of the employee when he returns to the job
   D. punish the employee by imposing a hardship on him

7. A manager has had difficulty in getting good clerical employees to staff a filing section under his supervision. To add to his problems, one of his most competent senior clerks requests a transfer to the accounting division so that he can utilize his new accounting skill, which he is acquiring by going to college at night. The manager attempts to keep the senior clerk in his filing section by calling the director of personnel and getting him to promise not to authorize any transfer.
   GENERALLY, this manager's action is
   A. *desirable*; he should not help his staff to develop themselves if it means losing good people
   B. *undesirable*; he should recommend that the senior clerk get a raise in the hope of preventing him from transferring to another section
   C. *desirable*; it shows that the manager is concerned about the senior clerk's future performance
   D. *undesirable*; it is good policy to transfer employees to the type of work they are interested in and for which they are acquiring training

8. One of your subordinates, a unit supervisor, comes to you, the division chief, because he feels that he is working out of title, and he suggests that his competitive class position should be reclassified to a higher title.
   Which one of the following statements that the subordinate has made is generally LEAST likely to be a valid support for his suggestion?
   A. The work he is doing conforms to the general statement of duties and responsibilities as described in the class specification for the next higher title in his occupational group.
   B. Most of the typical tasks he performs are listed in the class specification for a title with a higher salary range and are not listed for his current title.

C. His education and experience qualifications far exceed the minimum requirements for the position he holds.
D. His duties and responsibilities have changed recently and are now similar to those of his supervisor.

9. Assume that a class specification for a competitive title used exclusively by your agency is outdated, and that no examination for the title has been given since the specification was issued.
Of the following, the MOST appropriate action for your agency to take is to
   A. make the necessary changes and submit the revised class specification to the city civil service commission
   B. write the personnel director to recommend that the class specification be updated, giving the reasons and suggested revisions
   C. prepare a revised class specification and submit it to the office of management and budget for their approval
   D. secure approval of the state civil service commission to update the class specification, and then submit the revised specification to the city civil service commission

10. Assume that an appropriate eligible list has been established and certified to your agency for a title in which a large number of provisionals are serving in your agency.
In order to obtain permission from the personnel director to retain some of them beyond the usual time limit set by rules (two months) following certification of the list, which one of the following conditions MUST apply?
   A. The positions are sensitive and require investigation of eligibles prior to appointment.
   B. Replacement of all provisionals within two months would impair essential public service.
   C. Employees are required to work rotating shifts, including nights and weekends.
   D. The duties of the positions require unusual physical effort and endurance.

11. Under the federally-funded Comprehensive Employment and Training Act (CETA), the hiring by the city of non-civil servants for CETA jobs is PROHIBITED when the
   A. applicants are unemployed because of seasonal lay-offs in private industry
   B. applicants do not meet U.S. citizenship and city residence requirements
   C. jobs have minimum requirements of specialized professional or technical training and experience
   D. jobs are comparable to those performed by laid-off civil servants

12. Assume you are in charge of the duplicating service in your agency. Since employees assigned to this operation lack a sense of accomplishment because the work is highly specialized and repetitive, your superior proposes to enlarge the jobs of these workers and asks you about your reaction to this strategy.

The MOST appropriate response for you to make is that job enlargement would be
- A. *undesirable*, primarily because it would increase production costs
- B. *undesirable*, primarily because it would diminish the quality of the output
- C. *desirable*, primarily because it might make it possible to add an entire level of management to the organizational structure of your agency
- D. *desirable*, primarily because it might make it possible to decrease the amount of supervision the workers will require

13. According to civil service law, layoff or demotion must be made in inverse order of seniority among employees permanently serving in the same title and layoff unit.
Which one of the following is now the CORRECT formula for computing seniority?
Total continuous service in the
    - A. competitive class only
    - B. competitive, non-competitive, or labor class
    - C. classified or unclassified services
    - D. competitive, non-competitive, exempt, and labor classes

14. Under which of the following conditions would an appointing officer be permitted to consider the sex of a candidate in making an employment decision?
When
    - A. the duties of the position require considerable physical effort or strength
    - B. the duties of the position are considered inherently dangerous
    - C. separate toilet facilities and dressing rooms for the sexes are unavailable and/or cannot be provided in any event
    - D. the public has indicated a preference to be served by persons of a specified sex

15. Assume that an accountant under your supervision signs out to the field to make an agency audit. It is later discovered that, although he had reported himself at work until 5 P.M. that day, he had actually left for home at 3:30 P.M. Although this accountant has worked for the city for ten years and has had an excellent performance record, he is demoted to a lower title in punishment for this breach of duty.
According to generally accepted thinking on personnel management, the disciplinary action taken in this case should be considered
    - A. *appropriate*; a lesser penalty might encourage repetition of the offense
    - B. *inappropriate*; the correct penalty for such a breach of duty should be dismissal
    - C. *appropriate*; the accountant's abilities may be utilized better in the new assignment
    - D. *inappropriate*; the impact of a continuing stigma and loss of salary is not commensurate with the offense committed

16. Line managers often request more funds for their units than are actually required to attain their current objectives.
Which one of the following is the MOST important reason for such inflated budget requests?
The
    A. expectation that budget examiners will exercise their prerogative of budget cutting
    B. line manager's interest in improving the performance of his unit is thereby indicated to top management
    C. expectation that such requests will make it easier to obtain additional funds in future years
    D. opinion that it makes sense to obtain additional funds and decide later how to use them

17. Integrating budgeting with program planning and evaluation in a city agency is GENERALLY considered to be
    A. *undesirable*; budgeting must focus on the fiscal year at hand, whereas planning must concern itself with developments over a period of years
    B. *desirable*; budgeting facilitates the choice-making process by evaluating the financial implications of agency programs and forcing cost comparisons among them
    C. *undesirable*; accountants and statisticians with the required budgetary skills have little familiarity with the substantive programs that the agency is conducting
    D. *desirable*; such a partnership increases the budgetary skills of planners, thus promoting more effective use of public resources

18. An aspect of the managerial function, a budget is described BEST as a
    A. set of qualitative management controls over productivity
    B. tool based on historical accounting reports
    C. type of management plan expressed in quantitative terms
    D. precise estimate of future quantitative and qualitative contingencies

19. Which one of the following is generally accepted as the MAJOR immediate advantage of installing a system of program budgeting?
It
    A. encourages managers to relate their decisions to the agency's long-range goals
    B. is a replacement for the financial or fiscal budget
    C. decreases the need for managers to make trade-offs in the decision-making process
    D. helps to adjust budget figures to provide for unexpected developments

20. Of the following, the BEST means for assuring necessary responsiveness of a budgetary program to changing conditions is by
    A. overestimating budgetary expenditures by 15% and assigning the excess to unforeseen problem areas
    B. underestimating budgetary expenditures by at least 20% and setting aside a reserve account in the same amount

C. reviewing and revising the budget at regular intervals so that it retains its character as a current document
D. establishing *budget-by-exception* policies for each division in the agency

21. According to expert thought in the area of budgeting, participation in the preparation of a government agency's budget should GENERALLY involve
    A. only top management
    B. only lower levels of management
    C. all levels of the organization
    D. only a central budget office or bureau

22. Of the following, the MOST useful guide to analysis of budget estimates for the coming fiscal year is a comparison with
    A. appropriations as amended for the current fiscal year
    B. manpower requirements for the previous two years
    C. initial appropriations for the current fiscal year
    D. budget estimates for the preceding five years

23. A manager assigned to analyze the costs and benefits associated with a program which the agency head proposes to undertake may encounter certain factors which cannot be measured in dollar terms.
    In such a case, the manager should GENERALLY
    A. ignore the factors which cannot be quantified
    B. evaluate the factors in accordance with their degree of importance to the overall agency goals
    C. give the factors weight equal to the weight given to measurable costs and benefits
    D. assume that non-measurable costs and benefits will balance out against one another

24. If city employees believe that they are receiving adverse treatment in terms of training and disciplinary actions because of their national origin, they may file charges of discrimination with the Federal government's
    A. Human Rights Commission
    B. Public Employee Relations Board
    C. Equal Employment Opportunity Commission
    D. United States Department of Commerce

25. Under existing employment statutes, the city is obligated, as an employer, to take *affirmative action* in certain instances.
    This requirement has been imposed to ensure that
    A. employees who are members of minority groups, or women, be given special opportunities for training and promotion even though they are not available to other employees
    B. employees or applicants for employment are treated without regard to race, color, religion, sex, or national origin

C. proof exists to show that the city has acted with good intentions in any case where it has disregarded this requirement
D. men and women are treated alike except where State law provides special hour or working conditions for women

---

KEY (CORRECT ANSWERS)

1.	B		11.	D
2.	C		12.	D
3.	C		13.	D
4.	D		14.	C
5.	C		15.	D
6.	B		16.	A
7.	D		17.	B
8.	C		18.	C
9.	B		19.	A
10.	B		20.	D

21.	C
22.	A
23.	B
24.	C
25.	B

EXAMINATION SECTION
TEST 1

DIRECTIONS: Each question or incomplete statement is followed by several suggested answers or completions. Select the one that BEST answers the question or completes the statement. *PRINT THE LETTER OF THE CORRECT ANSWER IN THE SPACE AT THE RIGHT.*

1. A management approach widely used today is based on the belief that decisions should be made and actions should be taken by managers closest to the organization's problems.
   This style of management is MOST appropriately called _____ management.
   A. scientific
   B. means-end
   C. decentralized
   D. internal process

   1._____

2. As contrasted with tall organization structures with narrow spans of control, flat organization structures with wide spans of control MOST usually provide
   A. fast communication and information flows
   B. more levels in the organizational hierarchy
   C. fewer workers reporting to supervisors
   D. lower motivation because of tighter control standards

   2._____

3. Use of the systems approach is MOST likely to lead to
   A. consideration of the impact on the whole organization of actions taken in any part of that organization
   B. the placing of restrictions on departmental activity
   C. use of mathematical models to suboptimize production
   D. consideration of the activities of each unit of an organization as a totality without regard to the remainder of the organization

   3._____

4. An administrator, with overall responsibility for all administrative operations in a large operating agency, is considering organizing the agency's personnel office around either of the following two alternative concepts:
   Alternative I: A corps of specialists for each branch of personnel subject matter, whose skills, counsel, or work products are coordinated only by the agency personnel officer
   Alternative II: A crew of so-called *personnel generalists*, who individually work with particular segments of the organization but deal with all subspecialties of the personnel function
   The one of the following which MOST tends to be a DRAWBACK of Alternative I, as compared with Alternative II, is that
   A. training and employee relations work call for education, interests, and talents that differ from those required for classification and compensation work
   B. personnel office staff may develop only superficial familiarity with the specialized areas to which they have been assigned

   4._____

C. supervisors may fail to get continuing overall personnel advice on an integrated basis
D. the personnel specialists are likely to become so interested in and identified with the operating view as to particular cases that they lose their professional objectivity and become merely advocates of what some supervisor wants

5. The matrix summary or decision matrix is a useful tool for making choices. Its effectiveness is MOST dependent upon the user's ability to
   A. write a computer program (Fortran or Cobol)
   B. assign weights representing the relative importance of the objectives
   C. solve a set of two equations with two unknowns
   D. work with matrix algebra

6. An organizational form which is set up only on an *ad hoc* basis to meet specific goals is said PRIMARILY to use
   A. clean break departmentation
   B. matrix or task force organization
   C. scalar specialization
   D. geographic or area-wide decentralization

7. The concept of job enlargement would LEAST properly be implemented by
   A. permitting workers to follow through on tasks or projects from start to finish
   B. delegating the maximum authority possible for decision-making to lower levels in the hierarchy
   C. maximizing the number of professional classes in the classification plan
   D. training employees to grow beyond whatever tasks they have been performing

8. As used in the area of admission, the principle of *unity of command* MOST specifically means that
   A. an individual should report to only one superior for any single activity
   B. individuals make better decisions than do committees
   C. in large organizations, chains of command are normally too long
   D. an individual should not supervise over five subordinates

9. The method of operations research, statistical decision-making, and linear programming have been referred to as the tool kit of the manager. Utilization of these tools is LEAST useful in the performance of which of the following functions?
   A. Elimination of the need for using judgment when making decisions
   B. Facilitation of decision-making without the need for sub-optimization
   C. Quantifying problems for management study
   D. Research and analysis of management operations

10. When acting in their respective managerial capacities, the chief executive officer and the office supervisor both perform the fundamental functions of management.
    Of the following differences between the two, the one which is generally considered to be the LEAST significant is the
    A. breadth of the objectives
    B. complexity of measuring actual efficiency of performance
    C. number of decisions made
    D. organizational relationships affected by actions taken

    10._____

11. The ability of operations researchers to solve complicated problems rests on their use of models.
    These models can BEST be described as
    A. mathematical statements of the problem
    B. physical constructs that simulate a work layout
    C. toy-like representations of employees in work environments
    D. role-playing simulations

    11._____

12. Of the following, it is MOST likely to be proper for the agency head to allow the agency personnel officer to make final selection of appointees from certified eligible lists where there are
    A. *small* numbers of employees to be hired in newly-developed professional fields
    B. *large* numbers of persons to be hired for key managerial positions
    C. *large* numbers of persons to be hired in very routine occupations where the individual discretion of operating officials is not vital
    D. *small* numbers of persons to be hired in highly specialized professional occupations which are vital to the agency's operations

    12._____

13. Of the following, an operating agency personnel office is LEAST likely to be able to exert strong influence or control within the operating agency by
    A. interpreting to the operating agency head what is intended by the directives and rules emanating from the central personnel agency
    B. establishing the key objectives of those line divisions of the operating agency employing large numbers of staff and operating under the management-by-objectives approach
    C. formulating and proposing to the agency head the internal policies and procedures on personnel matters required within the operating agency
    D. exercising certain discretionary authority in the application of the agency head's general personnel policies to actual specific situations

    13._____

14. PERT is a recently developed system used PRIMARILY to
    A. evaluate the quality of applicants' background
    B. analyze and control the timing aspects of a major project
    C. control the total expenditure of agency funds within a monthly or quarterly time period
    D. analyze and control the differential effect on costs of purchasing different quantities

    14._____

15. Assume that an operating agency has among its vacant positions two positions, each of which encompasses mixed duties. Both require appointees to have considerable education and experience, but these requirements are essential only for the more difficult duties of these positions. In the place of these positions, an administrator creates two new positions, one in which the higher duties are concentrated and the other with the lesser functions requiring only minimum preparation.
Of the following, it is generally MOST appropriate to characterize the administrator's action as a(n)
    A. *undesirable* example of deliberate downgrading of standards and requirements
    B. *undesirable* manipulation of the classification system for non-merit purposes
    C. *desirable* broadening of the definition of a class of positions
    D. *desirable* example of job redesign

16. Of the following, the LEAST important stumbling block to the development of personnel mobility among governmental jurisdictions is the
    A. limitations on lateral entry above junior levels in many jurisdictions
    B. continued collection of filing fees for civil service tests by many governmental jurisdictions
    C. absence of reciprocal exchange of retirement benefit eligibility between governments
    D. disparities in salary scales between governments

17. Of the following, the MAJOR disadvantage of a personnel system that features the *selection out* (forced retirement) of those who have been passed over a number of times for promotion is that such a system
    A. wastes manpower which is perfectly competent at one level but unable to rise above that level
    B. wastes funds by requiring review boards
    C. leads to excessive recruiting of newcomers from outside the system
    D. may not be utilized in *closed* career systems with low maximum age limits for entrance

18. Of the following, the fields in which operating agency personnel offices generally exercise the MOST stringent controls over first line supervisors in the agency are
    A. methods analysis and work simplification
    B. selection and position classification
    C. vestibule training and Gantt chart
    D. suggestion systems and staff development

19. Of the following, computers are normally MOST effective in handling
    A. large masses of data requiring simple processing
    B. small amounts of data requiring constantly changing complex processing
    C. data for which reported values are often subject to inaccuracies
    D. large amounts of data requiring continual programming and reprocessing

20. Contingency planning, which has long been used by the military and is assuming increasing importance in other organizations, may BEST be described as a process which utilizes
    A. alternative plans based on varying assumptions
    B. *crash programs* by organizations departmentalized along process lines
    C. plans which mandate substitution of equipment for manpower at predetermined operational levels
    D. plans that individually and accurately predict future events

21. In the management of inventory, two kinds of costs normally determine when to order and in what amounts.
    The one of the following choices which includes BOTH of these kinds of costs is _____ costs and _____ costs.
    A. carrying; storage
    B. personnel; order
    C. computer; order
    D. personnel; computer

22. At top management levels, the one of the following which is generally the MOST important executive skill is skill in
    A. budgeting procedures
    B. a technical discipline
    C. controlling actions in accordance with previously approved plans
    D. seeing the organization as a whole

23. Of the following, the BEST way to facilitate the successful operation of a committee is to set guidelines establishing its
    A. budget exclusive of personnel costs
    B. location
    C. schedule of meetings or conferences
    D. scope of purpose

24. Executive training programs that single out particular managers and groom them for promotion create the so-called organizational *crown princes.*
    Of the following, the MOST serious problem that arises in connection with this practice is that
    A. the managers chosen for promotion seldom turn out to be the best managers since the future potential of persons cannot be predicted
    B. not enough effort is made to remove organizational obstacles in the way of their development and achievement
    C. the resentment of the managers not selected for the program has an adverse effect on the motivation of those managers not selected
    D. performance appraisal and review are not carried out systematically enough

25. Of the following, the LEAST likely result of the use of the concept of job enlargement is that
    A. coordination will be simplified
    B. the individual's job will become less challenging
    C. worker satisfaction will increase
    D. fewer people will have to give attention to each piece of work

KEY (CORRECT ANSWERS)

1.	C		11.	A
2.	A		12.	C
3.	A		13.	B
4.	C		14.	B
5.	B		15.	D
6.	B		16.	B
7.	C		17.	A
8.	A		18.	B
9.	A		19.	A
10.	C		20.	A

21. A
22. D
23. D
24. C
25. B

TEST 2

DIRECTIONS: Each question or incomplete statement is followed by several suggested answers or completions. Select the one that BEST answers the question or completes the statement. *PRINT THE LETTER OF THE CORRECT ANSWER IN THE SPACE AT THE RIGHT.*

1. The one of the following which is MOST likely to be emphasized in the use of the brainstorming technique is the
   A. early consideration of cost factors of all ideas which may be suggested
   B. avoidance of impractical suggestions
   C. separation of the generation of ideas from their evaluation
   D. appraisal of suggestions concurrently with their initial presentation

   1.____

2. Of the following, the BEST method for assessing managerial performance is generally to
   A. compare the manager's accomplishments against clear, specific, agreed-upon goals
   B. compare the manager's traits with those of his peers on a predetermined objective
   C. measure the manager's behavior against a listing of itemized personal traits
   D. measure the manager's success according to the enumeration of the *satisfaction* principle

   2.____

3. As compared with recruitment from outside, selection from within the service must generally show GREATER concern for the
   A. prestige in which the public service as a whole is held by the public
   B. morale of the candidate group compromising the recruitment field
   C. cost of examining per candidate
   D. benefits of the use of standardized and validated tests

   3.____

4. Performance budgeting focuses PRIMARY attention upon which one of the following? The
   A. things to be acquired, such as supplies and equipment
   B. general character and relative importance of the work to be done or the service to be rendered
   C. list of personnel to be employed, by specific title
   D. separation of employee performance evaluations from employee compensation

   4.____

5. Of the following, the FIRST step in the installation and operation of a performance budgeting system generally should be the
   A. identification of program costs in relationship to the accounting system and operating structure
   B. identification of the specific end results of past programs in other jurisdictions

   5.____

C. identification of work programs that are meaningful for management purposes
D. establishment of organizational structures each containing only one work program

6. Of the following, the MOST important purpose of a system of quarterly allotments of appropriated funds generally is to enable the
    A. head of the judicial branch to determine the legality of agency requests for budget increases
    B. operating agencies of government to upgrade the quality of their services without increasing costs
    C. head of the executive branch to control the rate at which the operating agencies obligate and expend funds
    D. operating agencies of government to avoid payment for services which have not been properly rendered by employees

6.____

7. In the preparation of the agency's budget, the agency's central budget office has two responsibilities: program review and management improvement. Which one of the following questions concerning an operating agency's program is MOST closely related to the agency budget officer's program review responsibility?
    A. Can expenditures for supplies, materials, or equipment be reduced?
    B. Will improved work methods contribute to a more effective program?
    C. What is the relative importance of this program as compared to a higher level of program performance?
    D. Will a realignment of responsibilities contribute to a higher level of program performance?

7.____

8. Of the following, the method of evaluating relative rates of return normally and generally thought to be MOST useful in evaluating government operations is _____ analysis.
    A. cost-benefit   B. budget variance
    C. investment capital   D. budget planning program

8.____

9. The one of the following assumptions that is LEAST likely to be made by a democratic or permissive type of leader is that
    A. commitment to goals is seldom a result of monetary rewards alone
    B. people can learn not only to accept, but also to seek, responsibility
    C. the average person prefers security over advancement
    D. creativity may be found in most segments of the population

9.____

10. In attempting to motivate subordinates, a manager should PRINCIPALLY be aware of the fact that
    A. the psychological qualities of people, in general, are easily predictable
    B. fear, as a traditional form of motivation, has lost much of its former power to motivate people in our modern industrial society
    C. fear is still the most potent force in motivating the behavior of subordinates in the public service
    D. the worker has very little control over the quality and quantity of his output

10.____

3 (#2)

11. Assume that the following figures represent the number of work-unit that were produced during a week by each of sixteen employees in a division:

    12   16   13   18
    21   12   16   13
    16   13   17   21
    13   15   18   20

    If all of the employees of the division who produced thirteen work-units during the week had instead produced fifteen work-units during that same week, then for that week the
    A. mean, median, and mode would all change
    B. mean and mode would change, but the median would remain the same
    C. mode and median would change, but the mean would remain the same
    D. mode, mean, and median would all still remain unchanged in value

12. An important law in motivation theory is called the *law of effect*. This law says that behavior which satisfies a person's needs tends to be repeated; behavior which does not satisfy a person's needs tends to be eliminated.
    The one of the following which is the BEST interpretation of this law is that
    A. productivity depends on personality traits
    B. diversity of goals leads to instability and motivation
    C. the greater the satisfaction, the more likely it is that the behavior will be reinforced
    D. extrinsic satisfaction is more important than intrinsic reward

13. Of the following, the MOST acceptable reason an administrator can give for taking advice from other employees in the organization only when he asks for it is that he wants to
    A. encourage creativity and high morale
    B. keep dysfunctional pressures and inconsistent recommendations to a minimum
    C. show his superiors and peers who is in charge
    D. show his subordinates who is in charge

14. A complete picture of the communication channels in an organization can BEST be revealed by
    A. observing the planned paperwork system
    B. recording the highly intermittent patterns of communication
    C. plotting the entire flow of information over a period of time
    D. monitoring the *grapevine*

Questions 15-16.

DIRECTIONS: Questions 15 and 16 are to be answered SOLELY on the basis of the following passage.

Management by objectives (MBO) may be defined as the process by which the superior and the subordinate managers of an organization jointly define its common goals, define each individual's major areas of responsibility in terms of the results expected of him and use these measures as guides for operating the unit and assessing the contribution of each of its members.

The MBO approach requires that after organizational goals are established and communicated, targets must be set for each individual position which are congruent with organizational goals. Periodic performance reviews and a final review using the objectives set as criteria are also basic to this approach.

Recent studies have shown that MBO programs are influenced by attitudes and perceptions of the boss, the company, the reward-punishment system, and the program itself. In addition, the manner in which the MBO program is carried out can influence the success of the program. A study done in the late sixties indicates that the best results are obtained when the manager sets goals which deal with significant problem areas in the organizational unit, or with the subordinate's personal deficiencies. These goals must be clear with regard to what is expected of the subordinate. The frequency of feedback is also important in the success of a management-by-objectives program. Generally, the greater the amount of feedback, the more successful the MBO program.

15. According to the above passage, the expected output for individual employees should be determined
    A. after a number of reviews of work performance
    B. after common organizational goals are defined
    C. before common organizational goals are defined
    D. on the basis of an employee's personal qualities

16. According to the above passage, the management-by-objectives approach requires
    A. less feedback than other types of management programs
    B. little review of on-the-job performance after the initial setting of goals
    C. general conformance between individual goals and organizational goals
    D. the setting of goals which deal with minor problem area in the organization

Questions 17-19.

DIRECTIONS: Questions 17 through 19 are to be answered SOLELY on the basis of the following passage.

During the last decade, a great deal of interest has been generated around the phenomenon of organizational development, or the process of developing human resources through conscious organization effort. Organizational development (OD) stresses improving interpersonal relationships and organizational skills, such as communication, to a much greater degree than individual training ever did.

The kind of training that an organization should emphasize depends upon the present and future structure of the organization. If future organizations are to be unstable, shifting coalitions, then individual skills and abilities, particularly those emphasizing innovativeness, creativity, flexibility, and the latest technological knowledge, are crucial, and individual training is most appropriate.

But if there is to be little change in organizational structure, then the main thrust of training should be group-oriented or organizational development. This approach seems better designed for overcoming hierarchical barriers, for developing a degree of interpersonal relationships which make communication along the chain of command possible, and for retaining a modicum of innovation and/or flexibility.

17. According to the above passage, group-oriented training is MOST useful in
    A. developing a communications system that will facilitate understanding through the chain of command
    B. highly flexible and mobile organizations
    C. preventing the crossing of hierarchical barriers within an organization
    D. saving energy otherwise wasted on developing methods of dealing with rigid hierarchies

17.____

18. The one of the following conclusions which can be drawn MOST appropriately from the above passage is that
    A. behavioral research supports the use of organizational development training method rather than individualized training
    B. it is easier to provide individualized training in specific skills than to set up sensitivity training programs
    C. organizational development eliminates innovative or flexible activity
    D. the nature of an organization greatly influences which training methods will be most effective

18.____

19. According to the above passage, the one of the following which is LEAST important for large-scale organizations geared to rapid and abrupt change is
    A. current technological information
    B. development of a high degree of interpersonal relationships
    C. development of individual skills and abilities
    D. emphasis on creativity

19.____

Questions 20-25.

DIRECTIONS: Each of Questions 20 through 25 consist of a statement which contains one word that is incorrectly used because it is not in keeping with the meaning that the quotation is evidently intended to convey. Determine which word is INCORRECTLY used. Select from the choices lettered A, B, C, and D the word which, when substituted for the incorrectly used word, would BEST help to convey the meaning of the statement.

20. One of the considerations likely to affect the currency of classification, particularly in professional and managerial occupations, is the impact of the incumbent's capacities on the job. Some work is highly susceptible to change as the result of the special talents or interests of the classifier. Organization should never be so rigid as not to capitalize on the innovative or unusual proclivities of its key employees. While a machine operator may not be able, even subtly, to change the character or level of his job, the design engineer, the attorney, or the organization and methods analyst might readily do so. Reliance on his judgment and the scope of his assignments may both grow as the result of his skill, insight, and capacity.
    A. unlikely   B. incumbent   C. directly   D. scope

20.____

21. The supply of services by the state is not governed by market price. The aim is to supply such services to all who need them and to treat all consumers equally. This objective especially compels the civil servant to maintain a role f strict impartiality, based on the principle of equality of individual citizens vis-à-vis their government. However, there is a clear difference between being neutral and impartial. If the requirement is construed to mean that all civil servants should be political eunuchs, devoid of the drive and motivation essential to dynamic administration, then the concept of impartiality is being seriously utilized. Modern governments should not be stopped from demanding that their hirelings have not only the technical but the emotional qualifications necessary for whole-hearted effort.
    A. determined   B. rule   C. stable   D. misapplied

21.____

22. The manager was barely listening. Recently, at the divisional level, several new fronts of troubles had erupted, including a requirement to increase production yet hold down operating costs and somehow raise quality standards. Though the three objectives were basically obsolete, top departmental management was insisting on the simultaneous attainment of them, an insistence not helping the manager's ulcer, an old enemy within. Thus, the manager could not find time for interest in individuals—only in statistics which regiment of individuals, like unconsidered Army privates, added up to.
    A. quantity   B. battalion   C. incompatible   D. quiet

22.____

23. When a large volume of data flows directly between operators and first-line supervisors, senior executives tend to be out of the mainstream of work. Summary reports can increase their remoteness. An executive needs to know the volume, quality, and cost of completed work, and exceptional problems. In addition, he may desire information on key operating conditions. Summary reports on these matters are, therefore, essential features of a communications network and make delegation without loss of control possible.
    A. unimportant   B. quantity   C. offset   D. incomplete

23.____

24. Of major significance in management is harmony between the overall objectives of the organization and the managerial objectives within that organization. In addition, harmony among goals of managers is impossible; they should not be at cross-purposes. Each manager's goal should supplement and assist the goals of his colleagues. Likewise, the objectives of individuals or non-management members should be harmonized with those of the manager. When this is accomplished, genuine teamwork is the result, and human relations are aided materially. The integration of managers' and individuals' goals aids in achieving greater work satisfaction at all levels.
    A. competition   B. dominate   C. incremental   D. vital

25. Change constantly challenges the manager. Some of this change is evolutionary, some revolutionary, some recognizable, some non-recognizable. Both forces within an enterprise and forces outside the enterprise cause managers to act and react in initiating changes in their immediate working environment. Change invalidates existing operations. Goals are not being accomplished in the best manner, problems develop, and frequently because of the lack of time, only patched-up solutions are followed. The result is that the mode of management is profound in nature and temporary in effectiveness. A complete overhaul of managerial operations should take place. It appears quite likely that we are just beginning to see the real effects of change in our society; the pace probably will accelerate in ways that few really understand or know how to handle.
    A. confirms   B. decline   C. instituting   D. superficial

KEY (CORRECT ANSWERS)

1.	C		11.	B
2.	A		12.	C
3.	B		13.	B
4.	B		14.	C
5.	C		15.	B
6.	C		16.	C
7.	C		17.	A
8.	A		18.	D
9.	C		19.	B
10.	B		20.	B

21.	D
22.	C
23.	C
24.	D
25.	D

EVALUATING INFORMATION AND EVIDENCE
EXAMINATION SECTION
TEST 1

DIRECTIONS: Each question or incomplete statement is followed by several suggested answers or completions. Select the one that BEST answers the question or completes the statement. *PRINT THE LETTER OF THE CORRECT ANSWER IN THE SPACE AT THE RIGHT.*

Questions 1-9.

DIRECTIONS: Questions 1 through 9 measure your ability to (1) determine whether statements from witnesses say essentially the same thing and (2) determine the evidence needed to make it reasonably certain that a particular conclusion is true.

1. Which of the following pairs of statements say essentially the same thing in two different ways?
   I. If you get your feet wet, you will catch a cold.
      If you catch a cold, you must have gotten your feet wet.
   II. If I am nominated, I will run for office.
      I will run for office only if I am nominated.
   The CORRECT answer is:
   A. I only   B. I and II   C. II only   D. Neither I nor II

   1.____

2. Which of the following pairs of statements say essentially the same thing in two different ways?
   I. The enzyme Rhopsin cannot be present if the bacterium Trilox is absent.
      Rhopsin and Trilox always appear together.
   II. A member of PENSA has an IQ of at least 175.
      A person with an IQ of less than 175 is not a member of PENSA
   The CORRECT answer is;
   A. I only   B. I and II   C. II only   D. Neither I nor II

   2.____

3. Which of the following pairs of statements say essentially the same thing in two different ways?
   I. None of Finer High School's sophomores will be going to the prom.
      No student at Finer High School who is going to the prom is a sophomore.
   II. If you have 20/20 vision, you may carry a firearm.
      You may not carry a firearm unless you have 20/20 vision.
   The CORRECT answer is:
   A. I only   B. I and II   C. II only   D. Neither I nor II

   3.____

91

4. Which of the following pairs of statements say essentially the same thing in two different ways?
   I. If the family doesn't pay the ransom, they will never see their son again.
      It is necessary for the family to pay the ransom in order for them to see their son again.
   II. If it is raining, I am carrying an umbrella.
       If I am carrying an umbrella, it is raining.
   The CORRECT answer is:
   A. I only   B. I and II   C. II only   D. Neither I nor II

5. Summary of Evidence Collected to Date:
   In the county's maternity wards, over the past year, only one baby was born who did not share a birthday with any other baby.
   Prematurely Drawn Conclusion: At least one baby was born on the same day as another baby in the county's maternity wards.
   Which of the following pieces of evidence, if any, would make it reasonably certain that the conclusion drawn is true?
   A. More than 365 babies were born in the county's maternity wards over the past year.
   B. No pairs of twins were born over the past year in the county's maternity wards.
   C. More than one baby was born in the county's maternity wards over the past year.
   D. None of the above

6. Summary of Evidence Collected to Date:
   Every claims adjustor for MetroLife drives only a Ford sedan when on the job.
   Prematurely Drawn Conclusion: A person who works for MetroLife and drives a Ford sedan is a claims adjustor.
   Which of the following pieces of evidence, if any, would make it reasonably certain that the conclusion drawn is true?
   A. Most people who work for MetroLife are claims adjustors.
   B. Some people who work for MetroLife are not claims adjustors.
   C. Most people who work for MetroLife drive Ford sedans
   D. None of the above

7. Summary of Evidence Collected to Date:
   Mason will speak to Zisk if Zisk will speak to Ronaldson.
   Prematurely Drawn Conclusion: Jones will not speak to Zisk if Zisk will speak to Ronaldson.
   Which of the following pieces of evidence, if any, would make it reasonably certain that the conclusion drawn is true?
   A. If Zisk will speak to Mason, then Ronaldson will not speak to Jones.
   B. If Mason will speak to Zisk, then Jones will not speak to Zisk.
   C. If Ronaldson will speak to Jones, then Jones will speak to Ronaldson.
   D. None of the above

8. <u>Summary of Evidence Collected to Date</u>:
   No blue lights on the machine are indicators for the belt drive status.
   <u>Prematurely Drawn Conclusion</u>: Some of the lights on the lower panel are not indicators for the belt drive status.
   Which of the following pieces of evidence, if any, would make it reasonably certain that the conclusion drawn is true?
   - A. No lights on the machine's lower panel are blue.
   - B. An indicator light for the machine's belt drive status is either green or red.
   - C. Some lights on the machine's lower panel are blue.
   - D. None of the above

8.____

9. <u>Summary of Evidence Collected to Date</u>:
   Of the four Sweeney sisters, two are married, three have brown eyes, and three are doctors.
   <u>Prematurely Drawn Conclusion</u>: Two of the Sweeney sisters are brown-eyed, married doctors.
   Which of the following pieces of evidence, if any, would make it reasonably certain that the conclusion is true?
   - A. The sister who does not have brown eyes is married.
   - B. The sister who does not have brown eyes is not a doctor, and one who is not married is not a doctor.
   - C. Every Sweeney sister with brown eyes is a doctor.
   - D. None of the above

9.____

Questions 10-14.

DIRECTIONS: Questions 10 through 14 refer to Map #5 and measure your ability to orient yourself within a given section of town, neighborhood or particular area. Each of the questions describes a starting point and a destination. Assume that you are driving a car in the area shown on the map accompanying the questions. Use the map as a basis for the shortest way to get from one point to another without breaking the law.

On the map, a street marked by arrows, or by arrows and the words "One Way," indicates one-way travel and should be assumed to be one-way for the entire length, even when there are breaks or jogs in the street. EXCEPTION: A street that does not have the same name over the full length.

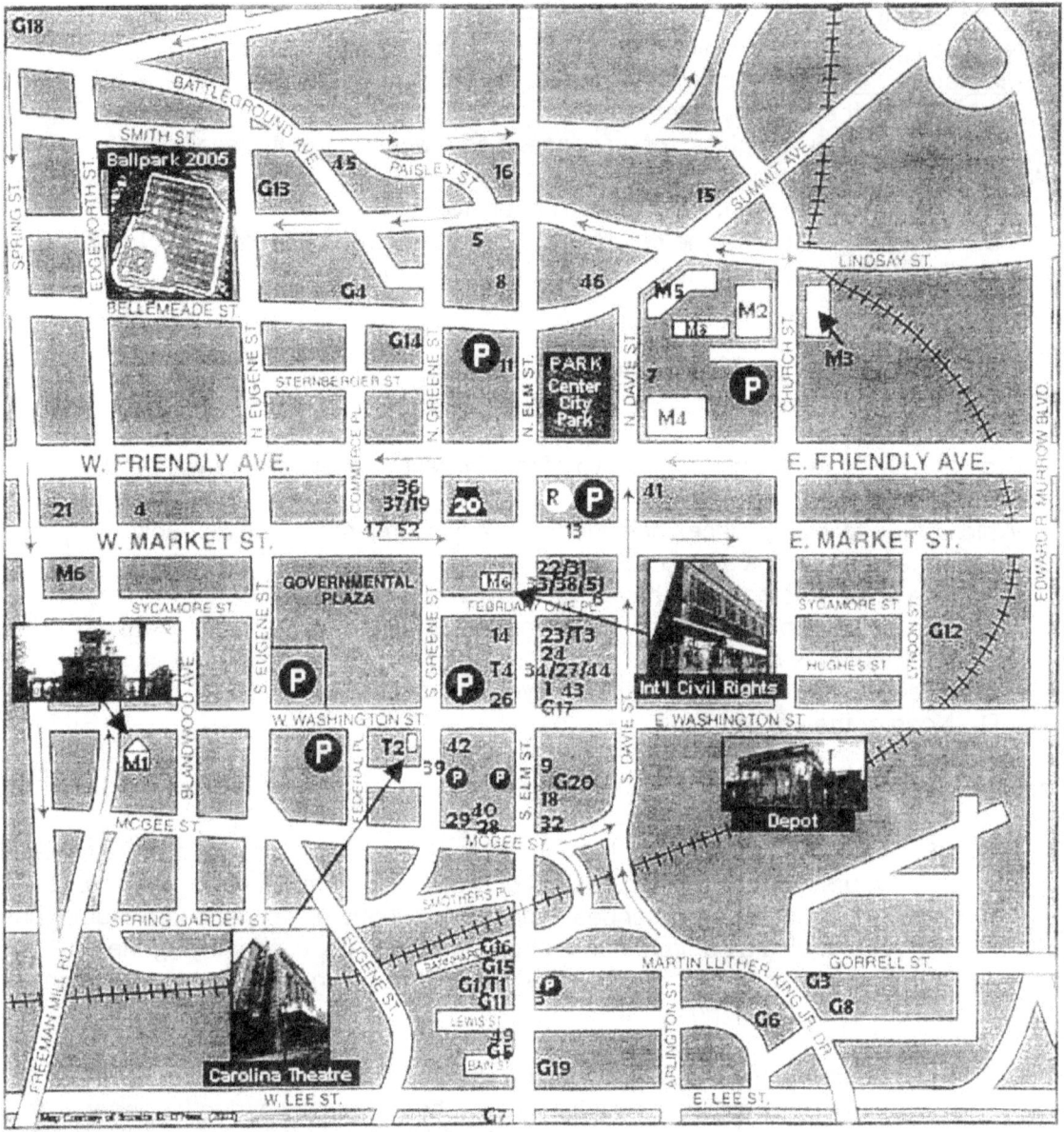

Map #5

10. The SHORTEST legal way from the depot to Center City Park is
    A. north on Church, west on Market, north on Elm
    B. east on Washington, north on Edward R. Murrow Blvd., west on Friendly Ave.
    C. west on Washington, north on Greene, east on Market, north on Davie
    D. north on Church, west on Friendly Ave.

11. The SHORTEST legal way from the Governmental Plaza to the Ballpark is 11.____
    A. west on Market, north on Edgeworth
    B. west on Market, north on Eugene
    C. north on Greene, west on Lindsay
    D. north on Commerce Place, west on Bellemeade

12. The SHORTEST legal way from the International Civil Rights Building to the building marked "M3" on the map is 12.____
    A. east on February One Place, north on Davie, east on Friendly Ave., north on Church
    B. south on Elm, west on Washington, north on Greene, east on Market, north on Church
    C. north on Elm, east on Market, north on Church
    D. north on Elm, east on Lindsay, south on Church

13. The SHORTEST legal way from the Ballpark to the Carolina Theatre is 13.____
    A. east on Lindsay, south on Greene
    B. south on Edgeworth, east on Friendly Ave., south on Greene
    C. east on Bellemeade, south on Elm, west on Washington

14. A car traveling north or south on Church Street may NOT go 14.____
    A. west onto Friendly Ave.   B. west onto Lindsay
    C. east onto Market   D. west onto Smith

Questions 15-19.

DIRECTIONS: Questions 15 through 19 refer to Figure #3, on the following page, and measure your ability to understand written descriptions of events. Each question presents a description of an accident or event and asks you which of the following five drawings in Figure #3 BEST represents it.
In the drawings, the following symbols are used:
Moving vehicle ⌂   Non-moving vehicle ♦
Pedestrian or bicyclist •
The path and direction of travel of a vehicle or pedestrian is indicated by a solid line.
The path and direction of travel of each vehicle or pedestrian directly involved in a collision from the point of impact is indicated by a dotted line.

6 (#1)

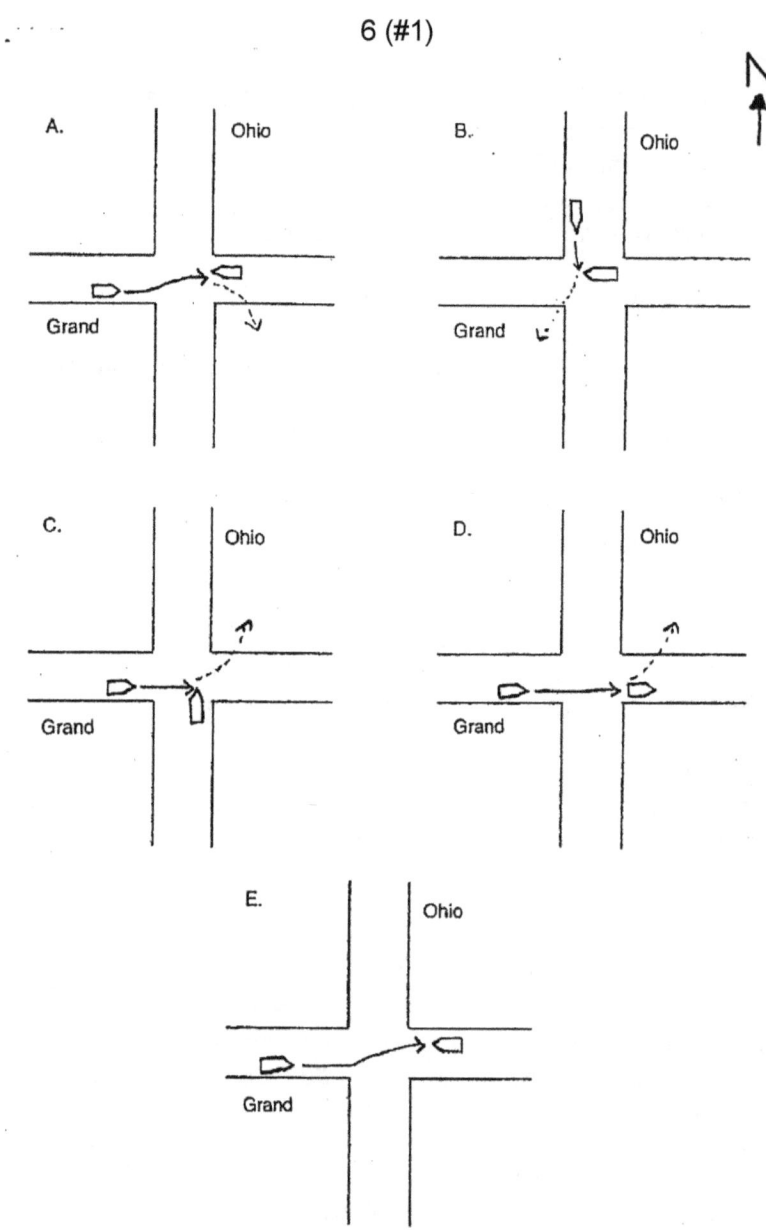

In the space at the right, print the letter of the drawing that BEST fit the descriptions written below.

15. A driver headed south on Ohio runs a red light and strikes the front of a car headed west on Grand. He glances off and leaves the roadway at the southwest corner of Grand and Ohio.   15.____

16. A driver heading east on Grand drifts into the oncoming lane as it travels through the intersection of Grand and Ohio, and strikes an oncoming car head-on   16.____

17. A driver heading east on Grand veers into the oncoming lane, sideswipes a westbound car and overcorrects as he swerves back into his lane. He leaves the roadway near the southeast corner of Grand and Ohio.

17._____

18. A driver heading east on Grand strikes the front of a car that is traveling north on Ohio and has run a red light. After striking the front of the northbound car, the driver veers left and leaves the roadway at the northeast corner of Grand and Ohio.

18._____

19. A driver heading east on Grand is traveling above the speed limit and clips the rear end of another eastbound car. The driver then veers to the left and leaves the roadway at the northeast corner of Grand and Ohio.

19._____

Questions 20-22.

DIRECTIONS: In Questions 20 through 22, choose the word or phrase CLOSEST in meaning to the word or phrase printed in capital letters.

20. PETITION
    A. appeal   B. law   C. oath   D. opposition

20._____

21. MALPRACTICE
    A. commission   B. mayhem   C. error   D. misconduct

21._____

22. EXONERATE
    A. incriminate   B. accuse   C. lengthen   D. acquit

22._____

Questions 23-25.

DIRECTIONS: Questions 23 through 25 measure your ability to do fieldwork-related arithmetic. Each question presents a separate arithmetic problem for you to solve.

23. Officers Lane and Bryant visited another city as part of an investigation. Because each is from a different precinct, they agree to split all expenses. With her credit card, Lane paid $70 for food and $150 for lodging. Bryant wrote checks for gas ($50) and entertainment ($40).
How much does Bryant owe Lane?
    A. $65   B. $90   C. $155   D. $210

23._____

24. In a remote mountain pass, two search-and-rescue teams, one from Silverton and one from Durango, combine to look for a family that disappeared in a recent snowstorm. The combined team is composed of 20 members.
Which of the following statements could NOT be true?
    A. The Durango team has a dozen members.
    B. The Silverton team has only one member.
    C. The Durango team has two more members than the Silverton team.
    D. The Silverton team has one more member than the Durango team.

24._____

25. Three people in the department share a vehicle for a period of one year. The average number of miles traveled per month by each person is 150. How many miles will be added to the car's odometer at the end of the year? 25.____
    A. 1,800   B. 2,400   C. 3,600   D. 5,400

KEY (CORRECT ANSWERS)

1.	D		11.	D
2.	C		12.	C
3.	A		13.	D
4.	A		14.	D
5.	A		15.	B
6.	A		16.	E
7.	B		17.	A
8.	C		18.	C
9.	B		19.	D
10.	D		20.	A

21. D
22. D
23. A
24. D
25. D

SOLUTIONS TO QUESTIONS 1-9

P implies Q = original statement

Not Q implies not P = contrapositive of the original statement. A statement and its contrapositive are logically equivalent.

Q implies P = converse of the original statement

Not P implies not Q = inverse of the original statement. The converse and inverse of an original statement are logically equivalent.

P implies Q = Not P or Q.

1. The CORRECT answer is D.
   In items I and II, each statement is the converses of the other. A converse of a statement is not equivalent to its original statement.

2. The CORRECT answer is C.
   In item I, the first statement is equivalent to "If Trilox is absent, then Rhopsin is also absent." But this does NOT imply that if Trilox is present, so too must Rhopsin be present. In item II, each statement is the contrapositive of the other. Thus, they are equivalent.

3. The CORRECT answer is A.
   In item I, the first sentence tells us that if a student is a sophomore, he/she will not go the prom. The second statement is equivalent to "If a student does attend the prom, he/she is not a sophomore." This is the contrapositive of the first statement, (so it is equivalent to it).

4. The CORRECT answer is A.
   In item I, the second statement can be written as "If the family sees their son again, then they must have paid the ransom." This is the contrapositive of the first statement. In item II, these statements are converses of each other; thus, they are not equivalent.

5. The CORRECT answer is A.
   If more than 365 babies were born in the county in one year, then at least two babies must share the same birthday.

6. The CORRECT answer is A.
   Given that most people who work for MetroLife are claims adjustors, plus the fact that all claims adjustors drive only a Ford sedan, it is a reasonable conclusion that any person who drives a Ford sedan and works for MetroLife is a claims adjustor.

7. The CORRECT answer is B.
   Jones will not speak to Zisk if Zisk will speak to Ronaldson, which will happen if Mason will speak to Zisk.

8. The CORRECT answer is C.
We are given that blue lights are never an indicator for the drive belt status. If some of the lights on the lower panel of the machine are blue, then it is reasonable to conclude that some of the lights on the lower panel are not indicators for the drive belt status.

9. The CORRECT answer is B.
There is only one sister that does not have brown eyes and only one sister that is not a doctor, and if the information in answer B is correct, then we learn that the same sister is a non-doctor without brown eyes. We also learn that this same non-doctor is not married. Since this all describes the same sister, we can conclude that two of the other sisters must be married doctors with brown eyes.

TEST 2

DIRECTIONS: Each question or incomplete statement is followed by several suggested answers or completions. Select the one that BEST answers the question or completes the statement. *PRINT THE LETTER OF THE CORRECT ANSWER IN THE SPACE AT THE RIGHT.*

Questions 1-9.

DIRECTIONS: Questions 1 through 9 measure your ability to (1) determine whether statements from witnesses say essentially the same thing and (2) determine the evidence needed to make it reasonably certain that a particular conclusion is true.
To do well on this part of the test, you do NOT have to have a working knowledge of police procedures and techniques. Nor do you have to have any more familiarity with criminals and criminal behavior than that acquired from reading newspapers, listening to radio or watching TV. To do well in this part, you must read and reason carefully.

1. Which of the following pairs of statements say essentially the same thing in two different ways?   1.____
   I. If there is life on Mars, we should fund NASA.
      Either there is life on Mars, or we should not fund NASA.
   II. All Eagle Scouts are teenage boys.
      All teenage boy are Eagle Scouts.
   The CORRECT answer is:
   A. I only   B. I and II   C. II only   D. Neither I nor II

2. Which of the following pairs of statements say essentially the same thing in two different ways?   2.____
   I. If that notebook is missing its front cover, it definitely belongs to Carter.
      Carter's notebook is the only one missing its front cover.
   II. If it's hot, the pool is open.
      The pool is open if it's hot.
   The CORRECT answer is:
   A. I only   B. I and II   C. II only   D. Neither I nor II

3 Which of the following pairs of statements say essentially the same thing in two different ways?   3.____
   I. Nobody who works at the mill is without benefits.
      Everyone who works at the mill has benefits.
   II. We will fund the program only if at least 100 people sign the petition.
      Either we will fund the program or at least 100 people will sign the petition.
   The CORRECT answer is:
   A. I only   B. I and II   C. II only   D. Neither I nor II

4. Which of the following pairs of statements say essentially the same thing in two different ways?
   I. If the new parts arrive, Mr. Luther's request has been answered.
      Mr. Luther requested new parts to arrive.
   II. The machine's test cycle will not run unless the operation cycle is not running.
      The machine's test cycle must be running in order for the operation cycle to run.
   The CORRECT answer is:
   A. I only   B. I and II   C. II only   D. Neither I nor II

5. Summary of Evidence Collected to Date:
   I. To become a member of the East Side Crips, a kid must be either "jumped in" or steal a squad car without getting caught.
   II. Sid, a kid on the East Side, was caught stealing a squad car.
   Prematurely Drawn Conclusion: Sid did not become a member of the East Side Crips.
   Which of the following pieces of evidence, if any, would make it reasonably certain that the conclusion drawn is true?
   A. "Jumping in" is not allowed in prison.
   B. Sid was not "jumped in."
   C. Sid's stealing the squad car had nothing to do with wanting to join the East Side Crips.
   D. None of the above

6. Summary of Evidence Collected to Date:
   I. Jones, a Precinct 8 officer, has more arrests than Smith.
   II. Smith and Watson have exactly the same number of arrests.
   Prematurely Drawn Conclusion: Watson is not a Precinct 8 officer.
   Which of the following pieces of evidence, if any, would make it reasonably certain that the conclusion drawn is true?
   A. All the officers in Precinct 8 have more arrests than Watson.
   B. All the officers in Precinct 8 have fewer arrests than Watson.
   C. Watson has fewer arrests than Jones.
   D. None of the above

7. Summary of Evidence Collected to Date:
   I. Twenty one-dollar bills are divided among Frances, Kerry, and Brian.
   II. If Kerry gives her dollar bills to Frances, then Frances will have more money than Brian.
   Prematurely Drawn Conclusion: Frances has twelve dollars.
   Which of the following pieces of evidence, if any, would make it reasonably certain that the conclusion drawn is true?
   A. If Brian gives his dollars to Kerry, then Kerry will have more money than Frances.
   B. Brian has two dollars.
   C. If Kerry gives her dollars to Brian, Brian will still have less money than Frances.
   D. None of the above

8. Summary of Evidence Collected to Date: 8.____
   I. The street sweepers will be here at noon today.
   II. Residents on the west side of the street should move their cars before noon.
   Prematurely Drawn Conclusion: Today is Wednesday.
   Which of the following pieces of evidence, if any, would make it reasonably certain that the conclusion drawn is true?
   A. The street sweepers never sweep the east side of the street on Wednesday.
   B. The street sweepers arrive at noon every other day.
   C. There is no parking allowed on the west side of the street on Wednesday.
   D. None of the above

9. Summary of Evidence Collected to Date: 9.____
   The only time the warning light comes on is when there is a power surge.
   Prematurely Drawn Conclusion: The warning light does not come on if the air conditioner is not running.
   Which of the following pieces of evidence, if any, would make it reasonably certain that the conclusion drawn is true?
   A. The air conditioner does not turn on if the warning light is on.
   B. Sometimes a power surge is caused by the dishwasher.
   C. There is only a power surge when the air conditioner turns on.
   D. None of the above

Questions 10-14.

DIRECTIONS: Questions 10 through 14 refer to Map #3 and measure your ability to orient yourself within a given section of town, neighborhood or particular area. Each of the questions describes a starting point and a destination. Assume that you are driving a car in the area shown on the map accompanying the questions. Use the map as a basis for the shortest way to get from one point to another without breaking the law.
On the map, a street marked by arrows, or by arrows and the words "One Way," indicates one-way travel and should be assumed to be one-way for the entire length, even when there are breaks or jogs in the street. EXCEPTION: A street that does not have the same name over the full length.

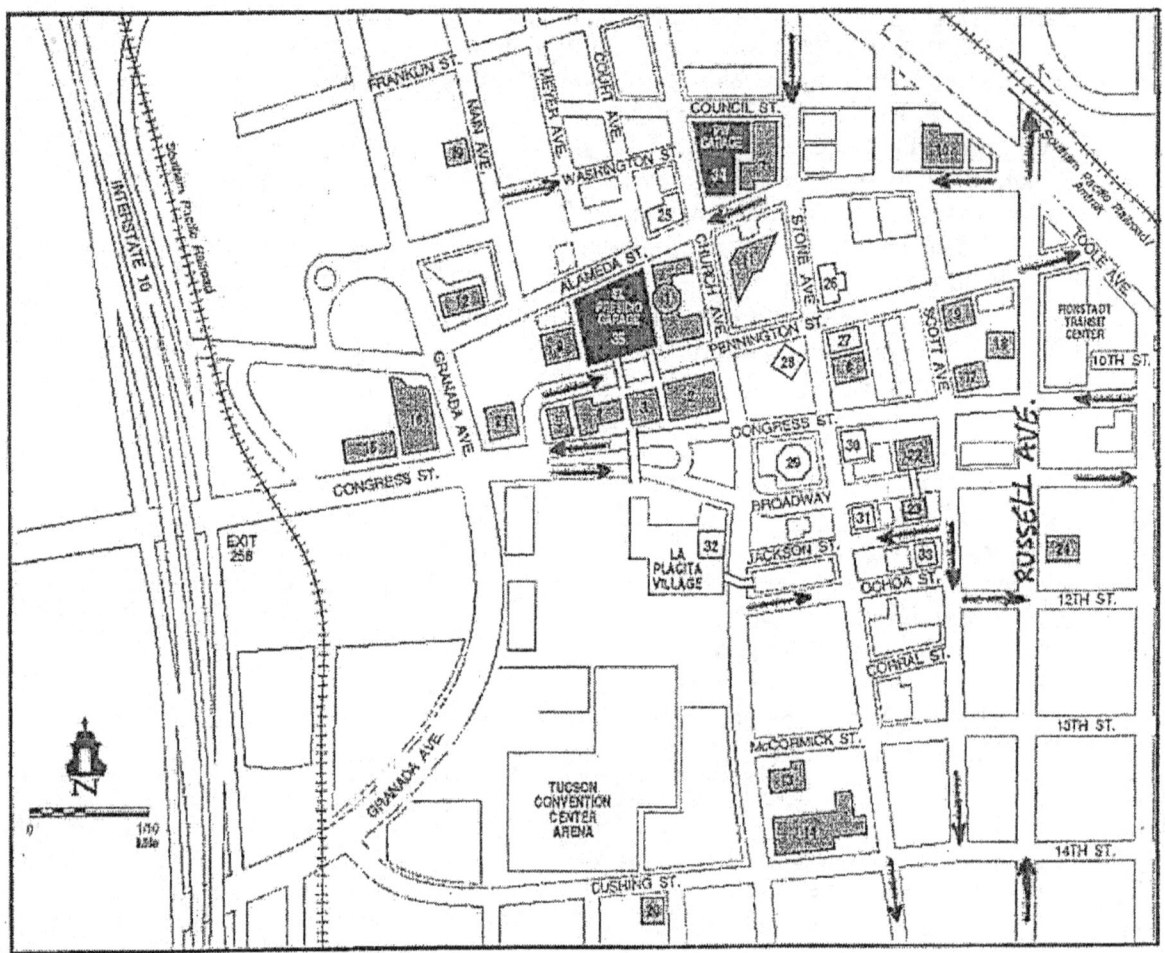

PIMA COUNTY
1. Old Courthouse
2. Superior Court Building
3. Administration Building
4. Health and Welfare Building
5. Mechanical Building
6. Legal Services Building
7. County/City Public Works Center

CITY OF TUCSON
8. City Hall
9. City Hall Annex
10. Alameda Plaza City Court Building
11. Public Library – Main Branch
12. Tucson Water Building
13. Fire Department Headquarters
14. Police Department Building

10. The SHORTEST legal way from the Public Library to the Alameda Plaza City Court Building is
    A. north on Stone Ave., east of Alameda
    B. south on Stone Ave., east on Congress, north on Russell Ave., west on Alameda
    C. south on Stone Ave., east on Pennington, north on Russell Ave., west on Alameda
    D. south on Church Ave., east on Pennington, north on Russell Ave., west on Alameda

10.____

5 (#2)

11. The SHORTEST legal way from City Hall to the Police Department is 11.____
    A. east on Congress, south on Scott Ave., west on 14th
    B. east on Pennington, south on Stone Ave.
    C. east on Congress, south on Stone Ave.
    D. east on Pennington, south on Church Ave.

12. The SHORTEST legal way from the Tucson Water Building to the Legal Service 12.____
    Building is
    A. south on Granada Ave., east on Congress, north to east on Pennington, south on Stone Ave.
    B. east on Alameda, south on Church Ave., east on Pennington, south on Stone Ave.
    C. north on Granada Ave., east on Washington, south on Church Ave., east on Pennington, south on Stone Ave.
    D. south on Granada Ave., east on Cushing, north on Stone Ave.

13. The SHORTEST legal way from the Tucson Convention Center Arena to the 13.____
    City Hall Annex is
    A. west on Cushing, north on Granada Ave., east on Congress east on Broadway
    B. east on Cushing, north on Church Ave., east on Pennington
    C. east on Cushing, north on Russel Ave., west on Pennington
    D. east on Cushing, north on Stone Ave., east on Pennington

14. The SHORTEST legal way from Ronstadt Transit Center to the Fire Department 14.____
    is
    A. west on Pennington, south on Stone Ave., west on McCormick
    B. west on Congress, south on Russell Ave., west on 13th
    C. west on Congress, south on Church Ave.
    D. west on Pennington, south on Church Ave.

Questions 15-19.

DIRECTIONS: Questions 15 through 19 refer to Figure #3, on the following page, and measure your ability to understand written descriptions of events. Each question presents a description of an accident or event and asks you which of the following five drawings in Figure #3 BEST represents it.
In the drawings, the following symbols are used:
Moving vehicle ⌂   Non-moving vehicle ▲
Pedestrian or bicyclist •
The path and direction of travel of a vehicle or pedestrian is indicated by a solid line.
The path and direction of travel of each vehicle or pedestrian directly involved in a collision from the point of impact is indicated by a dotted line.

In the space at the right, print the letter of the drawing that BEST fit the descriptions written below.

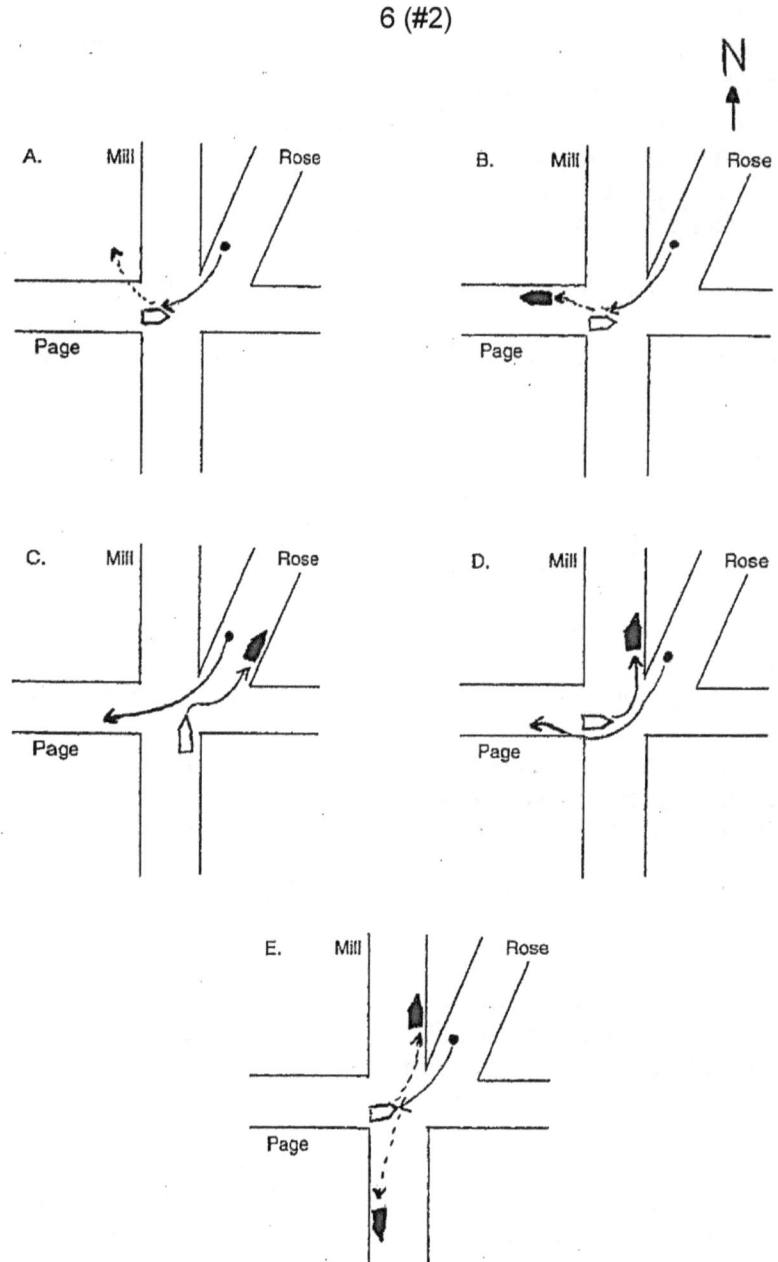

15. A bicyclist heading southwest on Rose travels into the intersection, sideswipes a car that is heading east on Page, and veers right, leaving the roadway at the northwest corner of Page and Mill. 15.____

16. A driver traveling north on Mill swerves right to avoid a bicyclist that is traveling southwest on Rose. The driver strikes the rear end of a car parked on Rose. The bicyclist continues through the intersection and travels west on Page. 16.____

17. A bicyclist heading southwest on Rose travels into the intersection, sideswipes a car that is heading east on Page, and veers right, striking the rear end of a car parked in the westbound lane on Page. 17.____

18. A driver traveling east on Page swerves left to avoid a bicyclist that is traveling   18._____
    southwest on Rose. The driver strikes the rear end of a car parked on Mill.
    The bicyclist continues through the intersection and travels west on Page.

19. A bicyclist heading southwest on Rose enters the intersection and sideswipes   19._____
    a car that is swerving left to avoid her. The bicyclist veers left and collides with
    a car parked in the southbound lane on Mill. The driver of the car veers left
    and collides with a car parked in the northbound lane on Mill.

Questions 20-22.

DIRECTIONS: In Questions 20 through 22, choose the word or phrase CLOSEST in meaning
             to the word or phrase printed in capital letters.

20. WAIVE   20._____
    A. cease   B. surrender   C. prevent   D. die

21. DEPOSITION   21._____
    A. settlement   B. deterioration C. testimony   D. character

22. IMMUNITY   22._____
    A. exposure   B. accusation   C. protection   D. exchange

Questions 23-25.

DIRECTIONS: Questions 23 through 25 measure your ability to do fieldwork-related
             arithmetic. Each question presents a separate arithmetic problem for you to
             solve.

23. Dean, a claims investigator, is reading a 445-page case record in his spare   23._____
    time at work. He has already read 157 pages.
    If Dean reads 24 pages a day, he should finish reading the rest of the record in
    _____ days.
    A. 7   B. 12   C. 19   D. 24

24. The Fire Department owns four cars. The Department of Sanitation owns twice   24._____
    as many cars as the Fire Department. The Department of Parks and
    Recreation owns one fewer car than the Department of Sanitation. The
    Department of Parks and Recreation is buying new tires for each of its cars.
    Each tire costs $100.
    How much is the Department of Parks and Recreation going to spend on tires?
    A. $400   B. $2,800   C. $3,200   D. $4,900

25. A dance hall is about 5,000 square feet. The local ordinance does not allow   25._____
    more than 50 people per every 100 square feet of commercial space.
    The maximum capacity of the hall is
    A. 500   B. 2,500   C. 5,000   D. 25,000

KEY (CORRECT ANSWERS)

1.	D		11.	D
2.	B		12.	A
3.	A		13.	B
4.	D		14.	C
5.	B		15.	A
6.	D		16.	C
7.	D		17.	B
8.	A		18.	D
9.	C		19.	E
10.	C		20.	B

21. C
22. C
23. B
24. B
25. B

SOLUTIONS TO QUESTIONS 1-9

P implies Q = original statement

Not Q implies not P = contrapositive of the original statement. A statement and its contrapositive are logically equivalent.

Q implies P = converse of the original statement

Not P implies not Q = inverse of the original statement. The converse and inverse of an original statement are logically equivalent.

P implies Q = Not P or Q.

1. The CORRECT answer is D.
   For item I, the second statement should be "Either there is no life on Mars or we should fund NASA" in order to be logically equivalent to the first statement. For item II, the statements are converses of each other; thus, they are not equivalent.

2. The CORRECT answer is B.
   In item I, this is an example of P implies Q and Q implies P. In this case, P = the notebook is missing its cover and Q = the notebook belongs to Carter. In item II, the ordering of the words is changed, but the If P then Q is exactly the same. P = it is hot and Q = the pool is open.

3. The CORRECT answer is A.
   For item I, if nobody is without benefits, then everybody has benefits. For item II, the second equivalent statement should be "either we will not fund the program or at least 100 people will sign the petition."

4. The CORRECT answer is D.
   For item I, the first statement is an implication, whereas the second statement mentions only one part of the implication (new parts are requested) and says nothing about the other part. For item II, the first statement is equivalent to "if the operating cycle is not running, then the test cycle will run." The second statement is equivalent to "if the operating cycle is running, then the test cycle will run." So, these statements in item II are not equivalent.

5. The CORRECT answer is B.
   Since Sid did not steal a car and avoid getting caught, the only other way he could become a Crips member would be "jumped in." Choice B tells us that Sid was not "jumped in," so we conclude that he did not become a member of the Crips.

6. The CORRECT answer is D.
   Since Smith and Watson have the same number of arrests, Watson must have fewer arrests than Jones. This means that each of choices A and B is impossible. Choice C would also not reveal whether or not Watson is a Precinct 8 officer.

7. The CORRECT answer is D.
   Exact dollar amounts still cannot be ascertained by using any of the other choices.

8. The CORRECT answer is A.
   The street sweepers never sweep on the east side of the street on Wednesday; however, they will be here at noon today. This implies that they will sweep on the west side of the street. Since the residents should move their cars before noon, we can conclude that today is Wednesday.

9. The CORRECT answer is C.
   We start with W implies P, where W = warning light comes on and P = power surge. Choice C would read as P implies A, where A = air conditioning is running. Combining these statements leads to W implies A. The conclusion can be read as: Not A implies Not W, which is equivalent to W implies A.

EVALUATING CONCLUSIONS IN LIGHT OF KNOWN FACTS
EXAMINATION SECTION
TEST 1

DIRECTIONS: Each question or incomplete statement is followed by several suggested answers or completions. Select the one that BEST answers the question or completes the statement. *PRINT THE LETTER OF THE CORRECT ANSWER IN THE SPACE AT THE RIGHT.*

Questions 1-9.

DIRECTIONS: In Questions 1 through 9, you will read a set of facts and a conclusion drawn from them. The conclusion may be valid or invalid, based on the facts—it's your task to determine the validity of the conclusion.

For each question, select the letter before the statement that BEST expresses the relationship between the given facts and the conclusion that has been drawn from them. Your choices are:
- A. The facts prove the conclusion;
- B. The facts disprove the conclusion; or
- C. The facts neither prove nor disprove the conclusion.

1. FACTS: If the supervisor retires, James, the assistant supervisor, will not be transferred to another department. James will be promoted to supervisor if he is not transferred. The supervisor retired.

    CONCLUSION: James will be promoted to supervisor.
    - A. The facts prove the conclusion.
    - B. The facts disprove the conclusion.
    - C. The facts neither prove nor disprove the conclusion.

    1.____

2. FACTS: In the town of Luray, every player on the softball team works at Luray National Bank. In addition, every player on the Luray softball team wear glasses.

    CONCLUSIONS: At least some of the people who work at Luray National Bank wear glasses.
    - A. The facts prove the conclusion.
    - B. The facts disprove the conclusion.
    - C. The facts neither prove nor disprove the conclusion.

    2.____

3. FACTS: The only time Henry and June go out to dinner is on an evening when they have childbirth classes. Their childbirth classes meet on Tuesdays and Thursdays.

    3.____

CONCLUSION: Henry and June never go out to dinner on Friday or Saturday.
  A. The facts prove the conclusion.
  B. The facts disprove the conclusion.
  C. The facts neither prove nor disprove the conclusion.

4. FACTS: Every player on the field hockey team has at least one bruise. Everyone on the field hockey team also has scarred knees.

   CONCLUSION: Most people with both bruises and scarred knees are field hockey players.
   A. The facts prove the conclusion.
   B. The facts disprove the conclusion.
   C. The facts neither prove nor disprove the conclusion.

4.____

5. FACTS: In the chess tournament, Lance will win his match against Jane if Jane wins her match against Mathias. If Lance wins his match against Jane, Christine will not win her match against Jane.

   CONCLUSION: Christine will not win her match against Jane if Jane wins her match against Mathias.
   A. The facts prove the conclusion.
   B. The facts disprove the conclusion.
   C. The facts neither prove nor disprove the conclusion.

5.____

6. FACTS: No green lights on the machine are indicators for the belt drive status. Not all of the lights on the machine's upper panel are green. Some lights on the machine's lower panel are green.

   CONCLUSION: The green lights on the machine's lower panel may be indicators for the belt drive status.
   A. The facts prove the conclusion.
   B. The facts disprove the conclusion.
   C. The facts neither prove nor disprove the conclusion.

6.____

7. FACTS: At a small, one-room country school, there are eight students: Amy, Ben, Carla, Dan, Elliot, Francine, Greg, and Hannah. Each student is in either the 6th, 7th, or 8th grade. Either two or three students are in each grade. Amy, Dan, and Francine are all in different grades. Ben and Elliot are both in the 7th grade. Hannah and Carl are in the same grade.

   CONCLUSION: Exactly three students are in the 7th grade.
   A. The facts prove the conclusion.
   B. The facts disprove the conclusion.
   C. The facts neither prove nor disprove the conclusion.

7.____

8. FACTS: Two married couples are having lunch together. Two of the four people are German and two are Russian, but in each couple the nationality of the spouse is not necessarily the same as the other's. One person in the group is a teacher, the other a lawyer, one an engineer, and the other a writer. The teacher is a Russian man. The writer is Russian, and her husband is an engineer. One of the people, Mr. Stern, is German.

   CONCLUSION: Mr. Stern's wife is a writer.
   A. The facts prove the conclusion.
   B. The facts disprove the conclusion.
   C. The facts neither prove nor disprove the conclusion.

   8.____

9. FACTS: The flume ride at the county fair is open only to children who are at least 36 inches tall. Lisa is 30 inches tall. John is shorter than Henry, but more than 10 inches taller than Lisa.

   CONCLUSION: Lisa is the only one who can't ride the flume ride.
   A. The facts prove the conclusion.
   B. The facts disprove the conclusion.
   C. The facts neither prove nor disprove the conclusion.

   9.____

Questions 10-17.

DIRECTIONS: Questions 10 through 17 are based on the following reading passage. It is not your knowledge of the particular topic that is being tested, but your ability to reason based on what you have read. The passage is likely to detail several proposed courses of action and factors affecting these proposals. The reading passage is followed by a conclusion or outcome based on the facts in the passage, or a description of a decision taken regarding the situation. The conclusion is followed by a number of statements that have a possible connection to the conclusion. For each statement, you are to determine whether:
   A. The statement proves the conclusion.
   B. The statement supports the conclusion but does not prove it.
   C. The statement disproves the conclusion.
   D. The statement weakens the conclusion but does not disprove it.
   E. The statement has no relevance to the conclusion.

Remember that the conclusion after the passage is to be accepted as the outcome of what actually happened, and that you are being asked to evaluate the impact each statement would have had on the conclusion.

PASSAGE:

The Grand Army of Foreign Wars, a national veteran's organization, is struggling to maintain its National Home, where the widowed spouses and orphans of deceased members are housed together in a small village-like community. The Home is open to spouses and children who are bereaved for any reason, regardless of whether the member's death was related to military service, but a new global conflict has led to a dramatic surge in the number of members' deaths: many veterans who re-enlisted for the conflict have been killed in action.

The Grand Army of Foreign Wars is considering several options for handling the increased number of applications for housing at the National Home, which has been traditionally supported by membership due. At its national convention, it will choose only one of the following:

The first idea is a one-time $50 tax on all members, above and beyond the dues they pay already. Since the organization has more than a million member, this tax should be sufficient for the construction and maintenance of new housing for applicants on the existing grounds of the National Home. The idea is opposed, however, by some older members who live on fixed incomes. These members object in principle to the taxation of Grand Army members. The Grand Army has never imposed a tax on its members.

The second idea is to launch a national fundraising drive the public relations campaign that will attract donations for the National Home. Several national celebrities are members of the organization, and other celebrities could be attracted to the cause. Many Grand Army members are wary of this approach, however: in the past, the net receipts of some fundraising efforts have been relatively insignificant, given the costs of staging them.

A third approach, suggested by many of the younger members, is to have new applicants share some of the costs of construction and maintenance. The spouses and children would pay an up-front "enrollment" fee, based on a sliding scale proportionate to their income and assets, and then a monthly fee adjusted similarly to contribute to maintenance costs. Many older members are strongly opposed to this idea, as it is in direct contradiction to the principles on which the organization was founded more than a century ago.

The fourth option is simply to maintain the status quo, focus the organization's efforts on supporting the families who already live at the National Home, and wait to accept new applicants based on attrition.

CONCLUSION: At its annual national convention, the Grand Army of Foreign Wars votes to impose a one-time tax of $10 on each member for the purpose of expanding and supporting the National Home to welcome a larger number of applicants. The tax is considered to be the solution most likely to produce the funds needed to accommodate the growing number of applicants.

10. Actuarial studies have shown that because the Grand Army's membership consists mostly of older veterans from earlier wars, the organization's membership will suffer a precipitous decline in numbers in about five years.
    A. The statement proves the conclusion.
    B. The statement supports the conclusion but does not prove it.
    C. The statement disproves the conclusion.
    D. The statement weakens the conclusion but does not disprove it.
    E. The statement has no relevance to the conclusion.

11. After passage of the funding measure, a splinter group of older members appeals for the "sliding scale" provision to be applied to the tax, so that some members may be allowed to contribute less based on their income.
    A. The statement proves the conclusion.
    B. The statement supports the conclusion but does not prove it.
    C. The statement disproves the conclusion.
    D. The statement weakens the conclusion but does not disprove it.
    E. The statement has no relevance to the conclusion.

12. The original charter of the Grand Army of Foreign Wars specifically states that the organization will not levy taxes or duties on its members beyond its modest annual dues. It takes a super-majority of attending delegates at the national convention to make alterations to the charter.
    A. The statement proves the conclusion.
    B. The statement supports the conclusion but does not prove it.
    C. The statement disproves the conclusion.
    D. The statement weakens the conclusion but does not disprove it.
    E. The statement has no relevance to the conclusion.

12.____

13. Six months before Grand Army of Foreign Wars' national convention, the Internal Revenue Service rules that because it is an organization that engages in political lobbying, the Grand Army must no longer enjoy its own federal tax-exempt status.
    A. The statement proves the conclusion.
    B. The statement supports the conclusion but does not prove it.
    C. The statement disproves the conclusion.
    D. The statement weakens the conclusion but does not disprove it.
    E. The statement has no relevance to the conclusion.

13.____

14. Two months before the national convention, Dirk Rockwell, arguably the country's most famous film actor, announces in a nationally televised interview that he has been saddened to learn of the plight of the National Home, and that he is going to make it his own personal crusade to see that it is able to house and support a greater number of widowed spouses and orphans in the future.
    A. The statement proves the conclusion.
    B. The statement supports the conclusion but does not prove it.
    C. The statement disproves the conclusion.
    D. The statement weakens the conclusion but does not disprove it.
    E. The statement has no relevance to the conclusion.

14.____

15. The Grand Army's final estimate is that the cost of expanding the National Home to accommodate the increased number of applicants will be about $61 million.
    A. The statement proves the conclusion.
    B. The statement supports the conclusion but does not prove it.
    C. The statement disproves the conclusion.
    D. The statement weakens the conclusion but does not disprove it.
    E. The statement has no relevance to the conclusion.

15.____

16. Just before the national convention, the Federal Department of Veterans Affairs announces steep cuts in the benefits package that is currently offered to the widowed spouses and orphans of veterans.
    A. The statement proves the conclusion.
    B. The statement supports the conclusion but does not prove it.
    C. The statement disproves the conclusion.
    D. The statement weakens the conclusion but does not disprove it.
    E. The statement has no relevance to the conclusion.

16.____

17. After the national convention, the Grand Army of Foreign Wars begins charging a modest "start-up" fee to all families who apply for residence at the national home. 17._____
   A. The statement proves the conclusion.
   B. The statement supports the conclusion but does not prove it.
   C. The statement disproves the conclusion.
   D. The statement weakens the conclusion but does not disprove it.
   E. The statement has no relevance to the conclusion.

Questions 18-25.

DIRECTIONS: Questions 18 through 25 each provide four factual statements and a conclusion based on these statements. After reading the entire question, you will decide whether:
   A. The conclusion is proved by statements I-IV;
   B. The conclusion is disproved by statements I-IV.
   C. The facts are not sufficient to prove or disprove the conclusion.

18. FACTUAL STATEMENTS: 18._____
   I. In the Field Day high jump competition, Martha jumped higher than Frank.
   II. Carl jumped higher than Ignacio.
   III. Ignacio jumped higher than Frank.
   IV. Dan jumped higher than Carl.

   CONCLUSION: Frank finished last in the high jump competition.
   A. The conclusion is proved by statements I-IV;
   B. The conclusion is disproved by statements I-IV.
   C. The facts are not sufficient to prove or disprove the conclusion.

19. FACTUAL STATEMENTS: 19._____
   I. The door to the hammer mill chamber is locked if light 6 is red.
   II. The door to the hammer mill chamber is locked only when the mill is operating.
   III. If the mill is not operating, light 6 is blue.
   IV. Light 6 is blue.

   CONCLUSION: The door to the hammer mill chamber is locked.
   A. The conclusion is proved by statements I-IV;
   B. The conclusion is disproved by statements I-IV.
   C. The facts are not sufficient to prove or disprove the conclusion.

20. FACTUAL STATEMENTS: 20._____
   I. Ziegfried, the lion tamer at the circus, has demanded ten additional minutes of performance time during each show.
   II. If Ziegfried is allowed his ten additional minutes per show, he will attempt to teach Kimba the tiger to shoot a basketball.
   III. If Kimba learns how to shoot a basketball, then Ziegfried was not given his ten additional minutes.
   IV. Ziegfried was given his ten additional minutes.

7 (#1)

CONCLUSION: Despite Ziegfried's efforts, Kimba did not learn how to shoot a basketball.
   A. The conclusion is proved by statements I-IV;
   B. The conclusion is disproved by statements I-IV.
   C. The facts are not sufficient to prove or disprove the conclusion.

21. FACTUAL STATEMENTS: 21.____
   I. If Stan goes to counseling, Sara won't divorce him.
   II. If Sara divorces Stan, she'll move back to Texas.
   III. If Sara doesn't divorce Stan, Irene will be disappointed.
   IV. Stan goes to counseling.

   CONCLUSION: Irene will be disappointed.
      A. The conclusion is proved by statements I-IV;
      B. The conclusion is disproved by statements I-IV.
      C. The facts are not sufficient to prove or disprove the conclusion.

22. FACTUAL STATEMENTS: 22.____
   I. If Delia is promoted to district manager, Claudia will have to be promoted to team leader.
   II. Delia will be promoted to district manager unless she misses her fourth-quarter sales quota.
   III. If Claudia is promoted to team leader, Thomas will be promoted to assistant team leader.
   IV. Delia meets her fourth-quarter sales quota.

   CONCLUSION: Thomas is promoted to assistant team leader.
      A. The conclusion is proved by statements I-IV;
      B. The conclusion is disproved by statements I-IV.
      C. The facts are not sufficient to prove or disprove the conclusion.

23. FACTUAL STATEMENTS: 23.____
   I. Clone D is identical to Clone B.
   II. Clone B is not identical to Clone A.
   III. Clone D is not identical to Clone C.
   IV. Clone E is not identical to the clones that are identical to Clone B.

   CONCLUSION: Clone E is identical to Clone D.
      A. The conclusion is proved by statements I-IV;
      B. The conclusion is disproved by statements I-IV.
      C. The facts are not sufficient to prove or disprove the conclusion.

24. FACTUAL STATEMENTS: 24.____
   I. In the Stafford Tower, each floor is occupied by a single business.
   II. Big G Staffing is on a floor between CyberGraphics and MainEvent.
   III. Gasco is on the floor directly below CyberGraphics and three floors above Treehorn Audio.
   IV. MainEvent is five floors below EZ Tax and four floors below Treehorn Audio.

CONCLUSION: EZ Tax is on a floor between Gasco and MainEvent.
  A. The conclusion is proved by statements I-IV;
  B. The conclusion is disproved by statements I-IV.
  C. The facts are not sufficient to prove or disprove the conclusion.

25. FACTUAL STATEMENTS:
  I. Only county roads lead to Nicodemus.
  II. All the roads from Hill City to Graham County are federal highways.
  III. Some of the roads from Plainville lead to Nicodemus.
  IV. Some of the roads running from Hill City lead to Strong City.

  CONCLUSION: Some of the roads from Plainville are county roads.
  A. The conclusion is proved by statements I-IV;
  B. The conclusion is disproved by statements I-IV.
  C. The facts are not sufficient to prove or disprove the conclusion.

KEY (CORRECT ANSWERS)

1.	A		11.	A
2.	A		12.	D
3.	A		13.	E
4.	C		14.	D
5.	A		15.	B
6.	B		16.	B
7.	A		17.	C
8.	A		18.	A
9.	A		19.	B
10.	E		20.	A

21. A
22. A
23. B
24. A
25. A

SOLUTIONS TO PROBLEMS

1. **CORRECT ANSWER: A**
   Given Statement 3, we deduce that James will not be transferred to another department. By Statement 2, we can conclude that James will be promoted.

2. **CORRECT ANSWER: A**
   Since every player on the softball team wears glasses, these individuals compose some of the people who work at the bank. Although not every person who works at the bank plays softball, those bank employees who do play softball wear glasses.

3. **CORRECT ANSWER: A**
   If Henry and June go out to dinner, we conclude that it must be on Tuesday or Thursday, which are the only two days when they have childbirth classes. This implies that if it is not Tuesday or Thursday, then this couple does not go out to dinner.

4. **CORRECT ANSWER: C**
   We can only conclude that if a person plays on the field hockey team, then he or she has both bruises and scarred knees. But there are probably a great number of people who have both bruises and scarred knees but do not play on the field hockey team. The given conclusion can neither be proven or disproven.

5. **CORRECT ANSWER: A**
   From statement 1, if Jane beats Mathias, then Lance will beat Jane. Using statement 2, we can then conclude that Christine will not win her match against Jane.

6. **CORRECT ANSWER: B**
   Statement 1 tells us that no green light can be an indicator of the belt drive status. Thus, the given conclusion must be false.

7. **CORRECT ANSWER: A**
   We already know that Ben and Elliot are in the 7th grade. Even though Hannah and Carl are in the same grade, it cannot be the 7th grade because we would then have at least four students in this 7th grade. This would contradict the third statement, which states that either two or three students are in each grade. Since Amy, Dan, and Francine are in different grade, exactly one of them must be in the 7th grade. Thus, Ben, Elliot, and exactly one of Amy, Dan, and Francine are the three students in the 7th grade.

8. **CORRECT ANSWER: A**
   One man is a teacher, who is Russian. We know that the writer is female and is Russian. Since her husband is an engineer, he cannot be the Russian teacher. Thus, her husband is of German descent, namely Mr. Stern. This means that Mr. Stern's wife is the writer. Note that one couple consists of a male Russian teacher and a female German lawyer. The other couple consists of a male German engineer and a female Russian writer.

9. CORRECT ANSWER: A
Since John is more than 10 inches taller than Lisa, his height is at least 46 inches. Also, John is shorter than Henry, so Henry's height must be greater than 46 inches. Thus, Lisa is the only one whose height is less than 36 inches. Therefore, she is the only one who is not allowed on the flume ride.

18. CORRECT ANSWER: A
Dan jumped higher than Carl, who jumped higher than Ignacio, who jumped higher than Frank. Since Martha jumped higher than Frank, every person jumped higher than Frank. Thus, Frank finished last.

19. CORRECT ANSWER: B
If the light is red, then the door is locked. If the door is locked, then the mill is operating. Reversing the logical sequence of these statements, if the mill is not operating, then the door is not locked, which means that the light is blue. Thus, the given conclusion is disproved.

20. CORRECT ANSWER: A
Using the contrapositive of statement III, Ziegfried was given his ten additional minutes, then Kimba did not learn how to shoot a basketball. Since statement IV is factual, the conclusion is proved.

21. CORRECT ANSWER: A
From Statements IV and I, we conclude that Sara doesn't divorce Stan. Then statement III reveals that Irene will be disappointed. Thus, the conclusion is proved.

22. CORRECT ANSWER: A
Statement II can be rewritten as "Delia is promoted to district manager or she misses her sales quota." Furthermore, this statement is equivalent to "If Delia makes her sales quota, then she is promoted to district manager." From statement I, we conclude that Claudia is promoted to team leader. Finally, by statement III, Thomas is promoted to assistant team leader.

23. CORRECT ANSWER: B
By statement IV, Clone E is not identical to any clones identical to Clone B. Statement I tells us that Clones B and D are identical. Therefore, Clone E cannot be identical to Clone D. The conclusion is disproved.

24. CORRECT ANSWER: A
Based on all four statements, CyberGraphics is somewhere below MainEvent. Gasco is one floor below CyberGraphics. EZ Tax is two floors below Gasco. Treehorn Audio is one floor below EZ Tax. MainEvent is four floors below Treehorn Audio. Thus, EZ Tax is two floors below Gasco and five floors above MainEvent. The conclusion is proved.

25. CORRECT ANSWER: A
From statement III, we know that some of the roads from Plainville lead to Nicodemus. But statement I tells us that only county roads lead to Nicodemus. Therefore, some of the roads from Plainville must be county roads. The conclusion is proved.

TEST 2

DIRECTIONS: Each question or incomplete statement is followed by several suggested answers or completions. Select the one that BEST answers the question or completes the statement. *PRINT THE LETTER OF THE CORRECT ANSWER IN THE SPACE AT THE RIGHT.*

Questions 1-9.

DIRECTIONS: In Questions 1 through 9, you will read a set of facts and a conclusion drawn from them. The conclusion may be valid or invalid, based on the facts—it's your task to determine the validity of the conclusion.

For each question, select the letter before the statement that BEST expresses the relationship between the given facts and the conclusion that has been drawn from them. Your choices are:
   A. The facts prove the conclusion;
   B. The facts disprove the conclusion; or
   C. The facts neither prove nor disprove the conclusion.

1. FACTS: Some employees in the testing department are statisticians. Most of the statisticians who work in the testing department are projection specialists. Tom Wilks works in the testing department.

   CONCLUSION: Tom Wilks is a statistician.
   A. The facts prove the conclusion.
   B. The facts disprove the conclusion.
   C. The facts neither prove nor disprove the conclusion.

   1.____

2. FACTS: Ten coins are split among Hank, Lawrence, and Gail. If Lawrence gives his coins to Hank, then Hank will have more coins than Gail. If Gail gives her coins to Lawrence, then Lawrence will have more coins than Hank.

   CONCLUSION: Hank has six coins.
   A. The facts prove the conclusion.
   B. The facts disprove the conclusion.
   C. The facts neither prove nor disprove the conclusion.

   2.____

3. FACTS: Nobody loves everybody. Janet loves Ken. Ken loves everybody who loves Janet.

   CONCLUSION: Everybody loves Janet.
   A. The facts prove the conclusion.
   B. The facts disprove the conclusion.
   C. The facts neither prove nor disprove the conclusion.

   3.____

4. FACTS: Most of the Torres family lives in East Los Angeles. Many people in East Los Angeles celebrate Cinco de Mayo. Joe is a member of the Torres family.

   CONCLUSION: Joe lives in East Los Angeles.
   A. The facts prove the conclusion.
   B. The facts disprove the conclusion.
   C. The facts neither prove nor disprove the conclusion.

   4.____

5. FACTS: Five professionals each occupy one story of a five-story office building. Dr. Kane's office is above Dr. Assad's. Dr. Johnson's office is between Dr. Kane's and Dr. Conlon's. Dr. Steen's office is between Dr. Conlon's and Dr. Assad's. Dr. Johnson is on the fourth story.

   CONCLUSION: Dr. Kane occupies the top story.
   A. The facts prove the conclusion.
   B. The facts disprove the conclusion.
   C. The facts neither prove nor disprove the conclusion.

   5.____

6. FACTS: To be eligible for membership in the Yukon Society, a person must be able to either tunnel through a snowbank while wearing only a T-shirt and short, or hold his breath for two minutes under water that is 50°F. Ray can only hold his breath for a minute and a half.

   CONCLUSION: Ray can still become a member of the Yukon Society by tunneling through a snowbank while wearing a T-shirt and shorts.
   A. The facts prove the conclusion.
   B. The facts disprove the conclusion.
   C. The facts neither prove nor disprove the conclusion.

   6.____

7. FACTS: A mark is worth five plunks. You can exchange four sharps for a tinplot. It takes eight marks to buy a sharp.

   CONCLUSION: A sharp is the most valuable.
   A. The facts prove the conclusion.
   B. The facts disprove the conclusion.
   C. The facts neither prove nor disprove the conclusion.

   7.____

8. FACTS: There are gibbons, as well as lemurs, who like to play in the trees at the monkey house. All those who like to play in the trees at the monkey house are fed lettuce and bananas.

   CONCLUSION: Lemurs and gibbons are types of monkeys.
   A. The facts prove the conclusion.
   B. The facts disprove the conclusion.
   C. The facts neither prove nor disprove the conclusion.

   8.____

9. FACTS: None of the Blackfoot tribes is a Salishan Indian tribe. Salishan Indians came from the northern Pacific Coast. All Salishan Indians live each of the Continental Divide.   9._____

   CONCLUSION: No Blackfoot tribes live east of the Continental Divide.
   A. The facts prove the conclusion.
   B. The facts disprove the conclusion.
   C. The facts neither prove nor disprove the conclusion.

Questions 10-17.

DIRECTIONS: Questions 10 through 17 are based on the following reading passage. It is not your knowledge of the particular topic that is being tested, but your ability to reason based on what you have read. The passage is likely to detail several proposed courses of action and factors affecting these proposals. The reading passage is followed by a conclusion or outcome based on the facts in the passage, or a description of a decision taken regarding the situation. The conclusion is followed by a number of statements that have a possible connection to the conclusion. For each statement, you are to determine whether:
   A. The statement proves the conclusion.
   B. The statement supports the conclusion but does not prove it.
   C. The statement disproves the conclusion.
   D. The statement weakens the conclusion but does not disprove it.
   E. The statement has no relevance to the conclusion.

Remember that the conclusion after the passage is to be accepted as the outcome of what actually happened, and that you are being asked to evaluate the impact each statement would have had on the conclusion.

PASSAGE:

On August 12, Beverly Willey reported that she was in the elevator late on the previous evening after leaving her office on the 16th floor of a large office building. In her report, she states that a man got on the elevator at the 11th floor, pulled her off the elevator, assaulted her, and stole her purse. Ms. Willey reported that she had seen the man in the elevators and hallways of the building before. She believes that the man works in the building. Her description of him is as follows: he is tall, unshaven, with wavy brown hair and a scar on his left cheek. He walks with a pronounced limp, often dragging his left foot behind his right.

CONCLUSION: After Beverly Willey makes her report, the police arrest a 43-year-old man, Barton Black, and charge him with her assault.

10. Barton Black is a former Marine who served in Vietnam, where he sustained shrapnel wounds to the left side of his face and suffered nerve damage in his left leg.
    A. The statement proves the conclusion.
    B. The statement supports the conclusion but does not prove it.
    C. The statement disproves the conclusion.
    D. The statement weakens the conclusion but does not disprove it.
    E. The statement has no relevance to the conclusion.

11. When they arrived at his residence to question him, detectives were greeted at the door by Barton Black, who was tall and clean-shaven.
    A. The statement proves the conclusion.
    B. The statement supports the conclusion but does not prove it.
    C. The statement disproves the conclusion.
    D. The statement weakens the conclusion but does not disprove it.
    E. The statement has no relevance to the conclusion.

12. Barton Black was booked into the county jail several days after Beverly Willey's assault.
    A. The statement proves the conclusion.
    B. The statement supports the conclusion but does not prove it.
    C. The statement disproves the conclusion.
    D. The statement weakens the conclusion but does not disprove it.
    E. The statement has no relevance to the conclusion.

13. Upon further investigation, detectives discover that Beverly Willey does not work at the office building.
    A. The statement proves the conclusion.
    B. The statement supports the conclusion but does not prove it.
    C. The statement disproves the conclusion.
    D. The statement weakens the conclusion but does not disprove it.
    E. The statement has no relevance to the conclusion.

14. Upon further investigation, detectives discover that Barton Black does not work at the office building.
    A. The statement proves the conclusion.
    B. The statement supports the conclusion but does not prove it.
    C. The statement disproves the conclusion.
    D. The statement weakens the conclusion but does not disprove it.
    E. The statement has no relevance to the conclusion.

15. In the spring of the following year, Barton Black is convicted of assaulting Beverly Willey on August 11.
    A. The statement proves the conclusion.
    B. The statement supports the conclusion but does not prove it.
    C. The statement disproves the conclusion.
    D. The statement weakens the conclusion but does not disprove it.
    E. The statement has no relevance to the conclusion.

16. During their investigation of the assault, detectives determine that Beverly Willey   16.____
was assaulted on the 12th floor of the office building.
    A. The statement proves the conclusion.
    B. The statement supports the conclusion but does not prove it.
    C. The statement disproves the conclusion.
    D. The statement weakens the conclusion but does not disprove it.
    E. The statement has no relevance to the conclusion.

17. The day after Beverly Willey's assault, Barton Black fled the area and was never   17.____
seen again.
    A. The statement proves the conclusion.
    B. The statement supports the conclusion but does not prove it.
    C. The statement disproves the conclusion.
    D. The statement weakens the conclusion but does not disprove it.
    E. The statement has no relevance to the conclusion.

Questions 18-25.

DIRECTIONS: Questions 18 through 25 each provide four factual statements and a conclusion based on these statements. After reading the entire question, you will decide whether:
    A. The conclusion is proved by statements I-IV;
    B. The conclusion is disproved by statements I-IV.
    C. The facts are not sufficient to prove or disprove the conclusion.

18. FACTUAL STATEMENTS: 18.____
    I. Among five spice jars on the shelf, the sage is to the right of the parsley.
    II. The pepper is to the left of the basil.
    III. The nutmeg is between the sage and the pepper.
    IV. The pepper is the second spice from the left.

    CONCLUSION: The safe is the farthest to the right.
        A. The conclusion is proved by statements I-IV;
        B. The conclusion is disproved by statements I-IV.
        C. The facts are not sufficient to prove or disprove the conclusion.

19. FACTUAL STATEMENTS: 19.____
    I. Gear X rotates in a clockwise direction if Switch C is in the OFF position.
    II. Gear X will rotate in a counter-clockwise direction is Switch C is ON.
    III. If Gear X is rotating in a clockwise direction, then Gear Y will not be rotating at all.
    IV. Switch C is ON.

    CONCLUSION: Gear X is rotating in a counter-clockwise direction.
        A. The conclusion is proved by statements I-IV;
        B. The conclusion is disproved by statements I-IV.
        C. The facts are not sufficient to prove or disprove the conclusion.

20. FACTUAL STATEMENTS:
    I. Lane will leave for the Toronto meeting today only if Terence, Rourke, and Jackson all file their marketing reports by the end of the work day.
    II. Rourke will file her report on time only if Ganz submits last quarter's data.
    III. If Terence attends the security meeting, he will attend it with Jackson, and they will not file their marketing reports by the end of the work day.

    CONCLUSION: Lane will leave for the Toronto meeting today.
    A. The conclusion is proved by statements I-IV;
    B. The conclusion is disproved by statements I-IV.
    C. The facts are not sufficient to prove or disprove the conclusion.

20._____

21. FACTUAL STATEMENTS:
    I. Bob is in second place in the Boston Marathon.
    II. Gregory is winning the Boston Marathon.
    III. There are four miles to go in the race, and Bob is gaining on Gregory at the rate of 100 yards every minute.
    IV. There are 1760 yards in a mile and Gregory's usual pace during the Boston Marathon is one mile every six minutes.

    CONCLUSION: Bob wins the Boston Marathon.
    A. The conclusion is proved by statements I-IV;
    B. The conclusion is disproved by statements I-IV.
    C. The facts are not sufficient to prove or disprove the conclusion.

21._____

22. FACTUAL STATEMENTS:
    I. Four brothers are named Earl, John, Gary, and Pete.
    II. Earl and Pete are unmarried.
    III. John is shorter than the youngest of the four.
    IV. The oldest brother is married, and is also the tallest.

    CONCLUSION: Gary is the oldest brother.
    A. The conclusion is proved by statements I-IV;
    B. The conclusion is disproved by statements I-IV.
    C. The facts are not sufficient to prove or disprove the conclusion.

22._____

23. FACTUAL STATEMENTS:
    I. Brigade X is ten miles from the demilitarized zone.
    II. If General Woundwort gives the order, Brigade X will advance to the demilitarized zone, but not quickly enough to reach the zone before the conflict begins.
    III. Brigade Y, five miles behind Brigade X, will not advance unless General Woundwort gives the order.
    IV. Brigade Y advances.

23._____

7 (#2)

CONCLUSION: Brigade X reaches the demilitarized zone before the conflict begins.
  A. The conclusion is proved by statements I-IV;
  B. The conclusion is disproved by statements I-IV.
  C. The facts are not sufficient to prove or disprove the conclusion.

24. FACTUAL STATEMENTS: 24.____
  I. Jerry has decided to take a cab from Fullerton to Elverton.
  II. Chubby Cab charges $5 plus $3 a mile.
  III. Orange Cab charges $7.50 but gives free mileage for the first 5 miles.
  IV. After the first 5 miles, Orange Cab charges $2.50 a mile.

  CONCLUSION: Orange Cab is the cheaper fare from Fullerton to Elverton.
  A. The conclusion is proved by statements I-IV;
  B. The conclusion is disproved by statements I-IV.
  C. The facts are not sufficient to prove or disprove the conclusion.

25. FACTUAL STATEMENTS: 25.____
  I. Dan is never in class when his friend Lucy is absent.
  II. Lucy is never absent unless her mother is sick.
  III. If Lucy is in class, Sergio is in class also.
  IV. Sergio is never in class when Dalton is absent.

  CONCLUSION: If Lucy is absent, Dalton may be in class.
  A. The conclusion is proved by statements I-IV;
  B. The conclusion is disproved by statements I-IV.
  C. The facts are not sufficient to prove or disprove the conclusion.

KEY (CORRECT ANSWERS)

1.	C		11.	E
2.	B		12.	B
3.	B		13.	D
4.	C		14.	E
5.	A		15.	A
6.	A		16.	E
7.	B		17.	C
8.	C		18.	B
9.	C		19.	A
10.	B		20.	C

21. C
22. A
23. B
24. A
25. B

SOLUTIONS TO PROBLEMS

1. CORRECT ANSWER: C
   Statement 1 only tells us that some employees who work in the Testing Department are statisticians. This means that we need to allow the possibility that at least one person in this department is not a statistician. Thus, if a person works in the Testing Department, we cannot conclude whether or not this individual is a statistician.

2. CORRECT ANSWER: B
   If Hank had six coins, then the total of Gail's collection and Lawrence's collection would be four. Thus, if Gail gave all her coins to Lawrence, Lawrence would only have four coins. Thus, it would be impossible for Lawrence to have more coins than Hank.

3. CORRECT ANSWER: B
   Statement 1 tells us that nobody loves everybody. If everybody loved Janet, then Statement 3 would imply that Ken loves everybody. This would contradict statement 1. The conclusion is disproved.

4. CORRECT ANSWER: C
   Although most of the Torres family lives in East Los Angeles, we can assume that some members of this family do not live in East Los Angeles. Thus, we cannot prove or disprove that Joe, who is a member of the Torres family, lives in East Los Angeles.

5. CORRECT ANSWER: A
   Since Dr. Johnson is on the 4th floor, either (a) Dr. Kane is on the 5th floor and Dr. Conlon is on the 3rd floor, or (b) Dr. Kane is on the 3rd floor and Dr. Conlon is on the 5th floor. If option (b) were correct, then since Dr. Assad would be on the 1st floor, it would be impossible for Dr. Steen's office to be between Dr. Conlon and Dr. Assad's office. Therefore, Dr. Kane's office must be on the 5th floor. The order of the doctors' offices, from 5th floor down to the 1st floor is: Dr. Kane, Dr. Johnson, Dr. Conlon, Dr. Steen, Dr. Assad.

6. CORRECT ANSWER: A
   Ray does not satisfy the requirement of holding his breath for two minutes under water, since he can only hold is breath for one minute in that setting. But if he tunnels through a snowbank with just a T-shirt and shorts, he will satisfy the eligibility requirement. Note that the eligibility requirement contains the key word "or." So only one of the two clauses separated by "or" need to be fulfilled.

7. CORRECT ANSWER: B
   Statement 2 says that four sharps is equivalent to one tinplot. This means that a tinplot is worth more than a sharp. The conclusion is disproved. We note that the order of these items, from most valuable to least valuable are: tinplot, sharp, mark, plunk.

8. CORRECT ANSWER: C
   We can only conclude that gibbons and lemurs are fed lettuce and bananas. We can neither prove nor disprove that these animals are types of monkeys.

9. CORRECT ANSWER: C
We know that all Salishan Indians live east of the Continental Divide. But some non-members of this tribe of Indians may also live east of the Continental Divide. Since none of the members of the Blackfoot tribe belong to the Salishan Indian tribe, we cannot draw any conclusion about the location of the Blackfoot tribe with respect to the Continental Divide.

18. CORRECT ANSWER: B
Since the pepper is second from the left and the nutmeg is between the sage and the pepper, the positions 2, 3, and 4 (from the left) are pepper, nutmeg, sage. By statement II, the basil must be in position 5, which implies that the parsley is in position 1. Therefore, the basil, not the sage, is farthest to the right. The conclusion disproved.

19. CORRECT ANSWER: A
Statement II assures us that if switch C is ON, then Gear X is rotating in a counterclockwise direction. The conclusion is proved.

20. CORRECT ANSWER: C
Based on Statement IV, followed by Statement II, we conclude that Ganz and Rourke will file their reports on time. Statement III reveals that if Terence and Jackson attend the security meeting, they will fail to file their reports on time. We have no further information if Terence and Jackson attended the security meeting, so we are not able to either confirm or deny that their reports were filed on time. This implies that we cannot know for certain that Lane will leave for his meeting in Toronto.

21. CORRECT ANSWER: C
Although Bob is in second place behind Gregory, we cannot deduce how far behind Gregory he is running. At Gregory's current pace, he will cover four miles in 24 minutes. If Bob were only 100 yards behind Gregory, he would catch up to Gregory in one minute. But if Bob were very far behind Gregory, for example 5 miles, this is the equivalent of (5)(1760) = 8800 yards. Then Bob would need 8800/100 = 88 minutes to catch up to Gregory. Thus, the given facts are not sufficient to draw a conclusion.

22. CORRECT ANSWER: A
Statement II tells us that neither Earl nor Pete could be the oldest; also, either John or Gary is married. Statement IV reveals that the oldest brother is both married and the tallest. By Statement III, John cannot be the tallest. Since John is not the tallest, he is not the oldest. Thus, the oldest brother must be Gary. The conclusion is proved.

23. CORRECT ANSWER: B
By Statements III and IV, General Woundwort must have given the order to advance. Statement II then tells us that Brigade X will advance to the demilitarized zone, but not soon enough before the conflict begins. Thus, the conclusion is disproved.

24. CORRECT ANSWER: A
If the distance is 5 miles or less, then the cost for the Orange Cab is only $7.50, whereas the cost for the Chubby Cab is $5 + 3x, where x represents the number of miles traveled. For 1 to 5 miles, the cost of the Chubby Cab is between $8 and $20. This means that for a distance of 5 miles, the Orange Cab costs $7.50, whereas the Chubby Cab costs $20. After 5 miles, the cost per mile of the Chubby Cab exceeds the cost per mile of the Orange Cab. Thus, regardless of the actual distance between Fullerton and Elverton, the cost for the Orange Cab will be cheaper than that of the Chubby Cab.

25. CORRECT ANSWER: B
It looks like "Dalton" should be replaced by "Dan" in the conclusion. Then by statement I, if Lucy is absent, Dan is never in class. Thus, the conclusion is disproved.

LOGICAL REASONING
EVALUATING CONCLUSIONS IN LIGHT OF KNOWN FACTS
EXAMINATION SECTION
TEST 1

COMMENTARY

This section is designed to provide practice questions in evaluating conclusions when you are given specific data to work with.

We suggest you do the questions three at a time, consulting the answer key and then the solution section for any questions you may have missed. It's a good idea to try the questions again a week before the exam.

In the validity of conclusion type of question, you are first given a reading passage which describes a particular situation. The passage may be on any topic, as it is not your knowledge of the topic that is being tested, but your reasoning abilities. The passage is likely to detail several proposed courses of action and factors affecting these proposals. The reading passage is followed by a conclusion based on the facts in the passage, or a description of a decision taken regarding the situation. The conclusion is followed by a number of statements which have a possible connection to the conclusion. For each statement, you are to determine whether:

- A. The statement proves the conclusion.
- B. The statement supports the conclusion but does not prove it.
- C. The statement disproves the conclusion.
- D. The statement weakens the conclusion but does not disprove it.
- E. The statement has no relevance to the conclusion.

Remember that the conclusion after the passage is to be accepted as the outcome of what actually happened, and that you are being asked to evaluate the impact each statement would have had on the conclusion.

Questions 1-8.

DIRECTIONS: Questions 1 through 8 are based on the following paragraph.

In May of 2018, Mr. Bryan inherited a clothing store on Main Street in a small New England town. The store has specialized in selling quality men's and women's clothing since 1920. Business has been stable throughout the years, neither increasing nor decreasing. He has an opportunity to buy two adjacent stores which would enable him to add a wider range and style of clothing. In order to do this, he would have to borrow a substantial amount of money. He also risks losing the goodwill of his present clientele.

CONCLUSION: On November 7, 2018, Mr. Bryan tells the owner of the two adjacent stores that he has decided not to purchase them. He feels that it would be best to simply maintain his present marketing position, as there would not be enough new business to support an expansion.

A. The statement proves the conclusion.
B. The statement supports the conclusion but does not prove it.
C. The statement disproves the conclusion.
D. The statement weakens the conclusion.
E. The statement is irrelevant to the conclusion.

1. A large new branch of the county's community college holds its first classes in September. 1._____

2. The town's largest factory shuts down with no indication that it will reopen. 2._____

3. The United States Census showed that the number of children per household dropped from 2.4 to 2.1 since the last census. 3._____

4. Mr. Bryan's brother tells him of a new clothing boutique specializing in casual women's clothing which is opening soon. 4._____

5. Mr. Bryan's sister buys her baby several items for Christmas at Mr. Bryan's store. 5._____

6. Mrs. McIntyre, the President of the Town Council, brings Mr. Bryan a home-baked pumpkin pie in honor of his store's 100th anniversary. They discuss the changes that have taken place in the town, and she comments on how his store has maintained the same look and feel over the years. 6._____

7. In October, Mr. Bryan's aunt lends him $50,000. 7._____

8. The Town Council has just announced that the town is eligible for funding from a federal project designed to encourage the location of new businesses in the central districts of cities and towns. 8._____

Questions 9-18.

DIRECTIONS: Questions 9 through 18 are based on the following paragraph.

A proposal was put before the legislative body of a country to require air bags in all automobiles manufactured for domestic use in that country after 2019. The air bag, made of nylon or plastic, is designed to inflate automatically within a car at the impact of a collision, thus protecting front-seat occupants from being thrown forward. There has been much support of the measure from consumer groups, the insurance industry, key legislators, and the general public. The country's automobile manufacturers, who contend the new crash equipment would add up to $1,000 to car prices and provide no more protection than existing seat belts, are against the proposed legislation

CONCLUSION: On April 21, 2014, the legislation requiring air bags in all automobiles manufactured for domestic use in that country after 2019.

A. The statement proves the conclusion.
B. The statement supports the conclusion but does not prove it.
C. The statement disproves the conclusion.
D. The statement weakens the conclusion.
E. The statement is irrelevant to the conclusion.

9. A study has shown that 59% of car occupants do not use seat belts. 9._____

10. The country's Department of Transportation has estimated that the crash protection equipment would save up to 5,900 lives each year. 10._____

11. On April 27, 2013, Augusta Raneoni was named head of an advisory committee to gather and analyze data on the costs, benefits, and feasibility of the proposed legislation on air bags in automobiles. 11._____

12. Consumer groups and the insurance industry accuse the legislature of rejecting passage of the regulation for political reasons. 12._____

13. A study by the Committee on Imports and Exports projected that the sales of imported cars would rise dramatically in 2019 because imported cars do not have to include air bags, and can be sold more cheaply. 13._____

14. Research has shown that air bags, if produced on a large scale, would cost about $200 apiece, and would provide more reliable protection than any other type of seat belt. 14._____

15. Auto sales in 2011 increased 3% over the previous year. 15._____

16. A Department of Transportation report in July of 2020 credits a drop in automobile deaths of 4,100 to the use of air bags. 16._____

17. In June of 2014, the lobbyist of the largest insurance company receives a bonus for her work on the passage of the air bag legislation. 17._____

18. In 2020, the stock in crash protection equipment has risen three-fold over the previous year. 18._____

Questions 19-25.

DIRECTIONS: Questions 19 through 25 are based on the following paragraph.

On a national television talk show, Joan Rivera, a famous comedienne, has recently insulted the physical appearances of a famous actress and the dead wife of an ex-President. There has been a flurry of controversy over her comments, and much discussion of the incident has appeared in the press. Most of the comments have been negative. It appears that this tie she might have gone too far. There have been cancellations of two of her five scheduled performances in the two weeks since the show was televised, and Joan's been receiving a lot of negative mail. Because of the controversy, she has an interview with a national news magazine at the end of the week, and her press agent is strongly urging her to apologize publicly. She feels strongly that her comments were no worse than any other she has ever made, and that the whole incident will *blow over* soon. She respects her press agent's judgment, however, as his assessment of public sentiment tends to be very accurate.

CONCLUSION: Joan does not apologize publicly, and during the interview she challenges the actress to a weight-losing contest. For every pound the actress loses, Joan says she will donate $1 to the Cellulite Prevention League.

    A.   The statement proves the conclusion.
          B.   The statement supports the conclusion but does not prove it.
          C.   The statement disproves the conclusion.
          D.   The statement weakens the conclusion.
          E.   The statement is irrelevant to the conclusion.

19. Joan's mother, who she is very fond of, is very upset with Joan's comments.   19.____

20. Six months after the interview, Joan's income has doubled.   20.____

21. Joan's agent is pleased with the way Joan handles the interview.   21.____

22. Joan's sister has been appointed Treasurer of the Cellulite Prevention League In her report, she states that Joan's $12 contribution is the only amount that has been donated to the League in its first six months.   22.____

23. The magazine receives many letters commending Joan for the courage it took for her to apologize publicly in the interview.   23.____

24. Immediately after the interview appears, another one of Joan's performances is cancelled.   24.____

25. Due to a printers' strike, the article was not published until the following week.   25.____

Questions 26-30.

DIRECTIONS: Questions 25 through 30 are based on the following paragraph.

    The law-making body of Country X must decide what to do about the issue of recording television shows for home use. There is currently no law against recording shows directly from the TV as long as the DVDs are not used for commercial purposes. The increasing popularity of pay TV and satellite systems, combined with the increasing number of homes that own recording equipment, has caused a great deal of concern in some segments of the entertainment industry. Companies that own the rights to films, popular television shows, and sporting events feel that their copyright privileges are being violated, and they are seeking compensation or the banning of TV recording. Legislation has been introduced to make it illegal to record television programs for home use. Separate proposed legislation is also pending that would continue to allow recording of TV shows for home use, but would place a tax of 10% on each DVD that is purchased for home use. The income from that tax would then be proportionately distributed as royalties to those owning the rights to programs being aired. A weighted point system coupled with the averaging of several national viewing rating systems would be used to determine the royalties. There is a great deal of lobbying being done for both bills, as the manufacturers of DVDs and recording equipment are against the passage of the bills.

CONCLUSION: The legislature of Country X rejects both bills by a wide margin.

A. The statement proves the conclusion.
   B. The statement supports the conclusion but does not prove it.
   C. The statement disproves the conclusion.
   D. The statement weakens the conclusion.
   E. The statement is irrelevant to the conclusion.

26. Country X's Department of Taxation hires 500 new employees to handle the increased paperwork created by the new tax on DVDs.

27. A study conducted by the country's most prestigious accounting firm shows that the cost of implementing the proposed new DVD tax would be greater than the income expected from it.

28. It is estimated that 80% of all those working in the entertainment industry, excluding performers, own DVD recorders.

29. The head of Country X's law enforcement agency states that legislation banning the home recording of TV shows would be unenforceable.

30. Financial experts predict that unless a tax is placed on DVDs, several large companies in the entertainment industry will have to file for bankruptcy.

Questions 31-38.

DIRECTIONS: Questions 31 through 38 are variations on the type of question you just had. It is important that you read the question very carefully to determine exactly what is required.

31. In this question, select the choice that is MOST relevant to the conclusion.
    I. The Buffalo Bills football team is in second place in its division.
    II. The New England Patriots are in first place in the same division.
    III. There are two games left to play in the season, and the Bills will not play the Patriots again.
    IV. The New England Patriots won ten games and lost four games, and the Buffalo Bills have won eight games and lost six games.
CONCLUSION: The Buffalo Bills win their division.
    A. The conclusion is proved by sentences I-IV.
    B. The conclusion is disproved by sentences I-IV.
    C. The facts are not sufficient to prove or disprove the conclusion.

32. In this question, select the choice that is MOST relevant to the conclusion. 32.____
    I. On the planet of Zeinon there are only two different eye colors and only two different hair colors.
    II. Half of those beings with purple hair have golden eyes.
    III. There are more inhabitants with purple hair than there are inhabitants with silver hair.
    IV. One-third of those with silver hair have green eyes.
    CONCLUSION: There are more golden-eyed beings on Zeinon than green-eyed ones.
    A. The conclusion is proved by sentences I-IV.
    B. The conclusion is disproved by sentences I-IV.
    C. The facts are not sufficient to prove or disprove the conclusion.

33. In this question, select the choice that is MOST relevant to the conclusion. 33.____
    John and Kevin are leaving Amaranth to go to school in Bethany. They've decided to rent a small truck to move their possessions. Joe's Truck Rental charges $100 plus 30¢ a mile. National Movers charges $50 more but gives free mileage for the first 100 miles. After the first 100 miles, they charge 25¢ a mile.
    CONCLUSION: John and Kevin rent their truck from National Movers because it is cheaper.
    A. The conclusion is proved by the facts in the above paragraph.
    B. The conclusion is disproved by the facts in the above paragraph.
    C. The facts are not sufficient to prove or disprove the conclusion.

34. For this question, select the choice that supports the information given in the passage. 34.____
    Municipalities in Country X are divided into villages, towns, and cities. A village has a population of 5,000 or less. The population of a town ranges from 5,001 to 15,000. In order to be incorporated as a city, the municipality must have a population over 15,000. If, after a village becomes a town, or a town becomes a city, the population drops below the minimum required (for example, the population of a city goes below 15,000), and stays below the minimum for more than ten years, it loses its current status, and drops to the next category. As soon as a municipality rises in population to the next category (village to town, for example), however, it is immediately reclassified to the next category.
    In the 2000 census, Plainfield had a population of 12,000. Between 2000 and 2010, Plainfield grew 10%, and between 2010 and 2020 Plainfield grew another 20%. The population of Springdale doubled from 2000 to 2010, and increased 25% from 2010 to 2020. The city of Smallville's population, 20,283, has not changed significantly in recent years. Granton had a population of 25,000 people in 1990, and has decreased 25% in each ten year period since then. Ellenville had a population of 4,283 in 1990, and grew 5% in each ten year period since 1990.

7 (#1)

In 2020,
- A. Plainfield, Smallville, and Granton are cities.
- B. Smallville is a city, Granton is a town, and Ellenville is a village.
- C. Springdale, Granton, and Ellenville are towns.
- D. Plainfield and Smallville are cities, and Ellenville is a town.

35. For this question, select the choice that is MOST relevant to the conclusion.   35.____
    A study was done for a major food-distributing firm to determine if there is any difference in the kind of caffeine containing products used by people of different ages. A sample of one thousand people between the ages of twenty and fifty were drawn from selected areas in the country. They were divided equally into three groups.
    Those individuals who were 20-29 were designated Group A, those 30-39 were Group B, and those 40-50 were placed in Group C.
    It was found that on the average, Group A drank 1.8 cups of coffee, Group B 3.1, and Group C 2.5 cups of coffee daily. Group A drank 2.1 cups of tea, Group B drank 1.2, and Group C drank 2.6 cups of tea daily. Group A drank 3 1.8 ounces glasses of cola, Group B drank 1.9, and Group C drank 1.5 glasses of cola daily.
    CONCLUSION: According to the study, the average person in the 20-29 age group drinks less tea daily than the average person in the 40-50 age group, but drinks more coffee daily than the average person in the 30-39 age group drinks cola.
    - A. The conclusion is proved by the facts in the above paragraph.
    - B. The conclusion is disproved by the facts in the above paragraph.
    - C. The facts are not sufficient to prove or disprove the conclusion.

36. For this question, select the choice that is MOST relevant to the conclusion   36.____
    I. Mary is taller than Jane but shorter than Dale.
    II. Fred is taller than Mary but shorter than Steven.
    III. Dale is shorter than Steven but taller than Elizabeth.
    IV. Elizabeth is taller than Mary but not as tall as Fred.
    CONCLUSION: Dale is taller than Fred.
    - A. The conclusion is proved by sentences I-IV.
    - B. The conclusion is disproved by sentences I-IV.
    - C. The facts are not sufficient to prove or disprove the conclusion.

37. For this question, select the choice that is MOST relevant to the conclusion.   37.____
    I. Main Street is between Spring Street and Glenn Blvd.
    II. Hawley Avenue is one block south of Spring Street and three blocks north of Main Street.
    III. Glenn Street is five blocks south of Elm and four blocks south of Main.
    IV. All the streets mentioned are parallel to one another.
    CONCLUSION: Elm Street is between Hawley Avenue and Glenn Blvd.
    - A. The conclusion is proved by the facts in sentences I-IV.
    - B. The conclusion is disproved by the facts in sentences I-IV.
    - C. The facts are not sufficient to prove or disprove the conclusion.

38. For this question, select the choice that is MOST relevant to the conclusion. 38.____
    I. Train A leaves the town of Hampshire every day at 5:50 A.M. and arrives in New London at 6:42 A.M.
    II. Train A leaves New London at 7:00 A.M. and arrives in Kellogsville at 8:42 A.M.
    III. Train B leaves Kellogsville at 8:00 A.M. and arrives in Hampshire at 10:45 A.M.
    IV. Due to the need for repairs, there is just one railroad track between New London and Hampshire.
    CONCLUSION: It is impossible for Train A and Train B to follow these schedules without colliding.
    A. The conclusion is proved by the facts in sentences I-IV.
    B. The conclusion is disproved by the facts in sentences I-IV.
    C. The facts are not sufficient to prove or disprove the conclusion.

KEY (CORRECT ANSWERS)

1.	D	11.	C	21.	D	31.	C
2.	B	12.	C	22.	A	32.	A
3.	E	13.	D	23.	C	33.	C
4.	B	14.	B	24.	B	34.	B
5.	C	15.	E	25.	E	35.	B
6.	A	16.	B	26.	C	36.	C
7.	D	17.	A	27.	B	37.	A
8.	B	18.	B	28.	E	38.	B
9.	B	19.	D	29.	B		
10.	B	20.	E	30.	D		

SOLUTIONS TO QUESTIONS

1. The answer is D. This statement weakens the conclusion, but does not disprove it. If a new branch of the community college opened in September, it could possibly bring in new business for Mr. Bryant. Since it states in the conclusion that Mr. Bryant felt there would not be enough new business to support the additional stores, this would tend to disprove the conclusion. Choice C would not be correct because it's possible that he felt that the students would not have enough additional money to support his new venture, or would not be interested in his clothing styles. It's also possible that the majority of the students already live in the area, so that they wouldn't really be a new customer population. This type of question is tricky, and can initially be very confusing, so don't feel badly if you missed it. Most people need to practice with a few of these types of questions before they feel comfortable recognizing exactly what they're being asked to do.

2. The answer is B. It supports the conclusion because the closing of the factory would probably take money and customers out of the town, causing Mr. Bryant to lose some of his present business. It doesn't prove the conclusion, however, because we don't know how large the factory was. It's possible that only a small percentage of the population was employed there, or that they found other jobs.

3. The answer is E. The fact that the number of children per household dropped slightly nationwide in the decade is irrelevant. Statistics showing a drop nationwide doesn't mean that there was a drop in the number of children per household in Mr. Bryant's hometown. This is a tricky question, as choice B, supporting the conclusion but not proving it, may seem reasonable. If the number of children per household declined nationwide, then it may not seem unreasonable to feel that this would support Mr. Bryant's decision not to expand his business. However, we're preparing you for promotional exams, not "real life." One of the difficult things about taking exams is that sometimes you're forced to make a choice between two statements that both seem like they could be the possible answer. What you need to do in that case is choose the best choice. Becoming annoyed or frustrated with the question won't really help much. If there's a review of the exam, you can certainly appeal the question. There have been many cases where, after an appeal, two possible choices have been allowed as correct answers. We've included this question, however, to help you see what to do should you get a question like this. It's most important not to get rattled, and to select the BEST choice. In this case, the connection between the statistical information and Mr. Bryant's decision is pretty remote. If the question had said that the number of children in Mr. Bryant's town had decreased, then choice B would have been a more reasonable choice. It could also help in this situation to visualize the situation. Picture Mr. Bryant in his armchair reading that, nationwide, the average number of children per household has declined slightly. How likely would this be to influence his decision, especially since he sells men's and women's clothing? It would take a while for this decline in population to show up, and we're not even sure if it applies to Mr. Bryant's hometown. Don't feel badly if you missed this; it was tricky. The more of these you do, the more comfortable you'll feel.

4. The answer is B. If a new clothing boutique specializing in casual women's clothing were to open soon, this would lend support to Mr. Bryant's decision not to expand, but would not prove that he had actually made the decision to expand. A new women's clothing boutique would most likely be in competition with his existing business, thus making any possible expansion a riskier venture. We can't be sure from this, however, that he didn't go ahead and expand his business despite the increased competition. Choice A, proves the conclusion, would only be the answer if we could be absolutely sure from the statement that Mr. Bryant had actually <u>not</u> expanded his business.

5. The answer is C. This statement disproves the conclusion. In order for his sister to buy several items for her baby at Mr. Bryant's store, he would have to have changed his business to include children's clothing.

6. The answer is A. It definitely proves the conclusion. The passage states that Mr. Bryan's store had been in business since 1920. A pie baked in honor of his store's 100th anniversary would have to be presented sometime in 2020. The conclusion states that he made his decision not to expand on November 7, 2018. If, more than a year later Mrs. MacIntyre comments that his store has maintained the same look and feel over the years, it could not have been expanded, or otherwise significantly changed.

7. The answer is D. If Mr. Bryant's aunt lent him $50,000 in October, this would tend to weaken the conclusion, which took place in November. Because it was stated that Mr. Bryant would need to borrow money in order to expand his business, it would be logical to assume that if he borrowed money he had decided to expand his business, weakening the conclusion. The reason C, disproves the conclusion, is not the correct answer is because we can't be sure Mr. Bryant didn't borrow the money for another reason.

8. The answer is B. If Mr. Bryant's town is eligible for federal funds to encourage the location of new businesses in the central district, this would tend to support his decision not to expand his business. Funds to encourage new business would increase the likelihood of there being additional competition for Mr. Bryant's store to contend with. Since we can't say for sure that there would be direct competition from a new business, however, choice A would be incorrect. Note that this is also a tricky question. You might have thought that the new funds weakened the conclusion because it would mean that Mr. Bryant could easily get the money he needed. Mr. Bryant is expanding his present business, not creating a <u>new</u> business. Therefore, he is not eligible for the funding.

9. The answer is B. This is a very tricky question. It's stated that 59% of car occupants don't use seat belts. The legislature is considering the use of air bags because of safety issues. The advantage of air bags over seat belts is that they inflate upon impact, and don't require car occupants to do anything with them ahead of time. Since the population has strongly resisted using seat belts, the air bags could become even more important in saving lives. Since saving lives is the purpose of the proposed legislation, the information that a small percentage of people use seat belts could be helpful to the passage of the legislation. We can't be sure that this is reason enough for the legislature to vote for the legislation, however, so choice A in incorrect.

11 (#1)

10. The answer is B, as the information that 5,900 lives could be saved would tend to support the conclusion. Saving that many lives through the use of air bags could be a very persuasive reason to vote for the legislation. Since we don't know for sure that it's enough of a compelling reason for the legislature to vote for the legislation, however, choice A could not be the answer.

11. The answer is C, disproves the conclusion. If the legislation had been passed as stated in the conclusion, there would be no reason to appoint someone head of an advisory committee six days later to analyze the "feasibility of the proposed legislation." The key word here is "proposed." If it has been proposed, it means it hasn't been passed. This contradicts the conclusion and, therefore, disproves it.

12. The answer is C, disproves the conclusion. If the legislation had passed, there would be no reason for supporters of the legislation to accuse the legislature of rejecting the legislation for political reasons. This question may have seemed so obvious that you might have thought there was a trick to it. Exams usually have a few obvious questions, which will trip you up if you begin reading too much into them.

13. The answer is D, as this would tend to disprove the conclusion. A projected dramatic rise in imported cars could be very harmful to the country's economy and could be a very good reason for some legislators to vote against the proposed legislation. It would be assuming too much to choose C, however, because we don't know if they actually did vote against it.

14. The answer is B. This information would tend to support the passage of the legislation. The estimate of the cost of the air bags is $800 less than the cost estimated by opponents, and it's stated that the protection would be more reliable than any other type of seat belt. Both of these would be good arguments in favor of passing the legislation. Since we don't know for sure, however, how persuasive they actually were, choice A would not be the correct choice.

15. The answer is E, as this is irrelevant information. It really doesn't matter whether auto sales in 2001 have increased slightly over the previous year. If the air bag legislation were to go into effect in 2004, that might make the information somehow more relevant. But the air bag legislation would not take effect until 2009, so the information is irrelevant, since it tells us nothing about the state of the auto industry then.

16. The answer is B, supports the conclusion. This is a tricky question. While at first it might seem to prove the conclusion, we can't be sure that the air bag legislation is responsible for the drop in automobile deaths. It's possible air bags came into popular use without the legislation, or with different legislation. There's no way we can be sure that it was the proposed legislation mandating the use of air bags that was responsible.

17. The answer is A. If, in June of 2009, the lobbyist received a bonus "for her work on the air bag legislation," we can be sure that the legislation passed. This proves the conclusion.

18. The answer is B. This is another tricky question. A three-fold stock increase would strongly suggest that the legislation had been passed, but it's possible that factors other than the air bag legislation caused the increase. Note that the stock is in "crash protection

equipment." Nowhere in the statement does it say air bags. Seat belts, motorcycle helmets, and collapsible bumpers are all crash protection equipment and could have contributed to the increase. This is just another reminder to read carefully because the questions are often designed to mislead you.

19. The answer is D. This would tend to weaken the conclusion because Joan is very fond of her mother and she would not want to upset her unnecessarily. It does not prove it, however, because if Joan strongly feels she is right, she probably wouldn't let her mother's opinion sway her. Choice E would also not be correct, because we cannot assume that Joan's mother's opinion is of so little importance to her as to be considered irrelevant.

20. The answer is E. The statement is irrelevant. We are told that Joan's income has doubled but we are not old why. The phrase "six months after the interview" can be misleading in that it leads us to assume that the increase and the interview are related. Her income could have doubled because she regained her popularity but it could also have come from stocks or some other business venture. Because we are not given any reason for her income doubling, it would be impossible to say whether or not this statement proves or disproves the conclusion. Choice E is the best choice of the five possible choices. One of the problems with promotional exams is that sometimes you need to select a choice you're not crazy about. In this case, "not having enough information to made a determination" would be the best choice. However, that's not an option, so you're forced to work with what you've got. On these exams it's sometimes like voting for President; you have to pick the "lesser of the two evils" or the least awful choice. In this case, the information is more irrelevant to the conclusion than it is anything else.

21. The answer is D, weakens the conclusion. We've been told that Joan's agent feels that she should apologize. If he is pleased with her interview, then it would tend to weaken the conclusion but not disprove it. We can't be sure that he hasn't had a change of heart, or that there weren't other parts of the interview he liked so much that they outweighed her unwillingness to apologize.

22. The answer is A. The conclusion states that Joan will donate $1 to the Cellulite Prevention League for every pound the actress loses. Joan's sister's financial report on the League's activities directly supports and proves the conclusion.

23. The answer is C, disproves the conclusion. If the magazine receives many letters commending Joan for her courage in apologizing, this directly contradicts the conclusion, which states that Joan didn't apologize.

24. The answer is B. It was stated in the passage that two of Joan's performances were cancelled after the controversy first occurred. The cancellation of another performance immediately after her interview was published would tend to support the conclusion that she refused to apologize. Because we can't be sure, however, that her performance wasn't cancelled for another reason, choice A would be incorrect.

25. The answer is E, as this information is irrelevant. Postponing the article an extra week does not affect Joan's decision or the public's reaction to it.

13 (#1)

26. The answer is C. If 500 new employees are hired to handle the "increased paperwork created by the new tax on DVDs," this would directly contradict the conclusion, which states that the legislature defeated both bills. (They should all be this easy.)

27. The answer is B. The results of the study would support the conclusion. If implementing the legislation was going to be so costly, it is likely that the legislature would vote against it. Choice A is not the answer, however, because we can't be sure that the legislature didn't pass it anyway.

28. The answer is E. It's irrelevant to the conclusion that 80% of all those working in the entertainment industry own DVD recorders. Sometimes if you're not sure about these, it can help a lot to try and visualize the situation. Why would someone voting on this legislation care about this fact? It doesn't seem to be the kind of information that would make any difference or impact upon the conclusion.

29. The answer is B. The head of the law enforcement agency's statement that the legislation would be unenforceable would support the conclusion. It's possible that many legislators would question why they should bother to pass legislation that would be impossible to enforce. Choice A would be incorrect, however, because we can't be sure that the legislation wasn't passed in spite of his statement.

30. The answer is D. This would tend to weaken the conclusion because the prospect of several large companies going bankrupt would seem to be a good argument in favor of the legislation. The possible loss of jobs and businesses would be a good reason for some people to vote for the legislation. We can't be sure, however, that this would be a competing enough reason to ensure passage of the legislation so choice C is incorrect.

This concludes our section on the "Validity of Conclusion" type of questions. We hope these weren't too horrible for you. It's important to keep in mind exactly what you've been given and exactly what they want you to do with it. It's also necessary to remember that you may have to choose between two possible answers. In that case, you must choose the one that seems the best. Sometimes you may think there is no good answer. You will probably be right, but you can't let that upset you. Just choose the one you dislike the least.

We want to repeat that it is unlikely that this exact format will appear on the exam. The skills required to answer these questions, however, are the same as those you'll need for the exam so we suggest that you review this section before taking the actual exam.

31. The answer is C. This next set of questions requires you to "switch gears" slightly, and get used to different formats. In this type of question, you have to decide whether the conclusion is proved by the facts give, disproved by the facts given, or neither because note enough information has been provided. Fortunately, unlike the previous questions, you don't have to decide whether particular facts support or don't support the conclusion. This type of question is more straight forward, but the reasoning behind it is the same. We are told that the Bills have won two games less than the Patriots, and that the Patriots are in first place and the Bills are in second place. We are also told that there are two games left to play, and that they won't play each other again. The conclusion states that the Bills won the division. Is there anything in the four statements that would prove this? We have

no idea what the outcome of the last two games of the season was. The Bills and Patriots could have ended up tied at the end of the season, or the Bills could have lost both or one of their last games while the Patriots did the same. There might even be another team tied for first or second place with the Bills or Patriots. Since we don't know for sure, Choice A is incorrect. Choice B is trickier. It might seem at first glance that the best the Bills could do would be to tie the Patriots if the Patriots lost their last two games and the Bills won their last two games. But it would be too much to assume that there is no procedure for a tiebreaker that wouldn't give the Bills the division championship. Since we don't know what the rules are in the event of a tie (for example, what if a tie was decided on the results of what happened when the two teams had played each other, or on the best record in the division, or on most points scored?), we can't say for sure that it would be impossible for the Bills to win their division. For this reason, choice C is the answer, as we don't have enough information to prove or disprove the conclusion. This question looked more difficult than it actually was. It's important to disregard any factors outside of the actual question, and to focus only on what you've been given. In this case, as on all of these types of questions, what you know or don't know about a subject is actually irrelevant. It's best to concentrate only on the actual facts given.

32. The answer is A. The conclusion is proved by the facts given.

In this type of problem, it is usually best to pull as many facts as possible from the sentences and then put them into a simpler form. The phrasing and the order of exam questions are designed to be confusing so you need to restate things as clearly as possible by eliminating the extras.

Sentence I tells us that there are only two possible colors for eyes and two for hair. Looking at the other sentences we learn that eyes are either green or gold and that hair is either silver or purple. If half the beings with purple hair have golden eyes, then the other half must have green eyes since it is the only other eye color. Likewise, if one-third of those with silver hair have green eyes, the other two-thirds must have golden eyes.

This information makes it clear that there are more golden-eyed beings on Zeinon than green-eyed ones. It doesn't matter that we don't know exactly how many are actually living on the planet. The number of those with gold eyes (1/2 plus 2/3) will always be greater than the number of those with green eyes (1/2 plus 1/3), no matter what the actual figures might be. Sentence III is totally irrelevant because even if there were more silver-haired inhabitants it would not affect the conclusion.

33. The answer is C. The conclusion is neither proved nor disproved by the facts because we don't know how many miles Bethany is from Amoranth.

With this type of question, if you're not sure how to approach it, you can always substitute in a range of "real numbers" to see what the result would be. If they were 200 miles apart, Joe's Truck Rental would be cheaper because they would charge a total of $160 while National Movers would charge $175.

    Joe's - $100 plus .30 x 200 (or $60) = $160
    National - $150 plus .25 x 100 (or $25) = $175

If the towns were 600 miles apart, however, National Movers would be cheaper. The cost of renting from National would be $275 compared to the $280 charged by Joe's Trucking.

    Joe's - $100 plus .30 x 600 (or $180) = $280
    National - $150 plus .25 x 500 (or $125) = $275

15 (#1)

34. The answer is B. We've varied the format once more, but the reasoning is similar. This is a tedious question that is more like a math question, but we wanted to give you some practice with this type, just in case. You won't be able to do this question if you've forgotten how to do percents. Many exams require this knowledge, so if you feel you need a review we suggest you read Booklets 1, 2 or 3 in this series.

The only way to attack this problem is to go through each choice until you find the one that is correct. Choice A states that Plainfield, Smallville, and Granton are cities. Let's begin with Plainfield. The passage states that in 1990 Plainfield had a population of 12,000, and that it grew 10% between 1990 and 2000, and another 20% between 2000 and 2010. Ten percent of 12,000 is 1200 (12,000 x .10 = 1200). Therefore, the population grew from 12,000 in 1990 to 12,000 + 1200 between 1990 and 2000. At the time of the 2000 Census, Plainfield's population was 13,200. It then grew another 20% between 2000 and 2010, so, 13,200 x .20 = 2640. 13,200 plus the additional increase of 2640 would make the population of Plainfield 15,840. This would qualify it as a city, since its population is over 15,000. Since a change upward in the population of a municipality is re-classified immediately, Plainfield would have become a city right away. So far, statement A is true. The passage states that Smallville's population has not changed significantly in the last twenty years. Since Smallville's population was 20,283, Smallville would still be a city. Granton had a population of 25,000 (what a coincidence that so any of these places have such nice, even numbers) in 1980. The population has decreased 25% in each ten year period since that time. So from 1980 to 1990, the population decreased 25%. 25,000 x .25 = 6,250. 25,000 minus 6,250 = 18,750. So the population of Granton in 1990 would have been 18,750. (Or, you could have saved a step and multiplied 25,000 by .75 to get 18,750.) The population from 1990 to 2000 decreased an additional 25%. So: 18,750 x .25 = 4,687.50. 18,750 minus 4,687.50 = 14,062.50. Or: 18,750 x .75 = 14,062.50. (Don't let the fact that a half of a person is involved confuse you; these are exam questions, not real life.) From 2000 to 2010 the population decreased an additional 25%. This would mean that Granton's population was below 15,000 for more than ten years, so it's status as a city would have changed to that of a town, which would make choice A incorrect.

Choice B states that Smallville is a city and Granton is a town, which we know to be true from the information above. Choice B is correct so far. We next need to determine if Ellenville is a village. Ellenville had a population of 4,283 in 1980, and increased 5% in each ten year period since 1980. 4,283 x .05 = 214.15. 4,283 plus 214.15 = 4,497.15, so Ellenville's population from 1980 to 1990 increased to 4,497.15. (Or: 4,283 x 1.05 – 4,497.15.) From 1990 to 2000 Ellenville's population increased another 5%: 4,497.15 x .05 = 224.86. 4,497.15 plus 224.86 = 4,772.01 (or: 4,497.15 x 1.05 = 4,722.01.) From 2000 to 2010, Ellenville's population increased another 5%: 4,722.01 x .05 = 236.10. 4,722.01 plus 236.10 = 4,958.11. (Or: 4,722.01 x 1.05 = 4,958.11.).

Ellenville's population is still under 5,000 in 2010, so it would continue to be classified as a village. Since all three statements in choice B are true, choice B must be the answer. However, we'll go through the other choices. Choice C states that Springdale is a town. The passage tells us that the population of Springdale doubled from 1990 to 2000, and increased 25% from 2000 to 2010. It doesn't give us any actual population figures, however, so it's impossible to know what the population of Springdale is, making choice C incorrect. Choice C also states that Granton is a town, which is true, and that Ellenville is a town, which is false (from choice B we know it's a village). Choice D states that Plainfield and Smallville are cities, which is information we already know is true, and that Ellenville is a town. Since Ellenville is a village, choice D is also incorrect.

This was a lot of work for just one question and we doubt you'll get one like this on this section of the exam, but we included it just in case. On an exam, you can always put a check mark next to a question like this and come back to it later, if you feel you're pressed for time and cold spend your time more productively on other, less time-consuming problems.

35. The answer is B. This question requires very careful reading. It's best to break the conclusion down into smaller parts in order to solve the problem. The first half of the conclusion states that the average person in the 20-29 age group (Group A) drinks less tea daily than the average person in the 40-50 age group (Group C). The average person in Group A drinks 2.1 cups of tea daily, while the average person in Group C drinks 2.6 cups of tea daily. Since 2.1 is less than 2.6, the conclusion is correct so far. The second half of the conclusion states that the average person in Group A drinks more coffee daily than the average person in the 30-39 age group (Group B) drinks cola. The average person in Group A drinks 1.8 cups of coffee daily, while the average person in Group B drinks 1.9 glasses of cola. This disproves the conclusion, which states that the average person in Group A drinks more coffee daily than the average person in Group B drinks cola.

36. The answer is C. The easiest way to approach a problem that deals with the relationship between a number of different people or things is to set up a diagram. This type of problem is usually too confusing to do in your head. For this particular problem, the "diagram" could be a line, one end of which would be labeled tall and the other end labeled short. Then, taking one sentence at a time, place the people on the line to see where they fall in relation to one another.

The diagram of the first sentence would look like this:

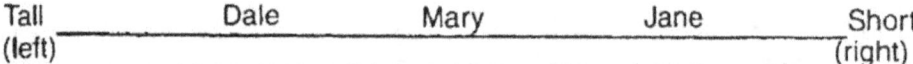

Mary is taller than Jane but shorter than Dale, so she would fall somewhere between the two of them. We have placed tall on the left and labeled it left just to make the explanation easier. You could just as easily have reversed the position.

The second sentence places Fred somewhere to the left of Mary because he is taller than she is. Steven would be to the left of Fred for the same reason. At this point we don't know whether Steven and Fred are taller or shorter than Dale. The new diagram would look like this:

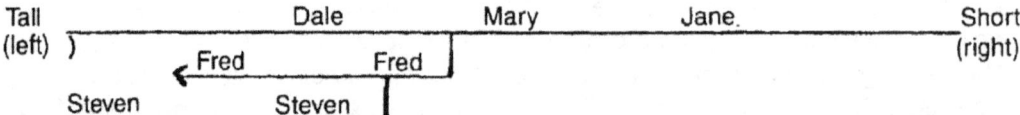

The third sentence introduces Elizabeth, presenting a new problem. Elizabeth can be anywhere to the right of Dale. Don't make the mistake of assuming she falls between Dale and Mary. At this point we don't know where she fits in relation to Mary, Jane, or even Fred.

We do get information about Steven, however. He is taller than Dale so he would be to the left of Dale. Since he is also taller than Fred (see sentence II), we know that Steven is the tallest person thus far. The diagram would now look like this:

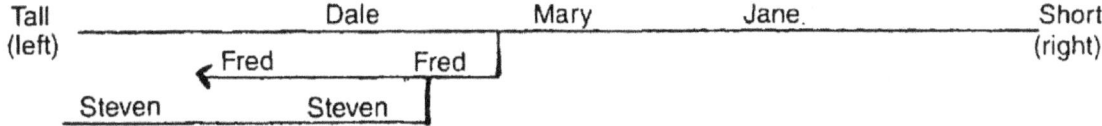

Fred's height is somewhere between Steven and Mary, Elizabeth's anywhere between Dale and the end of the line.

The fourth sentence tells us where Elizabeth stands, in relation to Fred and the others in the problem. The fact that she is taller than Mary means she is also taller than Jane. The final diagram would look like this:

We still don't know whether Dale or Fred is taller, however. Therefore, the conclusion that Dale is taller than Fred can't be proved. It also can't be disproved because we don't know for sure that he isn't. The answer has to be choice C, as the conclusion can't be proved or disproved.

37. The answer is A. This is another problem that is easiest for most people if they make a diagram. Sentence I states that Main Street is between Spring Street and Glenn Blvd. At this point we don't know if they are next to each other or if they are separated by a number of streets. Therefore, you should leave space between streets as you plot your first diagram.

The order of the streets could go either:

Spring St.	or	Glenn Blvd.
Main St.		Main St.
Glenn Blvd.		Spring St.

Sentence II states that Hawley Street is one block south of Spring Street and 3 blocks north of Main Street. Because most people think in terms of north as above and south as below and because it was stated that Hawley is one block south of Spring Street and three blocks north of Main Street, the next diagram could look like this:

Spring
Hawley
______
______
Main
Glenn

The third sentence states that Glenn Street is five blocks south of Elm and four blocks south of Main. It could look like this:

Spring
Hawley
______
Elm
Main
____
____
____
Glenn

The conclusion states that Elm Street is between Hawley Avenue and Glenn Blvd. From the above diagram, we can see that this is the case.

38. The answer is B. For most people, the best way to do this problem is to draw a diagram, plotting the course of both trains. Sentence I states that Train A leaves Hampshire at 5:50 A.M. and reaches New London at 6:42. Your first diagram might look like this:

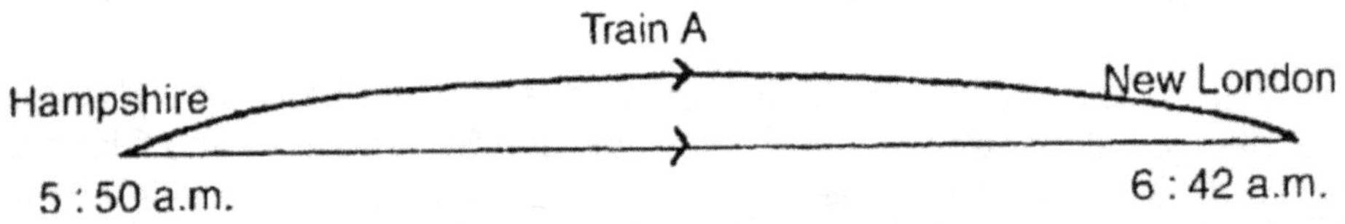

Sentence II states that the train leaves New London at 7:00 a.m. and arrives in Kellogsville at 8:42 a.m. The diagram might now look like this:

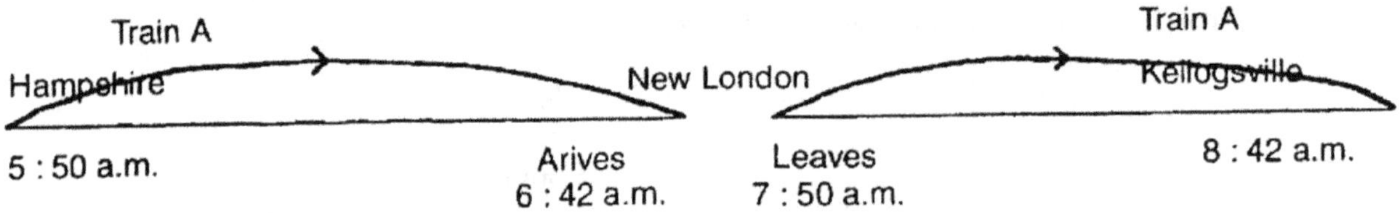

Sentence III gives us the rest of the information that must be included in the diagram. It introduces Train B, which moves in the opposite direction, leaving Kellogsville at 8:00 a.m. and arriving at Hampshire at 10:42 a.m. The final diagram might look like this:

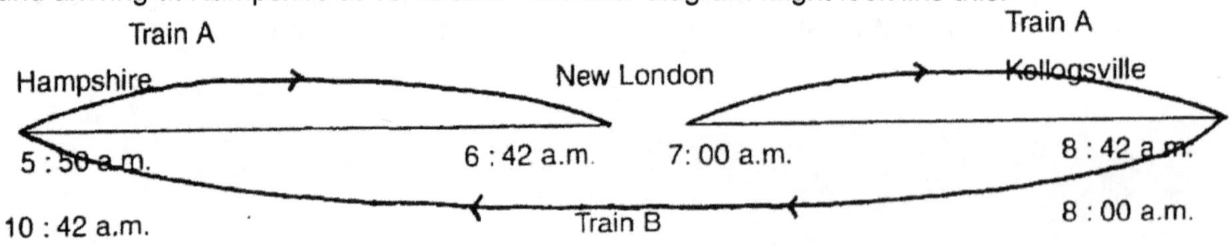

19 (#1)

As you can see from the diagram, the routes of the two trains will overlap somewhere between Kellogsville and New London. If you read sentence IV quickly and assumed that that was the section with only one track, you probably would have assumed that there would have had to be a collision. Sentence IV states, however, that there is only one railroad track between New London and Hampshire. That is the only section, then, where the two trains could collide. By the time Train B gets to that section, however, Train A will have passed it. The two trains will pass each other somewhere between New London and Kellogsville, not New London and Hampshire.

READING COMPREHENSION
UNDERSTANDING AND INTERPRETING WRITTEN MATERIAL

EXAMINATION SECTION

DIRECTIONS: Each question or incomplete statement is followed by several suggested answers or completions. Select the one that BEST answers the question or completes the statement. *PRINT THE LETTER OF THE CORRECT ANSWER IN THE SPACE AT THE RIGHT.*

TEST 1

Questions 1-2.

DIRECTIONS: Questions 1 and 2 are to be answered SOLELY on the basis of the following passage.

One of the biggest mistakes of government executives with substantial supervisory responsibility is failing to make careful appraisals of performance during employee probationary periods. Many a later headache could have been avoided by prompt and full appraisal during the early months of an employee's assignment. There is not much more to say about this except to emphasize the common prevalence of this oversight and to underscore that for its consequences, which are many and sad, the offending managers have no one to blame but themselves.

1. According to the above passage, probationary periods are
   A. a mistake and should not be used by supervisors with large responsibilities
   B. not used properly by government executives
   C. used only for those with supervisory responsibility
   D. the consequence of management mistakes

2. The one of the following conclusions that can MOST appropriately be drawn from the above passage is that
   A. management's failure to appraise employees during their probationary period is a common occurrence
   B. there is not much to say about probationary periods because they are unimportant
   C. managers should blame employees for failing to use their probationary periods properly
   D. probationary periods are a headache to most managers

Questions 3-7.

DIRECTIONS: Questions 3 through 7 are to be answered SOLELY on the basis of the passage preceding each question.

3. Things may not always be what they seem to be. Thus, the wise supervisor should analyze his problems and determine whether there is something there that does not meet the eye. For example, what may seem on the surface to be a personality clash between two subordinates may really be a problem of faulty organization, bad communication, or bad scheduling.
Which one of the following statements BEST supports this passage?
   A. The wise supervisor should avoid personality clashes.
   B. The smart supervisor should figure out what really is going on.
   C. Bad scheduling is the result of faulty organization.
   D. The best supervisor is the one who communicates effectively.

4. Some supervisors, under the pressure of meeting deadlines, become harsh and dictatorial to their subordinates. However, the supervisor most likely to be effective in meeting deadlines is one who absorbs or cushions pressures from above. According to the above passage, if a supervisor wishes to meet deadlines, it is MOST important that he
   A. be informative to his superiors
   B. encourage personal initiative among his subordinates
   C. become harsh and dictatorial to his subordinates
   D. protects his subordinates from pressures from above

5. When giving instructions, a supervisor must always make clear his meaning, leaving no room for misunderstanding. For example, a supervisor who tells a subordinate to do a task *as soon as possible* might legitimately be understood to mean either *it's top priority* or *do it when you can*. Which of the following statements is BEST supported by the above passage?
   A. Subordinates will attempt to avoid work by deliberately distorting instructions.
   B. Instructions should be short, since brief instructions are the clearest.
   C. Less educated subordinates are more likely to honestly misunderstand instructions.
   D. A supervisor should give precise instructions that cannot be misinterpreted.

6. Practical formulas are often suggested to simplify what a supervisor should know and how he should behave, such as the four F's (be firm, fair, friendly, and factual). But such simple formulas are really broad principles, not necessarily specific guides in a real situation. According to the above passage, simple formulas for supervisory behavior
   A. are superior to complicated theories and principles
   B. not always of practical use in actual situations
   C. useful only if they are fair and factual
   D. would be better understood if written in clear language

7. Many management decisions are made far removed from the actual place of operations. Therefore, there is a great need for reliable reports and records and, the larger the organization, the greater is the need for such reports and records. According to the above passage, management decisions made far from the place of operations are
   A. dependent to a great extent on reliable reports and records
   B. sometimes in error because of the great distances involved
   C. generally unreliable because of poor communications
   D. generally more accurate than on-the-scene decisions

Questions 8-9.

DIRECTIONS: Questions 8 and 9 are to be answered SOLELY on the basis of the following passage.

A supervisor who is seeking to influence the behavior of others, whether these others are subordinates, superiors, or colleagues, soon becomes aware of the importance of their attitudes. He may be surprised at some of the attitudes they have and wonder how they can hold some of the views they do - if these views differ from his own. He may be perplexed when others do not change their attitudes even after he has presented facts that obviously should cause them to change.

8. Of the following, the MAIN implication of the above passage is that
   A. behavior is influenced by factual data
   B. interaction with others is based on factual data
   C. rank and intelligence determine behavior
   D. interpretation of facts is controlled by attitude

9. The one of the following statements MOST directly supported by the above paragraph is:
   A. A competent supervisor is firm in his views yet retains an open mind
   B. Influencing the behavior of others is usually the most difficult problem in effective supervision
   C. A particular viewpoint may seem unusual to a supervisor holding a contrary opinion
   D. Organizational success depends upon supervisory motivation

Questions 10-13.

DIRECTIONS: Questions 10 through 13 are to be answered SOLELY on the basis of the following passage.

Top public officials, who feel they have tried to improve conditions for their employees, are often bewildered, hurt, or angered when these employees want to do something on their own through union membership. These officials gain little, however, by regarding unionization as an insult or as evidence of failure on their part. The real challenge and opportunity for top officials is to deal constructively with the labor organization which their employees have *duly* chosen to represent them.

10. The author of the above passage MOST likely considers top management to be
    A. corrupt   B. independent
    C. entrenched   D. paternalistic

11. The above passage points out that certain top public officials are LIKELY to be
    A. disturbed that employees wish to be unionized
    B. aware of the actual needs of their employees
    C. convinced that labor organizations are ineffectual in gaining benefits
    D. unable to deal constructively with individual employees

12. The tenor of the above passage suggests that
    A. top officials should deal positively with the labor organization
    B. intelligent management practices usually eliminate labor union activities
    C. the labor movement has often opposed enlightened management policies
    D. labor and management have had a long history of disagreement

13. As used in the above passage, the word *duly* means MOST NEARLY
    A. properly or legally   B. forcefully or sincerely
    C. openly or publicly   D. precisely or carefully

Questions 14-17.

DIRECTIONS: Questions 14 through 17 are to be answered SOLELY on the basis of the following passage.

The mental attitude of the employee toward safety is exceedingly important in preventing accidents. All efforts designed to keep safety on the employee's mind and to keep accident prevention a live subject in the office will help substantially in a safety program. Although it may seem strange, it is common for people to be careless. Therefore, safety education is a continuous process.

Safety rules should be explained, and the reasons for their rigid enforcement should be given to employees. Telling employees to be careful or giving similar general safety warnings and slogans is probably of little value. Employees should be informed of basic safety fundamentals. This can be done through staff meetings, informal suggestions to employees, movies, and safety instruction cards. Safety instruction cards provide the employees with specific suggestions about safety and serve as a series of timely reminders helping to keep safety on the minds of employees. Pictures, posters, and cartoon sketches on bulletin boards that are located in areas continually used by employees arouse the employees' interest in safety. It is usually good to supplement this type of safety promotion with intensive individual follow-up.

14. The above passage implies that the LEAST effective of the following safety measures is
    A. rigid enforcement of safety rules
    B. getting employees to think in terms of safety
    C. elimination of unsafe conditions in the office
    D. telling employees to stay alert at all times

15. The reason given by the above passage for maintaining ongoing safety education is that
    A. people are often careless
    B. office tasks are often dangerous
    C. the value of safety slogans increases with repetition
    D. safety rules change frequently

16. Which one of the following safety aids is MOST likely to be preferred by the above passage?
    A
    A. cartoon of a man tripping over a carton and yelling, *Keep aisles clear!*
    B. poster with a large number one and a caption saying, *Safety First*
    C. photograph of a very neatly arranged office
    D. large sign with the word *THINK* in capital letters

17. Of the following, the BEST title for the above passage is
    A. BASIC SAFETY FUNDAMENTALS
    B. ENFORCING SAFETY AMONG CARELESS EMPLOYEES
    C. ATTITUDES TOWARD SAFETY
    D. MAKING EMPLOYEES AWARE OF SAFETY

Questions 18-21.

DIRECTIONS: Questions 18 through 21 are to be answered SOLELY on the basis of the following passage.

An employee who has been a member of the retirement system continuously for at least two years may thereafter borrow an amount not exceeding forty percent of the amount of his accumulated contributions in the retirement system, provided that he can repay the amount borrowed, with interest, before he reaches age sixty-three by additional deductions of eight percent from his compensation at the time it is paid. The rate of interest payable on such loan shall be three percent higher than the rate of regular interest creditable to his retirement account. The amount borrowed, with interest, shall be repaid in equal installments by deduction from the member's compensation at the time it is paid, but such installments must be equal to at least four percent of the member's compensation.

Each loan shall be insured by the retirement system against the death of the member, as follows: from the twenty-fifth through the fiftieth day after making the loan, thirty percent of the present value of the loan is insured; from the fifty-first through the seventy-fifth day, sixty percent of the present value of the loan is insured; on and after the seventy-sixth day, all of the present value of the loan is insured. Upon the death of the member, the amount of insurance payable shall be credited to his accumulated contributions to the retirement system.

Instead of a loan, any member who cancels his rate of contribution may withdraw from his account, and may restore in any year he chooses, any sum in excess of the maximum in his annuity savings account and due to his account at the end of the calendar year in which he was entitled to cancel his rate of contribution.

18. Based on the information in the above passage, a member may obtain a loan
    A. in any amount not exceeding forty percent of his accumulated contributions in the system
    B. if he has contributions in excess of the maximum in his annuity savings account
    C. if he will remain a member of the retirement system until age 63
    D. once during his first two years of membership and then at any time thereafter

19. According to the information in the above passage, the interest rate paid by a member who borrows from the retirement system is
   A. 4% of his earnable compensation
   B. 8% of his earnable compensation
   C. lower than the interest rate creditable to his retirement account
   D. higher than the interest rate creditable to his retirement account

20. Suppose that a member of the retirement system obtained a loan on July 15 of this year and died on October 2 when the present value of her loan was $800. Based on the information in the above passage, this member will have _____ her accumulated contributions to the retirement system.
   A. $480 credited to   B. $480 deducted from
   C. $800 credited to   D. $800 deducted from

21. Based on the information in the above passage, a member who has excess funds in his retirement account may with- draw funds from the retirement system
   A. if he has cancelled his rate of contribution
   B. if he restores the funds within one year of withdrawal
   C. when he retires
   D. if he leaves city service

Questions 22-25.

DIRECTIONS: Questions 22 through 25 are to be answered SOLELY on the basis of the following passage.

Upon the death of a member or former member of the retirement system, there shall be paid to his estate, or to the person he had nominated by written designation, his accumulated deductions. In addition, if he is a member who is in city service, there shall be paid a sum consisting of: an amount equal to the compensation he earned while a member during the three months immediately preceding his death, or, if the total amount of years of allowable service exceeds five, there shall be paid an amount equal to the compensation he earned while a member during the six months immediately preceding his death; and the reserve-for-increased-take-home-pay, if any. Payment for the expense of burial, not exceeding two hundred and fifty dollars, may be made to the relative or friend who, in the absence or failure of the designated beneficiary, assumes this responsibility.

Until the first retirement benefit payment has been made, where a member has not selected an option, the member will be considered to be in city service, and the death benefits provided above will be paid instead of the retirement allowance. The member, or upon his death his designated beneficiary, may provide that the actuarial equivalent of the benefit otherwise payable in a lump sum shall be paid in the form of an annuity payable in installments; the amount of such annuity is determined at the time of the member's death on the basis of the age of the beneficiary at that time.

22. Suppose that a member who has applied for retirement benefits without selecting an option dies before receiving any payments.
According to the information in the above passage, this member's beneficiary would be entitled to receive
    A. an annuity based on the member's age at the time of his death
    B. a death benefit only
    C. the member's retirement allowance only
    D. the member's retirement allowance, plus a death benefit payment in a lump sum

22._____

23. According to the information in the above passage, the amount of the benefit payable upon the death of a member is based, in part, on the
    A. length of city service during which the deceased person was a member
    B. number of beneficiaries the deceased member had nominated
    C. percent of the deceased member's deductions for social security
    D. type of retirement plan to which the deceased member belonged

23._____

24. According to the information in the above passage, which one of the following statements concerning the payment of death benefits is CORRECT?
    A. In order for a death benefit to be paid, the deceased member must have previously nominated, in writing, someone to receive the benefit.
    B. Death benefits are paid upon the death of members who are in city service.
    C. A death benefit must be paid in one lump sum.
    D. When a retired person dies, his retirement allowance is replaced by a death benefit payment.

24._____

25. According to the information in the above passage, the amount of annuity payments made to a beneficiary in monthly installments in lieu of a lump sum payment is determined by the
    A. length of member's service at the time of his death
    B. age of the beneficiary at the time of the member's death
    C. member's age at retirement
    D. member's age at the time of his death

25._____

KEY (CORRECT ANSWERS)

1.	B	11.	A	21.	A
2.	A	12.	A	22.	B
3.	B	13.	A	23.	A
4.	D	14.	D	24.	B
5.	D	15.	A	25.	B
6.	B	16.	A		
7.	A	17.	D		
8.	D	18.	A		
9.	C	19.	D		
10.	D	20.	C		

TEST 2

DIRECTIONS: Each question or incomplete statement is followed by several suggested answers or completions. Select the one that BEST answers the question or completes the statement. *PRINT THE LETTER OF THE CORRECT ANSWER IN THE SPACE AT THE RIGHT.*

Questions 1-4.

DIRECTIONS: Questions 1 through 4 are to be answered SOLELY on the basis of the following passage.

Depreciation -- Any reduction from the upper limit of value. An effect caused by deterioration and/or obsolescence. Deterioration is evidenced by wear and tear, decay, dry rot, cracks, encrustations, or structural defects. Obsolescence is divisible into two parts, functional or economic. Functional obsolescence may be due to poor planning, mechanical inadequacy or overadequacy, functional inadequacy or overadequacy due to size, style, or age. It is evidenced by conditions within the property. Economic obsolescence is caused by changes external to the property, such as neighborhood infiltrations of inharmonious groups or property uses, legislation, etc. It is also the actual decline in market value of the improvement to land from the time of purchase to the time of sale.

1. According to the above passage, a form of physical deterioration can be caused by
   A. termite infestation
   B. zoning regulations
   C. inadequate wiring
   D. extra high ceilings

2. According to the above passage, a form of economic obsolescence may be caused by
   A. structural defects
   B. poor architectural design
   C. changes in zoning regulations
   D. chemical reactions

3. According to the above passage, the statement which BEST explains the meaning of depreciation is that it is a loss in value
   A. caused only by economic obsolescence
   B. resulting from any cause
   C. caused only by wear and tear
   D. resulting from conditions or changes external to the property

4. According to the above passage, the lack of air conditioning in warm climates is
   A. a form of physical deterioration
   B. a form of functional obsolescence
   C. a form of economic obsolescence
   D. not a form of depreciation

Questions 5-8.

DIRECTIONS: Questions 5 through 8 are to be answered SOLELY on the basis of the following passage.

In determining the valuation of income-producing property, the capitalization of income is accepted as a proper approach to value. Income-producing property is bought and sold for the purpose of making money. How much an investor would pay would, of course, depend on how much he could earn on his investment. The amount he would earn on his investment is called a return. The amount of return depends on the degree of risk involved.

If one has $100,000 to invest, it can be put in a bank account at perhaps a 5 percent return. In the bank, the money is relatively safe so the return is lower. If the money were invested by purchasing a block of stores in a depressed area, of course, one would not be satisfied with a 5 percent return. This is what the capitalization of income comes down to - the better the return, the higher the risk. This is the approach an experienced real estate investor uses in determining what he would pay for property.

5. According to the above passage, which one of the following investments would an experienced real estate investor with $100,000 MOST likely choose? A(n)
   A. apartment building in a slum area yielding a 6 percent return
   B. office building rented to professionals yielding a 6 percent return
   C. shopping center in a depressed area yielding a 10 percent return
   D. warehouse rented on a long-term lease to a major corporation yielding a 10 percent return

5._____

6. According to the above passage, in the capitalization of income, the relationship between the degree of risk and the rate of return GENERALLY is expected to be
   A. indeterminate   B. variable
   C. inverse   D. direct

6._____

7. According to the above passage, in purchasing income-producing property, the one of the following which would NOT be a factor influencing an experienced real estate investor is the
   A. socio-economic characteristics of the area in which the property is located
   B. rate of return on investment
   C. original cost of the property
   D. degree of risk involved

7._____

8. According to the above passage, the property listed below which would be LEAST likely to be valued by the capitalization of income is a(n)
   A. apartment house with no vacancies
   B. office building rented to 70 percent of capacity
   C. shopping center with several new tenants
   D. vacant lot located next to a factory

8._____

Questions 9-12.

DIRECTIONS: Questions 9 through 12 are to be answered SOLELY on the basis of the following passage.

The cost approach is used by assessors mainly in valuing one-family homes and properties of a special nature which are not commonly bought and sold and do not produce an income.

There are three aspects to the cost approach to valuation. The first is the actual cost of construction. Where the property has recently been built, the cost of constructing the property is relevant. It, however, may not be a true test as to its value. The building may have been constructed so as to serve the special needs of the owner. What it costs to construct may not truly reflect its value; it may be worth more or less. If it is income-producing property, the income may be more or less than expected. It may be sold for more or less than it cost to build.

The second aspect is replacement cost and applies to older structures. It involves the construction of a similar type of building with the same purpose. It does not require the use of the same materials or design.

Reproduction cost is the third aspect, and it also applies to older structures. It involves construction with the exact same materials and design. The cost in the two latter aspects is construction at today's prices with an allowance made for depreciation from the day the original building was constructed.

9. According to the above passage, which one of the following is a CORRECT statement concerning the cost approach to valuation?
   A. In determining value by the replacement and reproduction cost methods, an allowance must be made for depreciation from the day the building was originally constructed.
   B. The cost approach method is the best method to apply in valuing an office building.
   C. When a structure has been recently built, its actual cost is the best method of determining its value.
   D. The fact that a structure has been built to meet the special needs of the occupant is a relevant factor in valuation.

10. An assessor, in valuing a ten-year-old apartment house, finds that its original construction cost was $1,200,000. In capitalizing its net income, he realizes a valuation of $800,000. In using the replacement cost method and allowing for depreciation, the assessor arrives at a valuation of $900,000.
    According to the above passage, which one of the following valuations is LEAST acceptable for this apartment house?
    A. $1,200,000 B. $800,000
    C. $900,000   D. $850,000

11. The construction cost of a recently built structure is relevant to value, but may not be a true test of value. According to the above passage, which one of the following statements CORRECTLY explains why this is true?
    A. The builder may not know how to construct economically.
    B. A building can depreciate very quickly.
    C. The building may have been built to satisfy certain unique specifications.
    D. Cost-of-construction is not an accepted method of valuation.

12. According to the above passage, which one of the following statements CORRECTLY defines the essential difference between the replacement cost and reproduction cost aspects of the cost approach?

    A. Replacement cost is used only in assessing older buildings; reproduction cost is used only when the building has been recently constructed.
    B. Reproduction cost does not include any allowance for depreciation; replacement cost allows for depreciation from the date of construction of the original building.
    C. Replacement cost involves construction with the same exact materials; reproduction cost does not require the use of the same materials.
    D. Reproduction cost involves construction with the exact same materials and design; replacement cost does not require the use of the same materials and design.

Questions 13-18.

DIRECTIONS: Questions 13 through 18 are to be answered SOLELY on the basis of the following passage.

Realty, because of fixity in investment, immobility in location, and necessity for shelter purposes, lends itself readily to economic controls when such are deemed essential to serve social or political ends, or where the interest of health, safety, and morality of community population or the nation at large warrants it. Realty has consistently been recognized as a form of private property which is sufficiently invested with public interest to warrant its control either under the police power of a sovereign state and its branches of government or by direct and statutory legislation enacted within the framework of the governmental constitution.

Whenever war or catastrophe causes a sudden shifting of population or suspension of building operations, or both, an imbalance is brought about in the supply and demand for housing. This imbalance in housing demand and supply creates conditions of insecurity and instability among the tenants who fear indiscriminate eviction or unwarranted upward rental adjustments. It is this background of possible exploitation during times of economic stress and strain that underlies the enactment of emergency rent control legislation.

Although rent control has been in effect in many communities, particularly the larger metropolitan communities, since the end of World War II, the attitude of all levels of government is to view this form of legislation as temporary and to hasten, as far as their power permits, a return to normal relations between landlords and tenants.

13. According to the above passage, the reason that realty can conveniently be subjected to controls is due to
    A. public interest   B. site immobility
    C. population shifts   D. moral considerations

14. The above passage includes as a justification for the imposition of economic controls all of the following EXCEPT
    A. threats to physical safety
    B. socio-political considerations
    C. dangers to health in the community
    D. requirements of police powers

15. According to the above passage, a LIKELY cause for a cessation of construction might be a
    A. natural disaster
    B. change in the demand for housing
    C. change in the supply of housing
    D. demographic fluctuations

15._____

16. According to the above passage, of the following, a tenant's insecurity would MOST likely result in his fear of
    A. reduction in necessary services
    B. loss in equity
    C. rent increases
    D. condemnation proceedings

16._____

17. According to the above passage, indiscriminate evictions by landlords during periods of economic difficulties constitute
    A. unlawful acts   B. justifiable measures
    C. desirable actions D. exploitation of tenants

17._____

18. According to the above passage, economic controls of realty have been in effect on a widespread basis since
    A. 1918   B. 1945
    C. 1953   D. 1964

18._____

Questions 19-22.

DIRECTIONS: Questions 19 through 22 are to be answered SOLELY on the basis of the following passage.

In capitalizing the net income of property to produce a value, certain expenses are permitted to be deducted from gross income. Even though the premises may be fully rented, it is proper to deduct from the gross income an allowance for vacancy. All expenses attributable to the maintenance and upkeep of the premises are deductible. These include heat, light and power, water and sewers, wages or employees and expenses attributable to wages, insurance, repairs and maintenance, supplies and materials, legal and accounting fees, telephone, rental commission, advertising, and so forth. If the premises are furnished, a reserve for the depreciation of personal property is deductible. A capital improvement to the building is not a deductible expense. Real estate taxes should not be deducted as an expense. Instead, taxes should be factored as part of the overall capitalization rate.

It is proper to allow an expense for management of the building even in cases where the owner himself is manager. But payments of interest and principal of the mortgage are not a properly deductible expense. Real property is appraised free and clear of all encumbrances. Otherwise, two identical buildings located next to each other might be valued differently because one has a greater mortgage than the other.

19. According to the above passage, the one of the following which is NOT a proper deductible expense during the year in which the expense is incurred is the cost for
    A. advertising to rent the premises
    B. accounting fees
    C. utilities
    D. putting in central air conditioning

20. According to the above passage, the one of the following statements concerning deductible expenses which is CORRECT is that
    A. a vacancy allowance is a proper deductible expense even though the premises may be fully rented
    B. real estate taxes are a proper deductible expense
    C. if the owner manages his own property, he cannot charge a management fee as a deductible expense
    D. payments for interest and principal of the mortgage are proper deductible expenses

21. According to the above passage, two identical adjacent buildings CANNOT receive different valuations because of differences in their
    A. mortgages   B. net income
    C. leases   D. management fees

22. According to the above passage, an owner of furnished premises may set aside a reserve as a deductible expense for all of the following EXCEPT
    A. refrigerators   B. carpeting
    C. bookcases   D. walls

Questions 23-25.

DIRECTIONS: Questions 23 through 25 are to be answered SOLELY on the basis of the following passage.

The standard for assessment in the state is contained in Section 306 of the Real Property Tax Law. It states that all real property in each assessing unit shall be assessed at the full value thereof. However, the courts of the state have not required assessors to assess at 100% of full value. Assessments of property for real estate tax purposes at less than full value are not invalid if they are made at a uniform percentage of full value throughout the assessing district. In assessing real property, full value is equivalent to market value.

In determining market value of real property for tax purposes, every element which can reasonably affect value of property ought to be considered, and the main considerations should be given to actual sales of the subject or similar property, cost to produce or reproduce the property, capitalization of income therefrom, and the combination of these factors.

23. According to the above passage, the one of the following statements which is INCORRECT is that all real property in each assessing unit
    A. must be assessed at full value
    B. shall be assessed at full value or at a uniform percentage of full value
    C. may be assessed at 50% of full value
    D. may be assessed at 100% of full value

24. According to the above passage, the one of the following elements of value which should be given the LEAST consideration in determining market value is
    A. actual or comparable sales
    B. reproduction cost
    C. amount of mortgage
    D. capitalization of income

25. According to the above passage, the basis for the legality of assessing units, making assessments at a uniform percentage of full value rather than at full value is
    A. Section 306 of the Real Property Tax Law
    B. decisions of the state courts
    C. judgments of individual assessors
    D. decisions of municipal executives

KEY (CORRECT ANSWERS)

1.	A	11.	C
2.	C	12.	D
3.	B	13.	B
4.	B	14.	D
5.	D	15.	A
6.	D	16.	C
7.	C	17.	D
8.	D	18.	B
9.	A	19.	D
10.	A	20.	A

21.	A
22.	D
23.	A
24.	C
25.	B

TEST 3

DIRECTIONS: Each question or incomplete statement is followed by several suggested answers or completions. Select the one that BEST answers the question or completes the statement. *PRINT THE LETTER OF THE CORRECT ANSWER IN THE SPACE AT THE RIGHT.*

Questions 1-4.

DIRECTIONS: Questions 1 through 4 are to be answered SOLELY on the basis of the following passage.

    Although zoning is a phase of city planning and is concerned with land use control of private property, zoning powers are better known and more generally applied than most city planning powers. Zoning powers predict the formulation of a master plan and even the formation of the planning commission itself. The widespread application of zoning powers is evident from a survey conducted by the International City Managers' Association. As reported in the 2015 MUNICIPAL YEARBOOK, 98 percent of all cities in excess of ten thousand population had enacted comprehensive zoning ordinances governing the utilization of privately owned land. Since 60 percent of all urban land is generally held under private ownership, the impact of zoning laws upon income and value of real property is most significant.

1. According to the above passage, in relation to the powers of city planning, zoning powers are
   - A. not as familiar to the general public
   - B. formulated subsequent to the establishment of the powers of the planning commission
   - C. more general in their application
   - D. likely to develop as a result of the community's master plan

2. According to the above passage, if there are 200 cities in the United States with a population exceeding 10,000 persons, the number of such cities LIKELY to have enacted comprehensive zoning laws is
   - A. 190
   - B. 192
   - C. 194
   - D. 196

3. According to the above passage, for each 400 acres of urban land, it is LIKELY that the amount of land which would be privately owned would be _____ acres.
   - A. 220
   - B. 240
   - C. 260
   - D. 280

4. Of the following, the one whose land use is MOST likely to be affected by zoning controls, according to the above passage, is
   - A. Sears Department Store
   - B. the Port Authority terminal
   - C. the New York Public Library at 42nd Street
   - D. the Federal Building

Questions 5-7.

DIRECTIONS: Questions 5 through 7 are to be answered SOLELY on the basis of the following passage.

    Apartments located in rehabilitated old law tenement houses are designated as *off-site apartments*. The purpose of such apartments is to provide temporary housing accommodations for the relocation of persons and families living on sites which are to be used for future housing projects who can not otherwise be relocated. A family shall be permitted to continue to occupy an off-site apartment for a period of two years from the date of its admission and shall be required to move out at the termination of such two-year period. However, no proceedings shall be undertaken to remove any tenant now in occupancy of an off-site apartment until after May 9, 2015.

A family shall, however, be required to remove from an off-site apartment prior to the expiration of the periods and date enumerated above if it refuses to accept an available apartment in a public housing project for which it is eligible; or, as a tenant in occupancy, it fails to execute any lease required by management or it fails to comply with other requirements, standard procedures, or rules promulgated by management.

5. A tenant occupying an off-site apartment refuses to renew his lease for one year because he expects to move into a new apartment house within six months. This tenant may
   A. be required to move before his new apartment is ready
   B. be required to move before his new apartment is ready only if his occupancy in the off-site apartment exceeds two years
   C. not be required to move before his new apartment is ready
   D. not be required to move prior to May 9, 2015

6. According to the above passage, if a family living on a site can be relocated to an apartment in a public housing project, it is
   A. eligible for an off-site apartment near its present dwelling
   B. not eligible for any off-site apartment
   C. eligible for an off-site apartment if it has been living in its present home for at least two years
   D. permitted to continue in occupancy for at least two more years

7. According to the above passage, a tenant admitted to an off-site apartment on October 1, 2013 is FIRST subject to removal after
   A. October 1, 2015
   B. May 9, 2015
   C. he has been investigated and found to be ineligible for an apartment in the public housing project
   D. he refuses to sign a lease on the apartment or after September 30, 2015, whichever comes first

Questions 8-14.

DIRECTIONS: Questions 8 through 14 are to be answered SOLELY on the basis of the following passage.

From a nationwide point of view, the need for new housing units during the years immediately ahead will be determined by four major factors. The most important factor is the net change in household formations -- that is, the difference between the number of new households that are formed and the number of existing households that are dissolved, whether by death or other circumstances. During the 2010's, as the children born during the '80's and 90's come of age and marry, the total number of households is expected to increase at a rate of more than 1,000,000 annually. The second factor affecting the need for new housing units is *removals* -- that is, existing units that are demolished, damaged beyond repair, or otherwise removed from the housing supply. A third factor is the number of existing vacancies. To some extent, vacancies can satisfy the housing demand caused by increases in total number of households or by removals, although population shifts that are already underway mean that some areas will have a surfeit of vacancies and other areas will be faced with serious shortages of housing. A final factor, and one that has only recently assumed major importance, is the increasing demand for second homes. These may take any form from a shack in the woods for a city dweller to a pied-a-terre in the city for a suburbanite. Whatever the form, however, it is certain that increasing leisure time, rising amounts of discretionary income, and improvements in transportation are leading more and more Americans to look on a second home not as a rich man's luxury but as the common man's right.

8. The above passage uses the term *housing units* to refer to
    A. residences of all kinds
    B. apartment buildings only
    C. one-family houses only
    D. the total number of families in the United States

9. The above passage uses the word *removals* to mean
    A. the shift of population from one area to another
    B. vacancies that occur when families move
    C. financial losses suffered when a building is damaged or destroyed
    D. former dwellings that are demolished or can no longer be used for housing

10. The expression *pied-a-terre* appears in the next-to-last sentence in the above passage.
    A person who is not familiar with the expression should be able to tell from the way it is used here that it PROBABLY means
    A. a suburban home owned by a commuter
    B. a shack in the woods
    C. a second home that is used from time to time
    D. overnight lodging for a traveler in a strange city

11. Of the factors described in the above passage as having an important influence on the demand for housing, which factor, taken alone, is LEAST likely to encourage the construction of new housing?
    The
    A. net change in household formations
    B. destruction of existing housing
    C. existence of vacancies
    D. use of second homes

12. Based on the above passage, the TOTAL increase in the number of households during the 2010's is expected to be MOST NEARLY
    A. 1,000,000   B. 10,000,000
    C. 100,000,000   D. 1,000,000,000

13. Which one of the following conclusions could MOST logically be drawn from the information given in the above passage?
    A. The population of the United States is increasing at the rate of about 1,000,000 people annually.
    B. There is already a severe housing shortage in all parts of the country.
    C. The need for additional housing units is greater in some parts of the country than in others.
    D. It is still true that only wealthy people can afford to keep up more than one home.

14. Which one of the following conclusions could NOT logically be drawn from the information given in the above passage?
    A. The need for new housing will be even greater in the 2020's than in the 2010's.
    B. Demolition of existing housing must be taken into account in calculating the need for new housing construction.
    C. Having a second home is more common today than it was in the 1970's.
    D. Part of the housing needs of the 2010's can be met by vacancies.

Questions 15-18.

DIRECTIONS: Questions 15 through 18 are to be answered SOLELY on the basis of the following passage.

A city may expand by growing vertically through the replacement of lower buildings with higher ones; or by filling in open spaces between settled areas; or by extending the existing settled area. When the settled area is expanded, growth may take several forms, the most important forms being concentric circle or ring growth around the central nucleus; axial growth, with prongs or fingerlike extensions moving out along main transportation routes; and suburban growth, with the establishment of islands of settlements before the expansion of the main city area. These types of expansion are characteristic of most large cities. Baltimore was for a long time a good example of ring growth, whereas New York, Chicago, and Detroit illustrate axial and suburban growth.

15. The title that BEST expresses the theme of the above passage is
    A. FORMS OF CITY EXPANSION
    B. MAJOR METROPOLITAN PROBLEMS
    C. METHODS OF URBAN PLANNING
    D. SUBURBAN GROWTH IN AMERICA

16. The one of the following which is an example of vertical growth is the
    A. settlement of year-round residents along the upper Hudson River
    B. restoration of former rooming houses to their original brownstone condition
    C. subdivision of large estates into small lot semidetached houses
    D. erection of the Empire State Building in New York City

17. A city that grew as a concentric circle is
    A. Baltimore   B. New York
    C. Chicago   D. Detroit

18. When the author speaks of axial growth, he refers to a situation where 18._____
    A. expansion is primarily into rural areas until suburbs are thereby created
    B. small towns and villages are consolidated by gradually growing until one large city is created
    C. the direction in which a city expands is determined by the location of major highways
    D. the number of new buildings is greater than the number of old buildings demolished

Questions 19-21.

DIRECTIONS: Questions 19 through 21 are to be answered SOLELY on the basis of the following passage.

Incentive zoning is an affirmative tool that has widespread applications. The Zoning Resolution which became effective in 1998 substantially reduced the amount of floor space that a developer could put up on a given size lot and increased the light and air. In the Trump Building, which was built under the old legislation, the floor space is 27 times the size of the lot. The maximum ratio allowed for buildings now without a special permit is 18.

The 1998 zoning ordinance provided incentives to developers to devote part of the plot to public plazas or arcades. This space is needed to supplement the sidewalks, which in many cases are as narrow as they were when the midtown area was lined with brownstone or brickfront houses.

While the newer zoning has produced plazas, it has not of itself proved to be a sufficient development control. Stretches of Third Avenue and the Avenue of the Americas, for example, have been almost completely redeveloped in the last few years. This massive private investment has produced several fine individual buildings. The total environment produced, however, has been disappointing in a number of respects, and there is nowhere near the amenity that there could have been.

19. According to the above passage, the use of incentive zoning has NOT been entirely successful because it 19._____
    A. has discouraged redevelopment
    B. has encouraged massive private development along Third Avenue
    C. has been ineffective in controlling overall redevelopment
    D. has not significantly increased the number of parks and plazas being built

20. According to the above passage, one might conclude that before the 1998 Zoning Resolution was passed, 20._____
    A. buildings on a given site were required to have greater setbacks
    B. the amount of private investment in development was significantly smaller than it is today
    C. no controls on development existed
    D. the provision of parks and plazas was less frequent

21. In the context of the above passage, the word *amenity* means
    A. compliance with regulations
    B. correction of undesirable environmental aspects
    C. responsiveness to guidelines and incentives
    D. pleasant or desirable features

Questions 22-24.

DIRECTIONS: Questions 22 through 24 are to be answered SOLELY on the basis of the following passage.

Physical design plays a very significant role in crime rate. Crime rate has been found to increase almost proportionately with building height. The average number of crimes is much greater in higher buildings than in lower ones (equal to or less than six stories). What is most interesting is that in buildings of six stories or less, the project size or total number of units does not make a difference. It seems that although larger projects encourage crime by fostering feelings of anonymity, isolation, irresponsibility, and lack of identity with surroundings, evidence indicates that larger projects encompassed in low buildings seem to offset what we may assume to be factors conducive to high crime rates. High-rise projects not only experience a higher rate of crime within the buildings, but a greater proportion of the crime occurs in the interior public spaces of these buildings as compared with those of the lower buildings. Lower buildings have more limited public space than higher ones. A criminal probably perceives that the interior public areas of buildings are where his victims are most vulnerable and where the possibility of his being seen or apprehended is minimal. Placement of elevators, entrance lobbies, fire stairs, and secondary exits all are factors related to the likelihood of crimes taking place in buildings. The study of all of these elements should bear some weight in the planning of new projects.

22. According to the above passage, which of the following BEST describes the relationship between building size and crime?
    A. Larger projects lead to a greater crime rate.
    B. Higher buildings tend to increase the crime rate.
    C. The smaller the number of project apartments in low buildings, the higher the crime rate.
    D. Anonymity and isolation serve to lower the crime rate in small buildings.

23. According to the above passage, the likelihood of a criminal attempting a mugging in the interior public portions of a high-rise building is GOOD because
    A. tenants will be constantly flowing in and out of the area
    B. there is easy access to fire stairs and secondary exits
    C. there is a good chance that no one will see him
    D. tenants may not recognize the victims of crime as their neighbors

24. Which of the following is IMPLIED by the above passage as an explanation for the fact that the crime rate is lower in large low-rise housing projects than in large high-rise projects?
    A. Tenants know each other better and take a greater interest in what happens in the project.
    B. There is more public space where tenants are likely to gather together.
    C. The total number of units in a low-rise project is fewer than the total number of units in a high-rise project.
    D. Elevators in low-rise buildings travel quickly, thus limiting the amount of time in which a criminal can act.

25. The financing of housing represents two distinct forms of costs. One is the actual capital invested, and the other is the interest rate which is charged for the use of capital. In fixing rents, the interest rate which capital is expected to yield plays a very important part. On the basis of this statement, it would be MOST correct to state that
    A. the financing of housing represents two distinct forms of capital investment
    B. reducing the interest rate charged for the use of capital is not as important as economies in construction in achieving lower rentals
    C. in fixing rents, the interest rate is expected to yield capital gains, justifying the investment
    D. the actual capital invested and the interest rate charged for use of this capital are factors in determining housing costs

KEY (CORRECT ANSWERS)

1.	C	11.	C
2.	D	12.	B
3.	B	13.	C
4.	A	14.	A
5.	A	15.	A
6.	B	16.	D
7.	D	17.	A
8.	A	18.	C
9.	D	19.	C
10.	C	20.	D

21.	D
22.	B
23.	C
24.	A
25.	D

INTERPRETING STATISTICAL DATA
GRAPHS, CHARTS AND TABLES
EXAMINATION SECTION
TEST 1

DIRECTIONS: Each questioner incomplete statement is followed by several suggested answers or completions. Select the one that BEST answers the question or completes the statement. *PRINT THE LETTER OF THE CORRECT ANSWER IN THE SPACE AT THE RIGHT.*

Questions 1-3.

DIRECTIONS: Questions 1 through 3 are to be answered SOLELY on the basis of the following table.

QUARTERLY SALES REPORTED BY MAJOR INDUSTRY GROUPS

DECEMBER 2021 – FEBRUARY 2023
Reported Sales, Taxable & Non-Taxable (in Millions)

Industry Groups	12/21-2/22	3/22-5/22	6/22-8/22	9/22-11/22	12/22-2/23
Retailers	2,802	2,711	2,475	2,793	2,974
Wholesalers	2,404	2,237	2,269	2,485	2,974
Manufacturers	3,016	2,888	3,001	3,518	3,293
Services	1,034	1,065	984	1,132	1,092

1. The trend in total reported sales may be described as

   A. downward
   B. downward and upward
   C. horizontal
   D. upward

2. The two industry groups that reveal a similar seasonal pattern for the period December 2021 through November 2022 are

   A. retailers and manufacturers
   B. retailers and wholesalers
   C. wholesalers and manufacturers
   D. wholesalers and service

3. Reported sales were at a MINIMUM between

   A. December 2021 and February 2022
   B. March 2022 and May 2022
   C. June 2022 and August 2022
   D. September 2022 and November 2022

TEST 2

DIRECTIONS: Each question or incomplete statement is followed by several suggested answers or completions. Select the one that BEST answers the question or completes the statement. *PRINT THE LETTER OF THE CORRECT ANSWER IN THE SPACE AT THE RIGHT*

Questions 1-4.

DIRECTIONS: Questions 1 through 4 are to be answered SOLELY on the basis of the following information.

The income elasticity of demand for selected items of consumer demand in the United States are:

Item	Elasticity
Airline Travel	5.66
Alcohol	.62
Dentist Fees	1.00
Electric Utilities	3.00
Gasoline	1.29
Intercity Bus	1.89
Local Bus	1.41
Restaurant Meals	.75

1. The demand for the item listed below that would be MOST adversely affected by a decrease in income is
   - A. alcohol
   - B. electric utilities
   - C. gasoline
   - D. restaurant meals

2. The item whose relative change in demand would be the same as the relative change in income would be
   - A. dentist fees
   - B. gasoline
   - C. restaurant meals
   - D. none of the above

3. If income increases by 12 percent, the demand for restaurant meals may be expected to increase by
   - A. 9 percent
   - B. 12 percent
   - C. 16 percent
   - D. none of the above

4. On the basis of the above information, the item whose demand would be MOST adversely affected by an increase in the sales tax from 7 percent to 8 percent to be passed on to the consumer in the form of higher prices
   - A. would be airline travel
   - B. would be alcohol
   - C. would be gasoline
   - D. cannot be determined

TEST 3

DIRECTIONS: Each question or incomplete statement is followed by several suggested answers or completions. Select the one that BEST answers the question or completes the statement. *PRINT THE LETTER OF THE CORRECT ANSWER IN THE SPACE AT THE RIGHT.*

Questions 1-3.

DIRECTIONS: Questions 1 through 3 are to be answered SOLELY on the basis of the following graphs depicting various relationships in a single retail store.

GRAPH 1
RELATIONSHIP BETWEEN NUMBER OF CUSTOMERS STORE AND TIME OF DAY

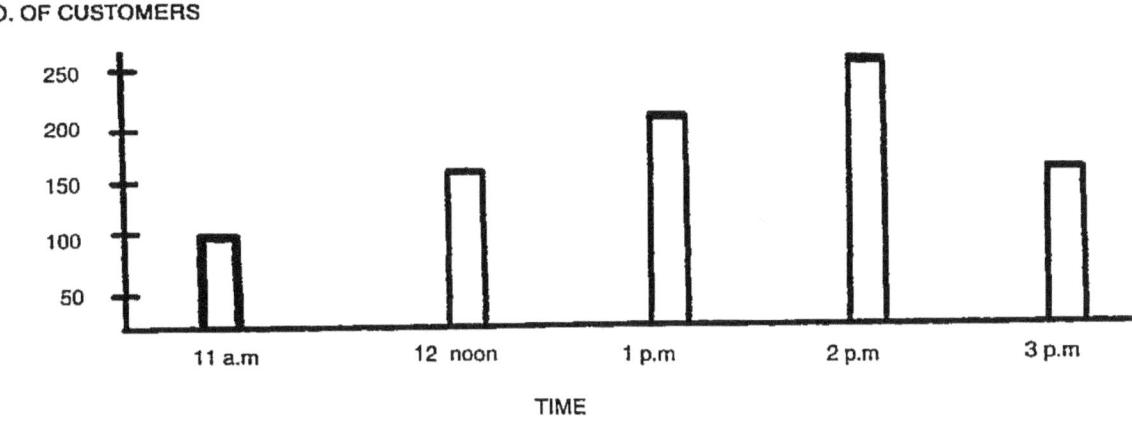

GRAPH II
RELATIONSHIP BETWEEN NUMBER OF CHECK-OUT LANES AVAILABLE IN STORE AND WAIT TIME FOR CHECK-OUT

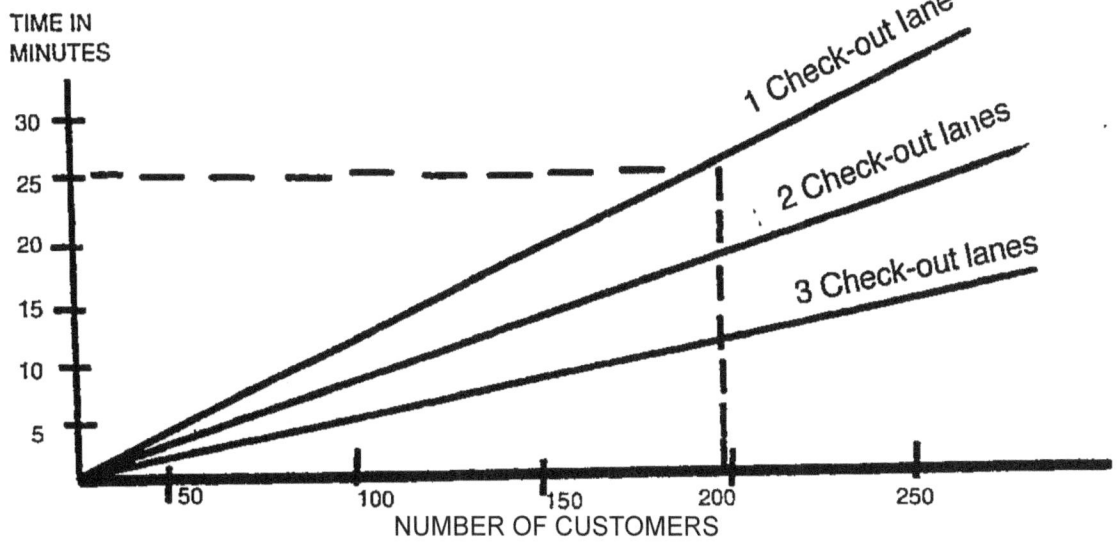

Note the dotted lines in Graph II. They demonstrate that, if there are 200 people in the store and only one check-out lane is open, the wait time will be 25 minutes.

1. At what time would a person be most likely NOT to have to wait more than 15 minutes if only one check-out lane is open?

    A. 11 A.M.　　　B. 12 Noon　　　C. 1 P.M.　　　D. 3 P.M.

2. At what time of day would a person have to wait the LONGEST to check out if three check-out lanes are available?

    A. 11 A.M.　　　B. 12 Noon　　　C. 1 P.M.　　　D. 2 P.M

3. The difference in wait times between 1 and 3 check-out lanes at 3 P.M. is MOST NEARLY

    A. 5　　　B. 10　　　C. 15　　　D. 20

TEST 4

DIRECTIONS: Each question or incomplete statement is followed by several suggested answers or completions. Select the one that BEST answers the question or completes the statement. *PRINT THE LETTER OF THE CORRECT ANSWER IN THE SPACE AT THE RIGHT.*

Questions 1-4.

DIRECTIONS: Questions 1 through 4 are to be answered SOLELY on the basis of the graph below.

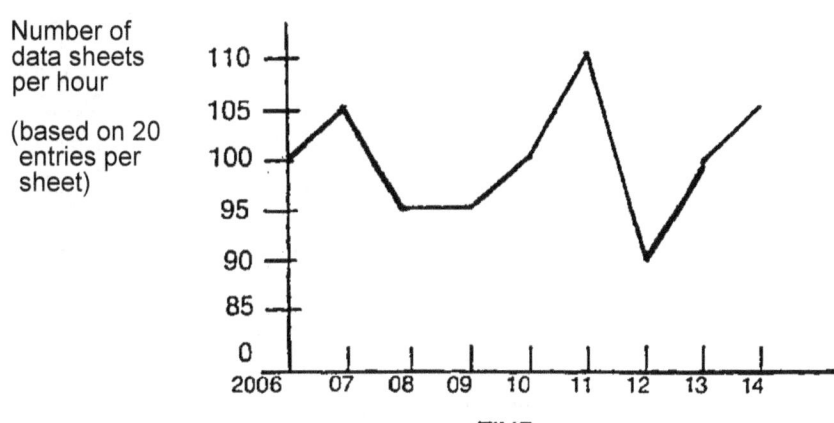

1. Of the following, during what four-year period did the average output of computer operators fall BELOW 100 sheets per hour?

   A. 2007-10   B. 2008-11   C. 2010-13   D. 2011-14

2. The average percentage change in output over the previous year's output for the years 2009 to 2012 is MOST NEARLY

   A. 2   B. 0   C. -5   D. -7

3. The difference between the actual output for 2012 and the projected figure based upon the average increase from 2006-2011 is MOST NEARLY

   A. 18   B. 20   C. 22   D. 24

4. Assume that after constructing the above graph you, an analyst, discovered that the average number of entries per sheet in 2012 was 25 (instead of 20) because of the complex nature of the work performed during that period.
   The average output in sheets per hour for the period 2010-13, expressed in terms of 20 items per sheet, would then be MOST NEARLY

   A. 95   B. 100   C. 105   D. 110

TEST 6

DIRECTIONS: Each question or incomplete statement is followed by several suggested answers or completions. Select the one that BEST answers the question or completes the statement. *PRINT THE LETTER OF THE CORRECT ANSWER IN THE SPACE AT THE RIGHT.*

Questions 1-3.

DIRECTIONS: Questions 1 through 3 are to be answered on the basis of the following data assembled for a cost-benefit analysis.

	Cost	Benefit
No program	0	0
Alternative W	$ 3,000	$ 6,000
Alternative X	$10,000	$17,000
Alternative Y	$17,000	$25,000
Alternative Z	$30,000	$32,000

1. From the point of view of selecting the alternative with the best cost benefit ratio, the BEST alternative is Alternative

    A. W   B. X   C. Y   D. Z

2. From the point of view of selecting the alternative with the best measure of net benefit, the BEST alternative is Alternative

    A. W   B. X   C. Y   D. Z

3. From the point of view of pushing public expenditure to the point where marginal benefit equals or exceeds marginal cost, the BEST alternative is Alternative

    A. W   B. X   C. Y   D. Z

TEST 6

DIRECTIONS: Each question or incomplete statement is followed by several suggested answers or completions. Select the one that BEST answers the question or completes the statement. *PRINT THE LETTER OF THE CORRECT ANSWER IN THE SPACE AT THE RIGHT.*

Questions 1-3.

DIRECTIONS: Questions 1 through 3 are to be answered SOLELY on the basis of the following data.

A series of cost-benefit studies of various alternative health programs yields the following results:

Program	Benefit	Cost
K	30	15
L	60	60
M	300	150
N	600	500

In answering Questions 1 and 2, assume that all programs can be increased or decreased in scale without affecting their individual benefit-to-cost ratios.

1. The benefit-to-cost ratio of Program M is

   A. 10:1   B. 5:1   C. 2:1   D. 1:2

2. The budget ceiling for one or more of the programs included in the study is set at 75 units. It may MOST logically be concluded that

   A. Programs K and L should be chosen to fit within the budget ceiling
   B. Program K would be the most desirable one that could be afforded
   C. Program M should be chosen rather than Program K
   D. the choice should be between Programs M and K

3. If no assumptions can be made regarding the effects of change of scale, the MOST logical conclusion, on the basis of the data available, is that

   A. more data are needed for a budget choice of program
   B. Program K is the most preferable because of its low cost and good benefit-to-cost ratio
   C. Program M is the most preferable because of its high benefits and good benefit-to-cost ratio
   D. there is no difference between Programs K and M, and either can be chosen for any purpose

TEST 7

DIRECTIONS: Each question or incomplete statement is followed by several suggested answers or completions. Select the one that BEST answers the question or completes the statement. *PRINT THE LETTER OF THE CORRECT ANSWER IN THE SPACE AT THE RIGHT.*

Questions 1-6.

DIRECTIONS: Questions 1 through 6 are to be answered SOLELY on the basis of the information contained in the charts below which relate to the budget allocations of City X, a small suburban community. The charts depict the annual budget allocations by Department and by expenditures over a five-year period.

CITY X BUDGET IN MILLIONS OF DOLLARS
TABLE I. Budget Allocations by Department

Department	2017	2018	2019	2020	2021
Public Safety	30	45	50	40	50
Health and Welfare	50	75	90	60	70
Engineering	5	8	10	5	8
Human Resources	10	12	20	10	22
Conservation & Environment	10	15	20	20	15
Education & Development	15	25	35	15	15
TOTAL BUDGET	120	180	225	150	180

TABLE II. Budget Allocations by Expenditures

Category	2017	2018	2019	2020	2021
Raw Materials & Machinery	36	63	68	30	98
Capital Outlay	12	27	56	15	18
Personal Services	72	90	101	105	64
TOTAL BUDGET	120	180	225	150	180

1. The year in which the SMALLEST percentage of the total annual budget was allocated to the Department of Education and Development is

   A. 2017   B. 2018   C. 2020   D. 2021

2. Assume that in 2020 the Department of Conservation and Environment divided its annual budget into the three categories of expenditures and in exactly the same proportion as the budget shown in Table II for the year 2020. The amount allocated for capital outlay in the Department of Conservation and Environment's 2020 budget was MOST NEARLY _____ million.

   A. $2   B. $4   C. $6   D. $10

3. From the year 2018 to the year 2020, the sum of the annual budgets for the Departments of Public Safety and Engineering showed an overall _____ million.

   A. decline; SB
   B. increase; $7
   C. decline; S15
   D. increase; S22

4. The LARGEST dollar increase in departmental budget allocations from one year to the next was in _____ from _____.

   A. Public Safety; 2017 to 2018
   B. Health and Welfare; 2017 to 2018
   C. Education and Development; 2019 to 2020
   D. Human Resources; 2019 to 2020

5. During the five-year period, the annual budget of the Department of Human Resources was GREATER than the annual budget for the Department of Conservation and Environment in _____ of the years.

   A. none
   B. one
   C. two
   D. three

6. If the total City X budget increases at the same rate from 2021 to 2022 as it did from 2020 to 2021, the total City X budget for 2022 will be MOST NEARLY _____ million.

   A. $180
   B. $200
   C. $210
   D. $215

TEST 8

DIRECTIONS: Each question or incomplete statement is followed by several suggested answers or completions. Select the one that BEST answers the question or completes the statement. *PRINT THE LETTER OF THE CORRECT ANSWER IN THE SPACE AT THE RIGHT.*

Questions 1-3.

DIRECTIONS: Questions 1 through 3 are to be answered SOLELY on the basis of the following information.

Assume that in order to encourage Program A, the State and Federal governments have agreed to make the following reimbursements for money spent on Program A, provided the unreimbursed balance is paid from City funds.

<u>During Fiscal Year 2021-2022</u> - For the first $2 million expended, 50% Federal reimbursement and 30% State reimbursement; for the next $3 million, 40% Federal reimbursement and 20% State reimbursement; for the next $5 million, 20% Federal reimbursement and 10% State reimbursement. Above $10 million expended, no Federal or State reimbursement.

<u>During Fiscal Year 2022-2023</u> - For the first $1 million expended, 30% Federal reimbursement and 20% State reimbursement; for the next $4 million, 15% Federal reimbursement and 10% State reimbursement. Above $5 million expended, no Federal or State reimbursement.

1. Assume that the Program A expenditures are such that the State reimbursement for Fiscal Year 2021-2022 will be $1 million.
   Then, the Federal reimbursement for Fiscal Year 2021-2022 will be

   A. $1,600,000 B. $1,800,000
   C. $2,000,000 D. $2,600,000

2. Assume that $8 million were to be spent on Program A in Fiscal Year 2022-2023.
   The TOTAL amount of unreimbursed City funds required would be

   A. $3,500,000 B. $4,500,000
   C. $5,500,000 D. $6,500,000

3. Assume that the City desires to have a combined total of $6 million spent in Program A during both the Fiscal Year 2021-2022 and the Fiscal Year 2022-2023.
   Of the following expenditure combinations, the one which results in the GREATEST reimbursement of City funds is _____ in Fiscal Year 2021-2022 and _____ in Fiscal Year 2022-2023.

   A. $5 million; $1 million   B. $4 million; $2 million
   C. $3 million; $3 million   D. $2 million; $4 million

KEY (CORRECT ANSWERS)

TEST 1	TEST 2	TEST 3	TEST 4
1. D	1. B	1. A	1. A
2. C	2. A	2. D	2. B
3. C	3. A	3. B	3. C
	4. D		4. C

TEST 5	TEST 6	TEST 7	TEST 8
1. A	1. C	1. D	1. B
2. C	2. D	2. A	2. D
3. C	3. A	3. A	3. A
		4. B	
		5. B	
		6. D	

PRINCIPLES AND PRACTICES, OF ADMINISTRATION, SUPERVISION AND MANAGEMENT

TABLE OF CONTENTS

	Page
GENERAL ADMINISTRATION	1
SEVEN BASIC FUNCTIONS OF THE SUPERVISOR	2
I. Planning	2
II. Organizing	3
III. Staffing	3
IV. Directing	3
V. Coordinating	3
VI. Reporting	3
VII. Budgeting	3
PLANNING TO MEET MANAGEMENT GOALS	4
I. What is Planning	4
II. Who Should Make Plans	4
III. What are the Results of Poor Planning	4
IV. Principles of Planning	4
MANAGEMENT PRINCIPLES	5
I. Management	5
II. Management Principles	5
III. Organization Structure	6
ORGANIZATION	8
I. Unity of Command	8
II. Span of Control	8
III. Uniformity of Assignment	9
IV. Assignment of Responsibility and Delegation of Authority	9
PRINCIPLES OF ORGANIZATION	9
I. Definition	9
II. Purpose of Organization	9
III. Basic Considerations in Organizational Planning	9
IV. Bases for Organization	10
V. Assignment of Functions	10
VI. Delegation of Authority and Responsibility	10
VII. Employee Relationships	11

DELEGATING		11
I.	WHAT IS DELEGATING:	11
II.	TO WHOM TO DELEGATE	11
REPORTS		12
I.	DEFINITION	12
II.	PURPOSE	12
III.	TYPES	12
IV.	FACTORS TO CONSIDER BEFORE WRITING REPORT	12
V.	PREPARATORY STEPS	12
VI.	OUTLINE FOR A RECOMMENDATION REPORT	12
MANAGEMENT CONTROLS		13
I.	Control	13
II.	Basis for Control	13
III.	Policy	13
IV.	Procedure	14
V.	Basis of Control	14
FRAMEWORK OF MANAGEMENT		14
I.	Elements	14
II.	Manager's Responsibility	15
III.	Control Techniques	16
IV.	Where Forecasts Fit	16
PROBLEM SOLVING		16
I.	Identify the Problem	16
II.	Gather Data	17
III.	List Possible Solutions	17
IV.	Test Possible Solutions	18
V.	Select the Best Solution	18
VI.	Put the Solution into Actual Practice	19
COMMUNICATION		19
I.	What is Communication?	19
II.	Why is Communication Needed?	19
III.	How is Communication Achieved?	20
IV.	Why Does Communication Fail?	21
V.	How to Improve Communication	21
VI.	How to Determine If You Are Getting Across	21
VII.	The Key Attitude	22
HOW ORDERS AND INSTRUCTIONS SHOULD BE GIVEN		22
I.	Characteristics of Good Orders and Instructions	22
FUNCTIONS OF A DEPARTMENT PERSONNEL OFFICE		23

SUPERVISION — 23
   I. Leadership — 23
      A. The Authoritarian Approach — 23
      B. The Laissez-Faire Approach — 24
      C. The Democratic Approach — 24
   II. Nine Points of Contrast Between Boss and Leader — 25

EMPLOYEE MORALE — 25
   I. Some Ways to Develop and Maintain Good Employee Morale — 25
   II. Some Indicators of Good Morale — 26

MOTIVATION — 26

EMPLOYEE PARTICIPATION — 27
   I. WHAT IS PARTICIPATION — 27
   II. WHY IS IT IMPORTANT? — 27
   III. HOW MAY SUPERVISORS OBTAIN IT? — 28

STEPS IN HANDLING A GRIEVANCE — 28

DISCIPLINE — 29
   I. THE DISCIPLINARY INTERVIEW — 29
   II. PLANNING THE INTERVIEW — 29
   III. CONDUCTING THE INTERVIEW — 30

PRINCIPLES AND PRACTICES, OF
ADMINISTRATION, SUPERVISION AND MANAGEMENT

Most people are inclined to think of administration as something that only a few persons are responsible for in a large organization. Perhaps this is true if you are thinking of Administration with a capital A, but administration with a lower case *a* is a responsibility of supervisors at all levels each working day.

All of us feel we are pretty good supervisors and that we do a good job of administering the workings of our agency. By and large, this is true, but every so often it is good to check up on ourselves. Checklists appear from time to time in various publications which psychologists say tell whether or not a person will make a good wife, husband, doctor, lawyer, or supervisor.

The following questions are an excellent checklist to test yourself as a supervisor and administrator.

Remember, Administration gives direction and points the way but administration carries the ideas to fruition. Each is dependent on the other for its success. Remember, too, that no unit is too small for these departmental functions to be carried out. These statements apply equally as well to the Chief Librarian as to the Department Head with but one or two persons to supervise.

GENERAL ADMINISTRATION: General Responsibilities of Supervisors

1. Have I prepared written statements of functions, activities, and duties for my organizational unit?

2. Have I prepared procedural guides for operating activities?

3. Have I established clearly in writing, lines of authority and responsibility for my organizational unit?

4. Do I make recommendations for improvements in organization, policies, administrative and operating routines and procedures, including simplification of work and elimination of non-essential operations?

5. Have I designated and trained an understudy to function in my absence?

6. Do I supervise and train personnel within the unit to effectively perform their assignments?

7. Do I assign personnel and distribute work on such a basis as to carry out the organizational unit's assignment or mission in the most effective and efficient manner?

8. Have I established administrative controls by:

    a. Fixing responsibility and accountability on all supervisors under my direction for the proper performance of their functions and duties.

b. Preparations and submitting periodic work load and progress reports covering the operations of the unit to my immediate superior.

c. Analysis and evaluation of such reports received from subordinate units.

d. Submission of significant developments and problems arising within the organizational unit to my immediate superior.

e. Conducting conferences, inspections, etc., as to the status and efficiency of unit operations.

9. Do I maintain an adequate and competent working force?

10. Have I fostered good employee-department relations, seeing that established rules, regulations, and instructions are being carried out properly?

11. Do I collaborate and consult with other organizational units performing related functions to insure harmonious and efficient working relationships?

12. Do I maintain liaison through prescribed channels with city departments and other governmental agencies concerned with the activities of the unit?

13. Do I maintain contact with and keep abreast of the latest developments and techniques of administration (professional societies, groups, periodicals, etc.) as to their applicability to the activities of the unit?

14. Do I communicate with superiors and subordinates through prescribed organizational channels?

15. Do I notify superiors and subordinates in instances where bypassing is necessary as soon thereafter as practicable?

16. Do I keep my superior informed of significant developments and problems?

SEVEN BASIC FUNCTIONS OF THE SUPERVISOR

I. PLANNING
This means working out goals and means to obtain goals. <u>What</u> needs to be done, <u>who</u> will do it, <u>how</u>, <u>when</u>, and <u>where</u> it is to be done.

SEVEN STEPS IN PLANNING

A. Define job or problem clearly.
B. Consider priority of job.
C. Consider time-limit—starting and completing.
D. Consider minimum distraction to, or interference with, other activities.
E. Consider and provide for contingencies—possible emergencies.
F. Break job down into components.

G. Consider the 5 W's and H:
   WHY..........is it necessary to do the job? (Is the purpose clearly defined?)
   WHAT........needs to be done to accomplish the defined purpose?
   ....is needed to do the job? (Money, materials, etc.)
   WHO..........is needed to do the job?
   ....will have responsibilities?
   WHERE......is the work to be done?
   WHEN........is the job to begin and end? (Schedules, etc.)
   HOW..........is the job to bed done? (Methods, controls, records, etc.)

II. ORGANIZING

This means dividing up the work, establishing clear lines of responsibility and authority and coordinating efforts to get the job done.

III. STAFFING

The whole personnel function of bringing in and <u>training</u> staff, getting the right man and fitting him to the right job—the job to which he is best suited.

In the normal situation, the supervisor's responsibility regarding staffing normally includes providing accurate job descriptions, that is, duties of the jobs, requirements, education and experience, skills, physical, etc.; assigning the work for maximum use of skills; and proper utilization of the probationary period to weed out unsatisfactory employees.

IV. DIRECTING

Providing the necessary leadership to the group supervised. Important work gets done to the supervisor's satisfaction.

V. COORDINATING

The all-important duty of inter-relating the various parts of the work.
The supervisor is also responsible for controlling the coordinated activities. This means measuring performance according to a time schedule and setting quotas to see that the goals previously set are being reached. Reports from workers should be analyzed, evaluated, and made part of all future plans.

VI. REPORTING

This means proper and effective communication to your superiors, subordinates, and your peers (in definition of the job of the supervisor). Reports should be read and information contained therein should be used, not be filed away and forgotten. Reports should be written in such a way that the desired action recommended by the report is forthcoming.

VII. BUDGETING
This means controlling current costs and forecasting future costs. This forecast is based on past experience, future plans and programs, as well as current costs.

You will note that these seven functions can fall under three topics:

- Planning) Make a plan
- Organizing)
- Staffing) Get things done
- Directing)
- Controlling)
- Reporting) Watch it work
- Budgeting)

PLANNING TO MEET MANAGEMENT GOALS

I. WHAT IS PLANNING?

   A. Thinking a job through before new work is done to determine the best way to do it
   B. A method of doing something
   C. Ways and means for achieving set goals
   D. A means of enabling a supervisor to deliver with a minimum of effort, all details involved in coordinating his work

II. WHO SHOULD MAKE PLANS?

   Everybody!
   All levels of supervision must plan work. (Top management, heads of divisions or bureaus, first line supervisors, and individual employees.) The higher the level, the more planning required.

III. WHAT ARE THE RESULTS OF POOR PLANNING?

   A. Failure to meet deadline
   B. Low employee morale
   C. Lack of job coordination
   D. Overtime is frequently necessary
   E. Excessive cost, waste of material and manhours

IV. PRINCIPLES OF PLANNING

   A. Getting a clear picture of your objectives. What exactly are you trying to accomplish?
   B. Plan the whole job, then the parts, in proper sequence.
   C. Delegate the planning of details to those responsible for executing them.
   D. Make your plan flexible.
   E. Coordinate your plan with the plans of others so that the work may be processed with a minimum of delay.
   F. Sell your plan before you execute it.
   G. Sell your plan to your superior, subordinate, in order to gain maximum participation and coordination.
   H. Your plan should take precedence. Use knowledge and skills that others have brought to a similar job.
   I. Your plan should take account of future contingencies; allow for future expansion.
   J. Plans should include minor details. Leave nothing to chance that can be anticipated.
   K. Your plan should be simple and provide standards and controls. Establish quality and quantity standards and set a standard method of doing the job. The controls will indicate whether the job is proceeding according to plan.
   L. Consider possible bottlenecks, breakdowns, or other difficulties that are likely to arise.

V. Q. WHAT ARE THE YARDSTICKS BY WHICH PLANNING SHOULD BE MEASURED?
   A. Any plan should:
   — Clearly state a definite course of action to be followed and goal to be achieved, with consideration for emergencies.
   — Be realistic and practical.
   — State what's to be done, when it's to be done, where, how, and by whom.
   — Establish the most efficient sequence of operating steps so that more is accomplished in less time, with the least effort, and with the best quality results.
   — Assure meeting deliveries without delays.
   — Establish the standard by which performance is to be judged.

   Q. WHAT KINDS OF PLANS DOES EFFECTIVE SUPERVISION REQUIRE?
   A. Plans should cover such factors as:
   — Manpower: right number of properly trained employees on the job
   — Materials: adequate supply of the right materials and supplies
   — Machines: full utilization of machines and equipment, with proper maintenance
   — Methods: most efficient handling of operations
   — Deliveries: making deliveries on time
   — Tools: sufficient well-conditioned tools
   — Layout: most effective use of space
   — Reports: maintaining proper records and reports
   — Supervision: planning work for employees and organizing supervisor's own time

MANAGEMENT PRINCIPLES

I. MANAGEMENT
   Q. What do we mean by management?
   A. Getting work done through others.

   Management could also be defined as planning, directing, and controlling the operations of a bureau or division so that all factors will function properly and all persons cooperate efficiently for a common objective.

II. MANAGEMENT PRINCIPLES

   A. There should be a hierarchy—wherein authority and responsibility run upward and downward through several levels—with a broad base at the bottom and a single head at the top.

   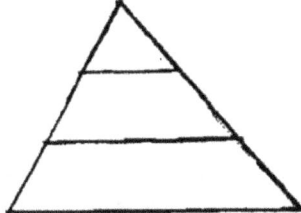

   B. Each and every unit or person in the organization should be answerable ultimately to the manager at the apex. In other words, *The buck stops here!*

C. Every necessary function involved in the bureau's objectives is assigned to a unit in that bureau.

D. Responsibilities assigned to a unit are specifically clear-cut and understood.

E. Consistent methods of organizational structure should be applied at each level of the organization.

F. Each member of the bureau from top to bottom knows: to whom he reports and who reports to him.

G. No member of one bureau reports to more than one supervisor. No dual functions.

H. Responsibility for a function is matched by authority necessary to perform that function. Weight of authority.

I. Individuals or units reporting to a supervisor do not exceed the number which can be feasibly and effectively coordinated and directed. Concept of *span of control*.

J. Channels of command (management) are not violated by staff units, although there should be staff services to facilitate and coordinate management functions.

K. Authority and responsibility should be decentralized to units and individuals who are responsible for the actual performance of operations.
Welfare – down to Welfare Centers
Hospitals – down to local hospitals

L. Management should exercise control through attention to policy problems of exceptional performance, rather than through review of routine actions of subordinates.

M. Organizations should never be permitted to grow so elaborate as to hinder work accomplishments.

III. ORGANIZATION STRUCTURE

Types of Organizations
The purest form is a leader and a few followers, such as:

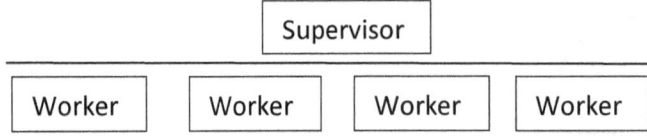

(Refer to organization chart) from supervisor to workers.

The line of authority is direct, The workers know exactly where they stand in relation to their boss, to whom they report for instructions and direction.

Unfortunately, in our present complex society, few organizations are similar to this example of a pure line organization. In this era of specialization, other people are often needed in the simplest of organizations. These specialists are known as staff. The sole purpose for their existence (staff) is to assist, advise, suggest, help or counsel line organizations. Staff has no authority to direct line people—nor do they give them direct instructions.

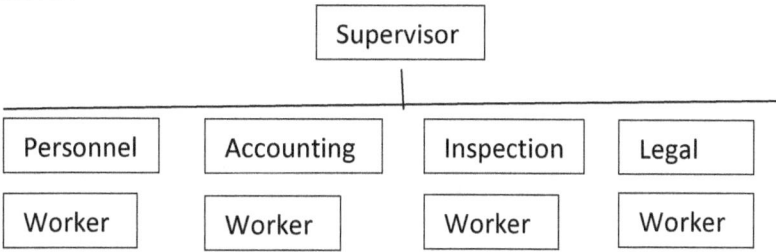

Line Functions
1. Directs
2. Orders
3. Responsibility for carrying out activities from beginning to end
4. Follows chain of command
5. Is identified with what it does
6. Decides when and how to use staff advice
7. Line executes

Staff Functions
1. Advises
2. Persuades and sells
3. Staff studies, reports, recommends but does not carry out
4. May advise across department lines
5. May find its ideas identified with others
6. Has to persuade line to want its advice
7. Staff: Conducts studies and research. Provides advice and instructions in technical matters. Serves as technical specialist to render specific services.

Types and Functions of Organization Charts
An organization chart is a picture of the arrangement and inter-relationship of the subdivisions of an organization.

A. Types of Charts:
   1. Structural: basic relationships only
   2. Functional: includes functions or duties
   3. Personnel: positions, salaries, status, etc.
   4. Process Chart: work performed
   5. Gantt Chart: actual performance against planned
   5. Flow Chart: flow and distribution of work

B. Functions of Charts:
   1. Assist in management planning and control
   2. Indicate duplication of functions
   3. Indicate incorrect stressing of functions
   4. Indicate neglect of important functions
   5. Correct unclear authority
   6. Establish proper span of control

C. Limitations of Charts:
1. Seldom maintained on current basis
2. Chart is oversimplified
3. Human factors cannot adequately be charted

D. Organization Charts should be:
1. Simple
2. Symmetrical
3. Indicate authority
4. Line and staff relationship differentiated
5. Chart should be dated and bear signature of approving officer
6. Chart should be displayed, not hidden

ORGANIZATION

There are four basic principles of organization:
1. Unity of command
2. Span of control
3. Uniformity of assignment
4. Assignment of responsibility and delegation of authority

I. UNITY OF COMMAND

Unity of command means that each person in the organization should receive orders from one, and only one, supervisor. When a person has to take orders from two or more people, (a) the orders may be in conflict and the employee is upset because he does not know which he should obey, or (b) different orders may reach him at the same time and he does not know which he should carry out first.

Equally as bad as having two bosses is the situation where the supervisor is bypassed. Let us suppose you are a supervisor whose boss bypasses you (deals directly with people reporting to you). To the worker, it is the same as having two bosses; but to you, the supervisor, it is equally serious. Bypassing on the part of your boss will undermine your authority, and the people under you will begin looking to your boss for decisions and even for routine orders.

You can prevent bypassing by telling the people you supervise that if anyone tries to give them orders, they should direct that person to you.

II. SPAN OF CONTROL

Span of control on a given level involves:
A. The number of people being supervised
B. The distance
C. The time involved in supervising the people. (One supervisor cannot supervise too many workers effectively.)

Span of control means that a supervisor has the right number (not too many and not too few) of subordinates that he can supervise well.

III. UNIFORMITY OF ASSIGNMENT

In assigning work, you as the supervisor should assign to each person jobs that are similar in nature. An employee who is assigned too many different types of jobs will waste time in going from one kind of work to another. It takes time for him to get to top production in one kind of task and, before he does so, he has to start on another.
When you assign work to people, remember that:

A. Job duties should be definite. Make it clear from the beginning <u>what</u> they are to do, <u>how</u> they are to do it, and <u>why</u> they are to do it. Let them know how much they are expected to do and how well they are expected to do it.
B. Check your assignments to be certain that there are no workers with too many unrelated duties, and that no two people have been given overlapping responsibilities. Your aim should be to have every task assigned to a specific person with the work fairly distributed and with each person doing his part.

IV. ASSIGNMENT OF RESPONSIBILITY AND DELEGATION OF AUTHORITY

A supervisor cannot delegate his final responsibility for the work of his department. The experienced supervisor knows that he gets his work done through people. He can't do it all himself. So he must assign the work and the responsibility for the work to his employees. Then they must be given the authority to carry out their responsibilities.

By assigning responsibility and delegating authority to carry out the responsibility, the supervisor builds in his workers initiative, resourcefulness, enthusiasm, and interest in their work. He is treating them as responsible adults. They can find satisfaction in their work, and they will respect the supervisor and be loyal to the supervisor.

PRINCIPLES OF ORGANIZATION

I. DEFINITION

Organization is the method of dividing up the work to provide the best channels for coordinated effort to get the agency's mission accomplished.

II. PURPOSE OF ORGANIZATION

A. To enable each employee within the organization to clearly know his responsibilities and relationships to his fellow employees and to organizational units
B. To avoid conflicts of authority and overlapping of jurisdiction.
C. To ensure teamwork.

III. BASIC CONSIDERATIONS IIN ORGANIZATIONAL PLANNING

A. The basic plans and objectives of the agency should be determined, and the organizational structure should be adapted to carry out effectively such plans and objectives.
B. The organization should be built around the major functions of the agency and not individuals or groups of individuals.

C. The organization should be sufficiently flexible to meet new and changing conditions which may be brought about from within or outside the department.
D. The organizational structure should be as simple as possible and the number of organizational units kept at a minimum.
E. The number of levels of authority should be kept at a minimum. Each additional management level lengthens the chain of authority and responsibility and increases the time for instructions to be distributed to operating levels and for decisions to be obtained from higher authority.
F. The form of organization should permit each executive to exercise maximum initiative within the limits of delegated authority.

IV. BASES FOR ORGANIZATION

A. Purpose (Examples: education, police, sanitation)
B. Process (Examples: accounting, legal, purchasing)
C. Clientele (Examples: welfare, parks, veteran)
D. Geographic (Examples: borough offices, precincts, libraries)

V. ASSIGNMENTS OF FUNCTIONS

A. Every function of the agency should be assigned to a specific organizational unit. Under normal circumstances, no single function should be assigned to more than one organizational unit.
B. There should be no overlapping, duplication, or conflict between organizational elements.
C. Line functions should be separated from staff functions, and proper emphasis should be placed on staff activities.
D. Functions which are closely related or similar should normally be assigned to a single organizational unit.
E. Functions should be properly distributed to promote balance, and to avoid overemphasis of less important functions and underemphasis of more essential functions.

VI. DELEGATION OF AUTHORITY AND RESPONSIBILITY

A. Responsibilities assigned to a specific individual or organizational unit should carry corresponding authority, and all statements of authority or limitations thereof should be as specific as possible.
B. Authority and responsibility for action should be decentralized to organizational units and individuals responsible for actual performance to the greatest extent possible, without relaxing necessary control over policy or the standardization of procedures. Delegation of authority will be consistent with decentralization of responsibility but such delegation will not divest an executive in higher authority of his overall responsibility.
C. The heads of organizational units should concern themselves with important matters and should delegate to the maximum extent details and routines performed in the ordinary course of business.
D. All responsibilities, authorities, and relationships should be stated in simple language to avoid misinterpretation.
E. Each individual or organizational unit charged with a specific responsibility will be held responsible for results.

VII. EMPLOYEE RELATIONSHIPS

   A. The employees reporting to one executive should not exceed the number which can be effectively directed and coordinated. The number will depend largely upon the scope and extent of the responsibilities of the subordinates.
   B. No person should report to more than one supervisor. Every supervisor should know who reports to him, and every employee should know to whom he reports. Channels of authority and responsibility should not be violated by staff units.
   C. Relationships between organizational units within the agency and with outside organizations and associations should be clearly stated and thoroughly understood to avoid misunderstanding.

DELEGATING

I. WHAT IS DELEGATING?
Delegating is assigning a job to an employee, giving him the authority to get that job done, and giving him the responsibility for seeing to it that the job is done.

   A. What To Delegate
      1. Routine details
      2. Jobs which may be necessary and take a lot of time, but do not have to be done by the supervisor personally (preparing reports, attending meetings, etc.)
      3. Routine decision-making (making decisions which do not require the supervisor's personal attention)

   B. What Not To Delegate
      1. Job details which are *executive functions* (setting goals, organizing employees into a good team, analyzing results so as to plan for the future)
      2. Disciplinary power (handling grievances, preparing service ratings, reprimands, etc.)
      3. Decision-making which involves large numbers of employees or other bureaus and departments
      4. Final and complete responsibility for the job done by the unit being supervised

   C. Why Delegate?
      1. To strengthen the organization by developing a greater number of skilled employees
      2. To improve the employee's performance by giving him the chance to learn more about the job, handle some responsibility, and become more interested in getting the job done
      3. To improve a supervisor's performance by relieving him of routine jobs and giving him more time for *executive functions* (planning, organizing, controlling, etc.) which cannot be delegated

II. TO WHOM TO DELEGATE
People with abilities not being used. Selection should be based on ability, not on favoritism.

REPORTS

I. DEFINITION
A report is an orderly presentation of factual information directed to a specific reader for a specific purpose

II. PURPOSE
The general purpose of a report is to bring to the reader useful and factual information about a condition or a problem. Some specific purposes of a report may be:

   A. To enable the reader to appraise the efficiency or effectiveness of a person or an operation
   B. To provide a basis for establishing standards
   C. To reflect the results of expenditures of time, effort, and money
   D. To provide a basis for developing or altering programs

III. TYPES

   A. Information Report: Contains facts arranged in sequence
   B. Summary (Examination) Report: Contains facts plus an analysis or discussion of the significance of the facts. Analysis may give advantages and disadvantages or give qualitative and quantitative comparisons
   C. Recommendation Report: Contains facts, analysis, and conclusion logically drawn from the facts and analysis, plus a recommendation based upon the facts, analysis, and conclusions

IV. FACTORS TO CONSIDER BEFORE WRITING REPORT

   A. _Why_ write the report?: The purpose of the report should be clearly defined.
   B. _Who_ will read the report?: What level of language should be used? Will the reader understand professional or technical language?
   C. _What_ should be said?: What does the reader need or want to know about the subject?
   D. _How_ should it be said?: Should the subject be presented tactfully? Convincingly? In a stimulating manner?

V. PREPARATORY STEPS

   A. Assemble the facts: Find out who, why, what, where, when, and how.
   B. Organize the facts: Eliminate unnecessary information
   C. Prepare an outline: Check for orderliness, logical sequence
   D. Prepare a draft: Check for correctness, clearness, completeness, conciseness, and tone
   E. Prepare it in final form: Check for grammar, punctuation, appearance

VI. OUTLINE FOR A RECOMMENDATION REPORT

   Is the report:
   A. Correct in information, grammar, and tone?
   B. Clear?
   C. Complete?

D. Concise?
E. Timely?
F. Worth its cost?

Will the report accomplish its purpose?

MANAGEMENT CONTROLS

I. CONTROL
What is control? What is controlled? Who controls?

The essence of control is action which adjusts operations to predetermined standards, and its basis is information in the hands of managers. Control is checking to determine whether plans are being observed and suitable progress toward stated objectives is being made, and action is taken, if necessary, to correct deviations.

We have a ready-made model for this concept of control in the automatic systems which are widely used for process control in the chemical land petroleum industries. A process control system works this way. Suppose, for example, it is desired to maintain a constant rate of flow of oil through a pipe at a predetermined or set-point value. A signal, whose strength represents the rate of flow, can be produced in a measuring device and transmitted to a control mechanism. The control mechanism, when it detects any deviation of the actual from the set-point signal, will reposition the value regulating flow rate.

II. BASIS FOR CONTROL

A process control mechanism thus acts to adjust operations to predetermined standards and does so on the basis of information it receives. In a parallel way, information reaching a manager gives him the opportunity for corrective action and is his basis for control. He cannot exercise control without such information, and he cannot do a complete job of managing without controlling.

III. POLICY

What is policy?

Policy is simply a statement of an organization's intention to act in certain ways when specified types of circumstances arise. It represents a general decision, predetermined and expressed as a principle or rule, establishing a normal pattern of conduct for dealing with given types of business events—usually recurrent. A statement is therefore useful in economizing the time of managers and in assisting them to discharge their responsibilities equitably and consistently.

Policy is not a means of control, but policy does generate the need for control.

Adherence to policies is not guaranteed nor can it be taken on faith. It has to be verified. Without verification, there is no basis for control. Policy and procedures, although closely related and interdependent to a certain extent, are not synonymous. A policy may be adopted, for example, to maintain a materials inventory not to exceed one million dollars.

A procedure for inventory control could interpret that policy and convert it into methods for keeping within that limit, with consideration, too, of possible but foreseeable expedient deviation.

IV. PROCEDURE

What is procedure?

A procedure specifically prescribes:
A. What work is to be performed by the various participants
B. Who are the respective participants
C. When and where the various steps in the different processes are to be performed
D. The sequence of operations that will insure uniform handling of recurring transactions
E. The paper that is involved, its origin, transition, and disposition

Necessary appurtenances to a procedure are:
A. Detailed organizational chart
B. Flow charts
C. Exhibits of forms, all presented in close proximity to the text of the procedure

V. BASIS OF CONTROL – INFORMATION IN THE HANDS OF MANAGERS

If the basis of control is information in the hands of managers, then reporting is elevated to a level of very considerable importance.

Types of reporting may include:
A. Special reports and routine reports
B. Written, oral, and graphic reports
C. Staff meetings
D. Conferences
E. Television screens
F. Non-receipt of information, as where management is by exception
G. Any other means whereby information is transmitted to a manager as a basis for control action

FRAMEWORK OF MANAGEMENT

I. ELEMENTS

   A. Policy: It has to be verified, controlled.

   B. Organization is part of the giving of an assignment. The organizational chart gives to each individual in his title, a first approximation of the nature of his assignment and orients him as being accountable to a certain individual. Organization is not in a true sense a means of control. Control is checking to ascertain whether the assignment is executed as intended and acting on the basis of that information.

   C. Budgets perform three functions:
      1. They present the objectives, plans, and programs of the organization in financial terms.

2. They report the progress of actual performance against these predetermined objectives, plans, and programs.
3. Like organizational charts, delegations of authority, procedures, and job descriptions, they define the assignments which have flowed from the Chief Executive. Budgets are a means of control in the respect that they report progress of actual performance against the program. They provide information which enables managers to take action directed toward bringing actual results into conformity with the program.

D. Internal Check provides in practice for the principle that the same person should not have responsibility for all phases of a transaction. This makes it clearly an aspect of organization rather than of control. Internal Check is static, or built-in.

E. Plans, Programs, Objectives
People must know what they are trying to do. Objectives fulfill this need. Without them, people may work industriously and yet, working aimlessly, accomplish little. Plans and Programs complement Objectives, since they propose how and according to what time schedule the objectives are to be reached.

F. Delegations of Authority
Among the ways we have for supplementing the titles and lines of authority of an organizational chart are delegations of authority. Delegations of authority clarify the extent of authority of individuals and in that way serve to define assignments. That they are not means of control is apparent from the very fact that wherever there has been a delegation of authority, the need for control increases. This could hardly be expected to happen if delegations of authority were themselves means of control.

II. MANAGER'S RESPONSIBILITY

Control becomes necessary whenever a manager delegates authority to a subordinate because he cannot delegate and then simply sit back and forget4 about it. A manager's accountability to his own superior has not diminished one whit as a result of delegating part of his authority to a subordinate. The manager must exercise control over actions taken under the authority so delegated. That means checking serves as a basis for possible corrective action.

Objectives, plans, programs, organizational charts, and other elements of the managerial system are not fruitfully regarded as either controls or means of control. They are pre-established standards or models of performance to which operations are adjusted by the exercise of management control. These standards or models of performance are dynamic in character for they are constantly altered, modified, or revised. Policies, organizational set-up, procedures, delegations, etc. are constantly altered but, like objectives and plans, they remain in force until they are either abandoned or revised. All of the elements (or standards or models of performance), objectives, plans, and programs, policies, organization, etc. can be regarded as a *framework of management*.

III. CONTROL TECHNIQUES

Examples of control techniques:
A. Compare against established standards
B. Compare with a similar operation
C. Compare with past operations
D. Compare with predictions of accomplishment

IV. WHERE FORECASTS FIT

Control is after-the-fact while forecasts are before. Forecasts and projections are important for setting objectives and formulating plans.

Information for aiming and planning does not have to be before-the-fact. It may be an after-the-fact analysis proving that a certain policy has been impolitic in its effect on the relation of the company or department with customer, employee, taxpayer, or stockholder; or that a certain plan is no longer practical, or that a certain procedure is unworkable.

The prescription here certainly would not be in control (in these cases, control would simply bring operations into conformity with obsolete standards) but the establishment of new standards, a new policy, a new plan, and a new procedure to be controlled too.

Information is, of course, the basis for all communication in addition to furnishing evidence to management of the need for reconstructing the framework of management.

PROBLEM SOLVING

The accepted concept in modern management for problem solving is the utilization of the following steps:

A. Identify the problem
B. Gather data
C. List possible solutions
D. Test possible solutions
E. Select the best solution
F. Put the solution into actual practice

Occasions might arise where you would have to apply the second step of gathering data before completing the first step.

You might also find that it will be necessary to work on several steps at the same time.

I. IDENTIFY THE PROBLEM

Your first step is to define as precisely as possible the problem to be solved. While this may sound easy, it is often the most difficult part of the process.

It has been said of problem solving that you are halfway to the solution when you can write out a clear statement of the problem itself.

Our job now is to get below the surface manifestations of the trouble and pinpoint the problem. This is usually accomplished by a logical analysis, by going from the general to the particular; from the obvious to the not-so-obvious cause.

Let us say that production is behind schedule. WHY? Absenteeism is high. Now, is absenteeism the basic problem to be tackled, or is it merely a symptom of low morale among the workforce? Under these circumstances, you may decide that production is not the problem; the problem is *employee morale*.

In trying to define the problem, remember there is seldom one simple reason why production is lagging, or reports are late, etc.

Analysis usually leads to the discovery that an apparent problem is really made up of several subproblems which must be attacked separately.

Another way is to limit the problem, and thereby ease the task of finding a solution, and concentrate on the elements which are within the scope of your control.

When you have gone this far, write out a tentative statement of the problem to be solved.

II. GATHER DATA

In the second step, you must set out to collect all the information that might have a bearing on the problem. Do not settle for an assumption when reasonable fact and figures are available.

If you merely go through the motions of problem-solving, you will probably shortcut the information-gathering step. Therefore, do not stack the evidence by confining your research to your own preconceived ideas.

As you collect facts, organize them in some form that helps you make sense of them and spot possible relationships between them. For example, plotting cost per unit figures on a graph can be more meaningful than a long column of figures.

Evaluate each item as you go along. Is the source material absolutely, reliable, probably reliable, or not to be trusted.

One of the best methods for gathering data is to go out and look the situation over carefully. Talk to the people on the job who are most affected by this problem.

Always keep in mind that a primary source is usually better than a secondary source of information.

III. LIST POSSIBLE SOLUTIONS

This is the creative thinking step of problem solving. This is a good time to bring into play whatever techniques of group dynamics the agency or bureau might have developed for a joint attack on problems.

Now the important thing for you to do is: Keep an open mind. Let your imagination roam freely over the facts you have collected. Jot down every possible solution that occurs to you. Resist the temptation to evaluate various proposals as you go along. List seemingly absurd ideas along with more plausible ones. The more possibilities you list during this step, the less risk you will run of settling for merely a workable, rather than the best, solution.

Keep studying the data as long as there seems to be any chance of deriving additional ideas, solutions, explanations, or patterns from it.

IV. TEST POSSIBLE SOLUTIONS

Now you begin to evaluate the possible solutions. Take pains to be objective. Up to this point, you have suspended judgment but you might be tempted to select a solution you secretly favored all along and proclaim it as the best of the lot.

The secret of objectivity in this phase is to test the possible solutions separately, measuring each against a common yardstick. To make this yardstick try to enumerate as many specific criteria as you can think of. Criteria are best phrased as questions which you ask of each possible solution. They can be drawn from these general categories:

Suitability –   Will this solution do the job?
                Will it solve the problem completely or partially?
                Is it a permanent or a stopgap solution?

Feasibility -   Will this plan work in actual practice?
                Can we afford this approach?
                How much will it cost?

Acceptability - Will the boss go along with the changes required in the plan?
                Are we trying to drive a tack with a sledge hammer?

V. SELECT THE BEST SOLUTION

This is the area of executive decision.

Occasionally, one clearly superior solution will stand out at the conclusion of the testing process. But often it is not that simple. You may find that no one solution has come through all the tests with flying colors.

You may also find that a proposal, which flunked miserably on one of the essential tests, racked up a very high score on others.

The best solution frequently will turn out to be a combination.

Try to arrange a marriage that will bring together the strong points of one possible solution with the particular virtues of another. The more skill and imagination that you apply, the greater is the likelihood that you will come out with a solution that is not merely adequate and workable, but is the best possible under the circumstances.

VI. PUT THE SOLUTION INTO ACTUAL PRACTICE

As every executive knows, a plan which works perfectly on paper may develop all sorts of bugs when put into actual practice.

Problem-solving does not stop with selecting the solution which looks best in theory. The next step is to put the chosen solution into action and watch the results. The results may point towards modifications.

If the problem disappears when you put your solution into effect, you know you have the right solution.

If it does not disappear, even after you have adjusted your plan to cover unforeseen difficulties that turned up in practice, work your way back through the problem-solving solutions.

> Would one of them have worked better?
> Did you overlook some vital piece of data which would have given you a different slant on the whole situation? Did you apply all necessary criteria in testing solutions? If no light dawns after this much rechecking, it is a pretty good bet that you defined the problem incorrectly in the first place.

You came up with the wrong solution because you tackled the wrong problem.

Thus, step six may become step one of a new problem-solving cycle.

COMMUNICATION

I. WHAT IS COMMUNICATION?
We communicate through writing, speaking, action, or inaction. In speaking to people face-to-face, there is opportunity to judge reactions and to adjust the message. This makes the supervisory chain one of the most, and in many instances the most, important channels of communication.

In an organization, communication means keeping employees informed about the organization's objectives, policies, problems, and progress. Communication is the free interchange of information, ideas, and desirable attitudes between and among employees and between employees and management.

II. WHY IS COMMUNICATION NEEDED?

   A. People have certain social needs
   B. Good communication is essential in meeting those social needs
   C. While people have similar basic needs, at the same time they differ from each other
   D. Communication must be adapted to these individual differences

An employee cannot do his best work unless he knows why he is doing it. If he has the feeling that he is being kept in the dark about what is going on, his enthusiasm and productivity suffer.

Effective communication is needed in an organization so that employees will understand what the organization is trying to accomplish; and how the work of one unit contributes to or affects the work of other units in the organization and other organizations.

III. HOW IS COMMUNICATION ACHIEVED?

Communication flows downward, upward, sideways.

A. Communication may come from top management down to employees. This is downward communication.

   Some means of downward communication are:
   1. Training (orientation, job instruction, supervision, public relations, etc.)
   2. Conferences
   3. Staff meetings
   4. Policy statements
   5. Bulletins
   6. Newsletters
   7. Memoranda
   8. Circulation of important letters

   In downward communication, it is important that employees be informed in advance of changes that will affect them.

B. Communications should also be developed so that the ideas, suggestions, and knowledge of employees will flow upward to top management.

   Some means of upward communication are:
   1. Personal discussion conferences
   2. Committees
   3. Memoranda
   4. Employees suggestion program
   5. Questionnaires to be filled in giving comments and suggestions about proposed actions that will affect field operations.

   Upward communication requires that management be willing to listen, to accept, and to make changes when good ideas are present. Upward communication succeeds when there is no fear of punishment for speaking out or lack of interest at the top. Employees will share their knowledge and ideas with management when interest is shown and recognition is given.

C. The advantages of downward communication:
   1. It enables the passing down of orders, policies, and plans necessary to the continued operation of the station.
   2. By making information available, it diminishes the fears and suspicions which result from misinformation and misunderstanding.
   3. It fosters the pride people want to have in their work when they are told of good work.
   4. It improves the morale and stature of the individual to be *in the know*.

5. It helps employees to understand, accept, and cooperate with changes when they know about them in advance.

D. The advantages of upward communication:
1. It enables the passing upward of information, attitudes, and feelings.
2. It makes it easier to find out how ready people are to receive downward communication.
3. It reveals the degree to which the downward communication is understood and accepted.
4. It helps to satisfy the basic social needs.
5. It stimulates employees to participate in the operation of their organization.
6. It encourage employees to contribute ideas for improving the efficiency and economy of operations.
7. It helps to solve problem situations before they reach the explosion point.

IV. WHY DOES COMMUNICATION FAIL?

A. The technical difficulties of conveying information clearly
B. The emotional content of communication which prevents complete transmission
C. The fact that there is a difference between what management needs to say, what it wants to day, and what it does say
D. The fact that there is a difference between what employees would like to say, what they think is profitable or safe to say, and what they do say

V. HOW TO IMPROVE COMMUNICATION

As a supervisor, you are a key figure in communication. To improve as a communicator, you should:
A. Know: Knowing your subordinates will help you to recognize and work with individual differences.
B. Like: If you like those who work for you and those for whom you work, this will foster the kind of friendly, warm, work atmosphere that will facilitate communication.
C. Trust: Showing a sincere desire to communicate will help to develop the mutual trust and confidence which are essential to the free flow of communication.
D. Tell: Tell your subordinates and superiors *what's doing*. Tell your subordinates *why* as well as *how*.
E. Listen: By listening, you help others to talk and you create good listeners. Don't forget that listening implies action.
F. Stimulate: Communication has to be stimulated and encouraged. Be receptive to ideas and suggestions and motivate your people so that each member of the team identifies himself with the job at hand.
G. Consult: The most effective way of consulting is to let your people participate, insofar as possible, in developing determinations which affect them or their work.

VI. HOW TO DETERMINE WHETHER YOU ARE GETTING ACROSS

A. Check to see that communication is received and understood
B. Judge this understanding by actions rather than words
C. Adapt or vary communication, when necessary
D. Remember that good communication cannot cure all problems

VII. THE KEY ATTITUDE

Try to see things from the other person's point of view. By doing this, you help to develop the permissive atmosphere and the shared confidence and understanding which are essential to effective two-way communication.

Communication is a two-way process:
A. The basic purpose of any communication is to get action.
B. The only way to get action is through acceptance.
C. In order to get acceptance, communication must be humanly satisfying as well as technically efficient.

HOW ORDERS AND INSTRUCTIONS SHOULD BE GIVEN

I. CHARACTERISTICS OF GOOD ORDERS AND INSTRUCTIONS

   A. Clear
      Orders should be definite as to
      —What is to be done
      —Who is to do it
      —When it is to be done
      —Where it is to be done
      —How it is to be done

   B. Concise
      Avoid wordiness. Orders should be brief and to the point.

   C. Timely
      Instructions and orders should be sent out at the proper time and not too long in advance of expected performance.

   D. Possibility of Performance
      Orders should be feasible:
      1. Investigate before giving orders
      2. Consult those who are to carry out instructions before formulating and issuing them

   E. Properly Directed
      Give the orders to the people concerned. Do not send orders to people who are not concerned. People who continually receive instructions that are not applicable to them get in the habit of neglecting instructions generally.

   F. Reviewed Before Issuance
      Orders should be reviewed before issuance:
      1. Test them by putting yourself in the position of the recipient
      2. If they involve new procedures, have the persons who are to do the work review them for suggestions.

   G. Reviewed After Issuance
      Persons who receive orders should be allowed to raise questions and to point out unforeseen consequences of orders.

H. Coordinated
Orders should be coordinated so that work runs smoothly.

I. Courteous
Make a request rather than a demand. There is no need to continually call attention to the fact that you are the boss.

J. Recognizable as an Order
Be sure that the order is recognizable as such.

K. Complete
Be sure recipient has knowledge and experience sufficient to carry out order. Give illustrations and examples.

A DEPARTMENTAL PERSONNEL OFFICE IS RESPONSIBLE FOR THE FOLLOWING FUNCTIONS

1. Policy
2. Personnel Programs
3. Recruitment and Placement
4. Position Classification
5. Salary and Wage Administration
6. Employee performance Standards and Evaluation
7. Employee Relations
8. Disciplinary Actions and Separations
9. Health and Safety
10. Staff Training and Development
11. Personnel Records, Procedures, and Reports
12. Employee Services
13. Personnel Research

SUPERVISION

I. LEADERSHIP

All leadership is based essentially on authority. This comes from two sources: It is received from higher management or it is earned by the supervisor through his methods of supervision. Although effective leadership has always depended upon the leader's using his authority in such a way as to appeal successfully to the motives of the people supervised, the conditions for making this appeal are continually changing. The key to today's problem of leadership is flexibility and resourcefulness on the part of the leader in meeting changes in conditions as they occur.

Three basic approaches to leadership are generally recognized:

A. The Authoritarian Approach
  1. The methods and techniques used in this approach emphasize the *I* in leadership and depend primarily on the formal authority of the leader. This authority is sometimes exercised in a hardboiled manner and sometimes in a benevolent

manner, but in either case the dominating role of the leader is reflected in the thinking, planning, and decisions of the group.
2. Group results are to a large degree dependent on close supervision by the leader. Usually, the individuals in the group will not show a high degree of initiative or acceptance of responsibility and their capacity to grow and develop probably will not be fully utilized. The group may react with resentment or submission, depending upon the manner and skill of the leader in using his authority.
3. This approach develops as a natural outgrowth of the authority that goes with the leader's job and his feeling of sole responsibility for getting the job done. It is relatively easy to use and does not require must resourcefulness.
4. The use of this approach is effective in times of emergencies, in meeting close deadline as a final resort, in settling some issues, in disciplinary matters, and with dependent individuals and groups.

B. The Laissez-Faire or Let 'em Alone Approach
1. This approach generally is characterized by an avoidance of leadership responsibility by the leader. The activities of the group depend largely on the choice of its members rather than the leader.
2. Group results probably will be poor. Generally, there will be disagreements over petty things, bickering, and confusion. Except for a few aggressive people, individuals will not show much initiative and growth and development will be retarded. There may be a tendency for informal leaders to take over leadership of the group.
3. This approach frequently results from the leader's dislike of responsibility, from his lack of confidence, from failure of other methods to work, from disappointment or criticism. It is usually the easiest of the three to use and requires both understanding and resourcefulness on the part of the leader.
4. This approach is occasionally useful and effective, particularly in forcing dependent individuals or groups to rely on themselves, to give someone a chance to save face by clearing his own difficulties, or when action should be delayed temporarily for good cause.

C. The Democratic Approach
1. The methods and techniques used in this approach emphasize the *we* in leadership and build up the responsibility of the group to attain its objectives. Reliance is placed largely on the earned authority of the leader.
2. Group results are likely to be good because most of the job motives of the people will be satisfied. Cooperation and teamwork, initiative, acceptance of responsibility, and the individual's capacity for growth probably will show a high degree of development.
3. This approach grows out of a desire or necessity of the leader to find ways to appeal effectively to the motivation of his group. It is the best approach to build up inside the person a strong desire to cooperate and apply himself to the job. It is the most difficult to develop, and requires both understanding and resourcefulness on the part of the leader.
4. The value of this approach increases over a long period where sustained efficiency and development of people are important. It may not be fully effective in all situations, however, particularly when there is not sufficient time to use it properly or where quick decisions must be made.

All three approaches are used by most leaders and have a place in supervising people. The extent of their use varies with individual leaders, with some using one approach predominantly. The leader who uses these three approaches, and varies their use with time and circumstance, is probably the most effective. Leadership which is used predominantly with a democratic approach requires more resourcefulness on the part of the leader but offers the greatest possibilities in terms of teamwork and cooperation.

The one best way of developing democratic leadership is to provide a real sense of participation on the part of the group, since this satisfies most of the chief job motives. Although there are many ways of providing participation, consulting as frequently as possible with individuals and groups on things that affect them seems to offer the most in building cooperation and responsibility. Consultation takes different forms, but it is most constructive when people feel they are actually helping in finding the answers to the problems on the job.

There are some requirements of leaders in respect to human relations which should be considered in their selection and development. Generally, the leader should be interested in working with other people, emotionally stable, self-confident, and sensitive to the reactions of others. In addition, his viewpoint should be one of getting the job done through people who work cooperatively in response to his leadership. He should have a knowledge of individual and group behavior, but, most important of all, he should work to combine all of these requirements into a definite, practical skill in leadership.

II. NINE POINTS OF CONTRAST BETWEEN *BOSS* AND *LEADER*

   A. The boss drives his men; the leader coaches them.
   B. The boss depends on authority; the leader on good will.
   C. The boss inspires fear; the leader inspires enthusiasm.
   D. The boss says I; the leader says *We*.
   E. The boss says *Get here on time*; the leader gets there ahead of time.
   F. The boss fixes the blame for the breakdown; the leader fixes the breakdown.
   G. The boss knows how it is done; the leader shows how.
   H. The boss makes work a drudgery; the leader makes work a game.
   I. The boss says *Go*; the leader says *Let's go*.

EMPLOYEE MORALE

Employee morale is the way employees feel about each other, the organization or unit in which they work, and the work they perform.

I. SOME WAYS TO DEVELOP AND MAINTAIN GOOD EMPLYEE MORALE

   A. Give adequate credit and praise when due.
   B. Recognize importance of all jobs and equalize load with proper assignments, always giving consideration to personality differences and abilities.
   C. Welcome suggestions and do not have an *all-wise* attitude. Request employees' assistance in solving problems and use assistants when conducting group meetings on certain subjects.
   D. Properly assign responsibilities and give adequate authority for fulfillment of such assignments.

E. Keep employees informed about matters that affect them.
F. Criticize and reprimand employees privately.
G. Be accessible and willing to listen.
H. Be fair.
I. Be alert to detect training possibilities so that you will not miss an opportunity to help each employee do a better job, and if possible with less effort on his part.
J. Set a good example.
K. Apply the golden rule.

II. SOME INDICATIONS OF GOOD MORALE

A. Good quality of work
B. Good quantity
C. Good attitude of employees
D. Good discipline
E. Teamwork
F. Good attendance
G. Employee participation

MOTIVATION

DRIVES

A drive, stated simply, is a desire or force which causes a person to do or say certain things. These are some of the most usual drives and some of their identifying characteristics recognizable in people motivated by such drives:

A. Security (desire to provide for the future)
Always on time for work
Works for the same employer for many years
Never takes unnecessary chances
Seldom resists doing what he is told

B. Recognition (desire to be rewarded for accomplishment)
Likes to be asked for his opinion
Becomes very disturbed when he makes a mistake
Does things to attract attention
Likes to see his name in print

C. Position (desire to hold certain status in relation to others)
Boasts about important people he knows
Wants to be known as a key man
Likes titles
Demands respect
Belongs to clubs, for prestige

D. Accomplishment (desire to get things done)
   Complains when things are held up
   Likes to do things that have tangible results
   Never lies down on the job
   Is proud of turning out good work

E. Companionship (desire to associate with other people)
   Likes to work with others
   Tells stories and jokes
   Indulges in horseplay
   Finds excuses to talk to others on the job

F. Possession (desire to collect and hoard objects)
   Likes to collect things
   Puts his name on things belonging to him
   Insists on the same location

Supervisors may find that identifying the drives of employees is a helpful step toward motivating them to self-improvement and better job performance. For example: An employee's job performance is below average. His supervisor, having previously determined that the employee is motivated by a drive for security, suggests that taking training courses will help the employee to improve, advance, and earn more money. Since earning more money can be a step toward greater security, the employee's drive for security would motivate him to take the training suggested by the supervisor. In essence, this is the process of charting an employee's future course by using his motivating drives to positive advantage.

EMPLOYEE PARTICIPATION

I. WHAT IS PARTICIPATION

Employee participation is the employee's giving freely of his time, skill, and knowledge to an extent which cannot be obtained by demand.

II. WHY IS IT IMPORTANT?

The supervisor's responsibility is to get the job done through people. A good supervisor gets the job done through people who work willingly and well. The participation of employees is important because:

A. Employees develop a greater sense of responsibility when they share in working out operating plans and goals.
B. Participation provides greater opportunity and stimulation for employees to learn, and to develop their ability.
C. Participation sometimes provides better solutions to problems because such solutions may combine the experience and knowledge of interested employees who want the solutions to work.
D. An employee or group may offer a solution which the supervisor might hesitate to make for fear of demanding too much.

E. Since the group wants to make the solution work, they exert pressure in a constructive way on each other.
F. Participation usually results in reducing the need for close supervision.

II. HOW MAY SUPERVISORS OBTAIN IT?

Participation is encouraged when employees feel that they share some responsibility for the work and that their ideas are sincerely wanted and valued. Some ways of obtaining employee participation are:

A. Conduct orientation programs for new employees to inform them about the organization and their rights and responsibilities as employees.
B. Explain the aims and objectives of the agency. On a continuing basis, be sure that the employees know what these aims and objectives are.
C. Share job successes and responsibilities and give credit for success.
D. Consult with employees, both as individuals and in groups, about things that affect them.
E. Encourage suggestions for job improvements. Help employees to develop good suggestions. The suggestions can bring them recognition. The city's suggestion program offers additional encouragement through cash awards.

The supervisor who encourages employee participation is not surrendering his authority. He must still make decisions and initiate action, and he must continue to be ultimately responsible for the work of those he supervises. But, through employee participation, he is helping his group to develop greater ability and a sense of responsibility while getting the job done faster and better.

STEPS IN HANDLING A GRIEVANCE

1. Get the Facts
   a. Listen sympathetically
   b. Let him talk himself out
   c. Get his story straight
   d. Get his point of view
   e. Don't argue with him
   f. Give him plenty of time
   g. Conduct the interview privately
   h. Don't try to shift the blame or pass the buck

2. Consider the Facts
   a. Consider the employee's viewpoint
   b. How will the decision affect similar cases
   c. Consider each decision as a possible precedent
   d. Avoid snap judgments—don't jump to conclusions

3. Make or Get a Decision
   a. Frame an effective counter-proposal
   b. Make sure it is fair to all
   c. Have confidence in your judgment
   d. Be sure you can substantiate your decision

4. Notify the Employee of Your Decision
   Be sure he is told; try to convince him that the decision is fair and just.

5. Take Action When Needed and If Within Your Authority
   Otherwise, tell employee that the matter will be called to the attention of the proper person or that nothing can be done, and why it cannot.

6. Follow through to see that the desired result is achieved.

7. Record key facts concerning the complaint and the action taken.

8. Leave the way open to him to appeal your decision to a higher authority.

9. Report all grievances to your superior, whether they are appealed or not.

DISCIPLINE

Discipline is training that develops self-control, orderly conduct, and efficiency.

To discipline does not necessarily mean to punish.

To discipline does mean to train, to regulate, and to govern conduct.

I. THE DISCIPLINARY INTERVIEW

Most employees sincerely want to do what is expected of them. In other words, they are self-disciplined. Some employees, however, fail to observe established rules and standards, and disciplinary action by the supervisor is required.

The primary purpose of disciplinary action is to improve conduct without creating dissatisfaction, bitterness, or resentment in the process.

Constructive disciplinary action is more concerned with causes and explanations of breaches of conduct than with punishment. The disciplinary interview is held to get at the causes of apparent misbehavior and to motivate better performance in the future.

It is important that the interview be kept on an impersonal a basis as possible. If the supervisor lets the interview descend to the plane of an argument, it loses its effectiveness.

II. PLANNING THE INTERVIEW

Get all pertinent facts concerning the situation so that you can talk in specific terms to the employee.

Review the employee's record, appraisal ratings, etc.

Consider what you know about the temperament of the employee. Consider your attitude toward the employee. Remember that the primary requisite of disciplinary action is fairness.

Don't enter upon the interview when angry.

Schedule the interview for a place which is private and out of hearing of others.

III. CONDUCTING THE INTERVIEW

    A. Make an effort to establish accord.
    B. Question the employee about the apparent breach of discipline. Be sure that the question is not so worded as to be itself an accusation.
    C. Give the employee a chance to tell his side of the story. Give him ample opportunity to talk.
    D. Use understanding—listening except where it is necessary to ask a question or to point out some details of which the employee may not be aware. If the employee misrepresents facts, make a plain, accurate statement of the facts, but don't argue and don't engage in personal controversy.
    E. Listen and try to understand the reasons for the employee's (mis)conduct. First of all, don't assume that there has been a breach of discipline. Evaluate the employee's reasons for his conduct in the light of his opinions and feelings concerning the consistency and reasonableness of the standards which he was expected to follow. Has the supervisor done his part in explaining the reasons for the rule? Was the employee's behavior unintentional or deliberate? Does he think he had real reasons for his actions? What new facts is he telling? Do the facts justify his actions? What causes, other than those mentioned, could have stimulated the behavior?
    F. After listening to the employee's version of the situation, and if censure of his actions is warranted, the supervisor should proceed with whatever criticism is justified. Emphasis should be placed on future improvement rather than exclusively on the employee's failure to measure up to expected standards of job conduct.
    G. Fit the criticism to the individual. With one employee, a word of correction may be all that is required.
    H. Attempt to distinguish between unintentional error and deliberate misbehavior. An error due to ignorance requires training and not censure.
    I. Administer criticism in a controlled, even tone of voice, never in anger. Make it clear that you are acting as an agent of the department. In general, criticism should refer to the job or the employee's actions and not to the person. Criticism of the employee's work is not an attack on the individual.
    J. Be sure the interview does not destroy the employee's self-confidence. Mention his good qualities and assure him that you feel confident that he can improve his performance.
    K. Wherever possible, before the employee leaves the interview, satisfy him that the incident is closed, that nothing more will be said on the subject unless the offense is repeated.